Key Customers

How to Manage Them Profitably

Malcolm McDonald
Beth Rogers
Diana Woodburn

*Published in association with
the Chartered Institute of Marketing*

BUTTERWORTH
HEINEMANN

OXFORD AUCKLAND BOSTON JOHANNESBURG MELBOURNE NEW DELHI

Butterworth-Heinemann
Linacre House, Jordan Hill, Oxford OX2 8DP
225 Wildwood Avenue, Woburn, MA 01801–2041
A division of Reed Educational and Professional Publishing Ltd

ℛ A member of the Reed Elsevier plc group

First published 2000

British Library Cataloguing in Publication Data
A catalogue record of this book is available from the British Library

Library of Congress Cataloguing in Publication Data
A catalogue record of this book is available from the Library of Congress

ISBN 0 7506 4615 2

Composition by Genesis Typesetting, Laser Quay, Rochester, Kent
Printed at Bath Press, Bath

314556

Contents

Foreword

The concept of pan-company marketing was first championed by Sir Michael Perry, then Chairman of Unilever and now Chairman of The Marketing Council and Vice-President of the Chartered Institute of Marketing.

Pan-company marketing is based on the idea of an organization which competes effectively for customer preference because it redefines its market with great customer insight, lives and breathes customer commitment from the top down and puts customer satisfaction ahead of shareholder, employee and supplier interests.

Such companies redefine work processes and systems around customers rather than according to traditional functional silos, they inspire their people to invest in even better standards of customer service and they judge their performance against clear customer satisfaction measures.

Their products and services also happen to be excellent and are normally associated with clear brand values. Little to disagree with there – many of us might want to review our own organization's performance against such criteria.

But is it really that simple?

Professor Malcolm McDonald, Beth Rogers and Diana Woodburn have researched the development of relationships between suppliers and customers from transaction-based relationships through to fully integrated relationships in which a joint team from both organizations works on areas such as research and development, manufacturing and distribution. The role of the key account manager is to coordinate the work of the multidisciplinary task groups from both companies.

How does a major world company like Dupont or 3M really maximize its added value to worldwide customers such as General Motors or AT&T? It is not easy and a pound to a penny the respective corporate structures do not fit.

The pan-company model acts as a framework, but the real answers, as this excellent book demonstrates, are infinitely more complex. Marketing – creating and keeping customers – is a multidimensional task. Two-dimensional models sometimes make it seem easier than it is.

John Stubbs
Chief Executive, The Chartered Institute of Marketing, Cookham, UK
April 2000

Preface

Throughout this book we use the expression 'key account management' (KAM), even though the title of the book is *Key Customers – How to Manage Them Profitably*. Why have we chosen a different title?

For a start, KAM has popularly come to mean *any* important customer, to the extent that almost *all* an organization's customers are classified as key accounts.

In one sense, of course, all customers are important. Yet there is a danger in this approach of spreading scarce resources too thinly and achieving little of the real intimacy required by those few customers who can help us make significant progress towards our long-term objectives. In a way, it is like expecting us to give to every one of our friends the time and devotion which makes just some of them so very special. Clearly, this is an unreasonable prospect.

Consequently, we decided to refer to these crucial accounts as 'key customers' in the title, in order to draw attention to what the book is really about.

Nonetheless, as much of what we say is relevant to any special customer, irrespective of size, we have chosen to use the more popular expression KAM throughout the book.

Innumerable mighty tomes have been written about the importance of customer focus and getting close to customers. There can be no closer focus than 'the segment of one'.

The growing complexity of business-to-business markets, which are in a state of metamorphosis from chains of value to integrated recipes of value, presents a great challenge. Add the internationalization of business and the growing sophistication of consumers and you can see why one of the key messages of our research into key account management is that it does have to be distinguished from its predecessor, key account selling.

In a traditional transactional focus the selling company is oriented to single sales focused on product features. The business outlook of the company is short term. There is a limited commitment to customer service, discontinuous customer contact and a belief that quality is the concern of production staff.

Companies which have adopted a key account approach, on the other hand, are oriented towards customer retention through continuous customer contact and a focus on delivering value to customers over an extended time-frame. They exhibit a high commitment to meeting customer expectations and believe that quality is the concern of all staff.

Key account strategy, of course, has to fit in with the company's overall marketing strategy. Key accounts will normally be the leading players in segments which have been identified as attractive to the selling company. Key accounts themselves can be distinguished by their relative attractiveness to the selling company and by the apparent fit of the company's strengths to the customer's requirements. We ask the reader in particular to consider customer profitability, which should grow as the customer is retained over many years.

Adopting a key account approach has implications for the way the company is organized. Customer focus can be achieved through highly skilled, consultative key account managers leading dedicated key account teams.

All the indications are that, in business-to-business marketing, key account management is not so much an option but a customer expectation. Maintaining the momentum of relationship marketing is a considerable challenge in every selling company.

This book is designed to provide a route through this most difficult of terrains. It is a route map which has emerged from the authors' extensive research into the practice of global key account management with some of the world's leading companies. Although there is still much to learn, we believe readers will find this book representative of the very best of best practice.

Professor Malcolm McDonald
Beth Rogers
Diana Woodburn
Cranfield University School of Management

Acknowledgements

We would like to acknowledge in particular the contribution of our colleague on the original key account management research report, Professor Tony Millman. Special thanks are due to him for his enthusiasm for the topic. His previous work and that of Dr Kevin Wilson was invaluable in creating frameworks for understanding the development of supplier–customer relationships. In our KAM Best Practice Research Clubs at Cranfield, we have been able to build on their groundbreaking research and push the frontiers of learning and practice forward even further. Our thanks also go to the work of other colleagues at Cranfield in the field of relationship marketing.

We are also extremely grateful to colleagues who have been instrumental in the production of this book, notably Lee Smith, Margrit Bass, Bernard Gracia and John Leppard, and to the world-leading companies who have contributed through participating in our research.

The purpose of this book

The Cranfield research into key account management from supplier and customer perspectives found the following:

- Key account management is a strategic approach distinguishable from key account selling. It is used to ensure the long-term development and retention of strategic customers.
- Key account management is fashionable, but difficult to do well.
- Key account management is appropriate for different types of relationships, but is most clearly a special function when supplier and customer have a mutually recognized partnership or have even achieved some degree of integration.
- There are mismatches between the way suppliers and customers perceive each other – communications and vigilance are vital.
- Where supplier and customer are partnering, cost reductions and quality improvements are achieved. However, regular monitoring of the profitability of individual customers by suppliers is quite rare because it is difficult to measure.
- Key account managers need a broad portfolio of business management skills to deal with interdependent or integrated customers.
- Key account management has structural implications for selling companies. Interdependence and integration can only be achieved where the key account manager has a considerable degree of control over staff and other resources devoted to their key account.
- Adopting key account management means change in the ways companies get things done across a broad spectrum.

This book will propose some ways of dealing with these findings, taking the reader to a level whereby they can implement some solutions. It is intended to help key account strategists and key account managers in capturing and developing a scientific basis for their company's practice. The scope of key account management (KAM) is widening and it is becoming more complex. For KAM to be successfully implemented, there is an urgent need for developing reliable diagnostic tools and measures of performance which support strategic marketing decisions. The skills of professionals involved in KAM at strategic and operational levels need to be constantly updated and developed. This book demonstrates how KAM can be implemented and describes the elements of best practice which can be adopted by all types and sizes of organization.

Chapter 1 sets KAM in the context of a dramatically changing business environment where increasingly complex relationships have altered the nature of marketing and imposed an urgent need for greater understanding and more appropriate treatment of key relationships.

Chapter 2 describes the evolution of the buyer–seller relationship leading to the trend towards partnership. KAM and partnership sourcing are seen to provide stepping-stones towards integrated value management.

Chapter 3 explores the interplay of trust and power in relationships between suppliers and customers and how they affect the potential for interdependence and integration.

Chapter 4 looks at the purchasing context from the buyer's perspective and emphasizes that progression towards *interdependent* or *integrated* relationships requires complementary buyer and seller strategies and mutual trust.

Chapter 5 explains how to select and categorize the most appropriate accounts to target for KAM.

Chapter 6 examines how to analyse key accounts in order to establish and prioritize their needs.

Chapter 7 introduces the processes for and the tools and techniques of key account planning. It describes how to set objectives and strategies for each targeted key account and how to measure their profitability.

Chapter 8 suggests how KAM might be positioned in organizations in order to achieve the status appropriate to the function.

Chapter 9 discusses the qualities and skills required of a key account manager and how they must be matched to the type of key account. The role of the key account manager as leader of a customer-focused team is included.

Chapter 10 explores the operations and processes necessary to take supply chain relationships to new levels of integration.

Chapter 11 offers a framework for developing business relationships proactively, based on targeted features of key relationships.

Learning features

In this Chapter:
Each chapter begins with bullet points which outline the main features and learning to be covered in the proceeding chapter.

Headlines:
Extracts taken from the text as marginalized notes bring important points to the attention of the reader.

Crucial Terms:
Concise definitions of important terms and vocabulary are provided in the margin to allow for a smoother, easier reading of the text.

Mini-cases:
Brief examples show how the theories work in real world companies.

Marketing Insights:
Real-life marketing anecdotes contextualize learning.

Key Concepts:
Principal marketing ideas and themes are highlighted as snapshots throughout the text.

xvi Learning features

Chapter Summary:
Condenses the main themes of the chapter.

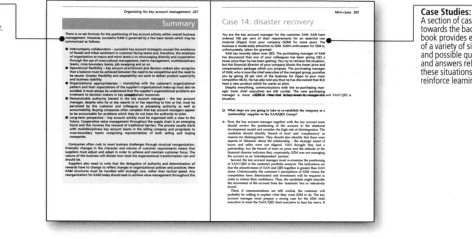

Case Studies:
A section of case studies towards the back of the book provides examples of a variety of situations and possible questions and answers related to these situations to reinforce learning.

Before you read this book!

Most readers of this book will have had at least some experience of managing key accounts. Some will have considerable experience, not only of managing key accounts, but also in managing others who have responsibility for key accounts. It should therefore be quite easy to answer the following questionnaire without having to spend too much time over it.

Please have a go at completing the questionnaire before you read this book. Rate your response to each question on a scale from 1 to 10 (1 = not very well, 10 = very well). Keep a record of each individual score and the total score.

You will be asked to complete the same questionnaire after you have read this book and to compare the individual questions and total scores to see to what extent the contents of this research-based book have caused you to reassess the efficacy of your key account processes.

How advanced is your key account practice?

How well do you know your key accounts?

Do you

Score out of ten:

- Know your company's proportion of customer spend? ☐
- Know their financial health (ratios, etc.)? ☐
- Know their strategic plan? ☐
- Know their business process (logistics, purchasing, manufacturing, etc.)? ☐
- Know their key customers/segments/products? ☐
- Know which of your competitors they use, why and how they rate you? ☐
- Know what they value/need from their suppliers? ☐
- Allocate attributable (interface) costs to accounts/ customer groups? ☐
- Know the real profitability of the top ten and bottom ten accounts/customer groups? ☐
- Know how long it takes to make a profit on a major new customer? ☐

List of figures and tables

Chapter 1
Why key account management?

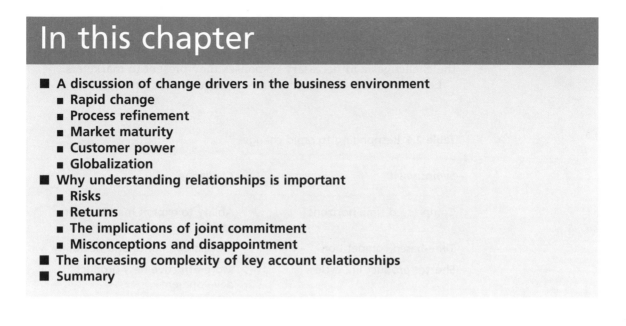
Introduction

While sales and marketing strategists have for some time been convinced that effective key account management (KAM) leads to increased sales, heightened profitability and improved sales productivity, the characteristics and techniques of KAM were not extensively explored beyond the need for a dedicated sales force until the 1990s. The impetus behind this unprecedented interest in the dynamics and mechanics of KAM comes from an awakening to the need to address changes in both the context and construct of marketing. The marketplace today is a different world from that which we have known before and the rules of engagement have likewise evolved significantly. Such rapid and radical transformation warrants attention.

> The characteristics and techniques of KAM were not extensively explored until the 1990s.

Cranfield's breakthrough research (McDonald, Millman and Rogers, 1996) closely examined the nature of KAM from both the supplier's and the customer's point of view. The findings demonstrated that specific forces were driving changes to the make up of the marketplace, which in turn were fuelling the growing complexity of the buyer–seller relationship.

Change drivers in the business environment

With hindsight, we can easily recognize those factors in the business environment which have led to the ascendancy of KAM as a separate and significant discipline. These influences were initially identified in a research report published by Cranfield and the Chartered Institute of Marketing entitled *Marketing, the Challenge of Change* (McDonald et al., 1994). Tables 1.1–1.5 summarize the apparent symptoms of change and the challenges and necessary responses they present to marketers.

Let us consider each of these five change drivers in turn.

Table 1.1 Responding to rapid change

Symptoms	Challenge
Compressed time horizons	Ability to exploit markets more rapidly
Time-based competition	Process excellence and flexibility
Shorter product life cycles	More effective new product development
Shorter technology life cycles	More investment in skills and understanding of applications of technology
Transient customer preferences	Flexibility in approach to markets, accuracy in demand forecasting, and optimization in price setting
Increasingly diverse business arena	Cultural sensitivity

Table 1.2 Refining the process

Symptoms	Challenge
Move to flexible manufacturing and control systems	Project orientation to deal with micro-segmentation
Materials substitution	Means to shift from single transaction focus to the forging of long-term relationships
Developments in technology (such as microelectronics and robotics)	More investment in skills to realize potential of technological innovations
Concentration on core business	Embrace opportunities for suppliers to run non-core aspects of customer's business
Quality focus	Widespread involvement in quality initiatives
Collaborative working practices	Create greater customer commitment

Table 1.3 Redefining the marketplace

Symptoms	Challenge
Commoditization	Need for product/process differentiation
Lack of growth and over capacity	Need to achieve growth within key accounts
Greater and stronger competition	Customer retention more vital than ever
Low margins	Greater pressure for cost reduction and quality improvement
Saturated markets	Need for new market creation and stimulation
Downsizing	Need to apply resource where it can deliver most value to customers

Table 1.4 Pleasing the customer

Symptoms	Challenge
Customers more demanding and more knowledgeable	Quality and traceability favour supply chain partnerships
Purchase behaviour strategic rather than tactical	A strategic and sympathetic approach to selling is required
Concentration of buying power	Selling companies need to add more value to succeed
Higher expectations	A greater investment and closer relationship to the customer is required
Customer identity and role more complex	Need to better manage the complexities of multiple market channels

Table 1.5 Coping with globalization

Symptoms	Challenge
Industry players differentiated by scope	Restructuring to achieve wider scope (restructuring of domestic operations to compete internationally)
Greater and stronger competition	Customer retention more vital than ever
Lower margins	Greater pressure for cost reduction and quality improvement
Greater customer choice	Need to customize offers
Larger and more complex markets	Need to become customer-focused in larger and more disparate markets

Rapid change

Any company which is complacent will be quickly overtaken.

Time has become a major determinant of competitive advantage. The drive towards lean production systems has increased interdependency in supply chains. Businesses need to be more in touch with the marketplace in order to adapt to change. Any company which is complacent will be quickly overtaken. Ironically, the shorter the opportunity for success, the more important it becomes for companies to think strategically and for the long term. In so doing, the potential for minimizing the risks inherent in rapidly changing markets through supply chain partnerships is often an attractive option.

Marketing managers understand that, for a product or service to be commercially advantageous to the provider, value must be added faster than cost. This concept has been labelled 'lean supply' by purchasing professionals.

Definition:
A supply chain defines the distribution chain between supplier and user.

Lean supply involves the study of the entire supply flow from raw materials to consumer as an integrated whole.

Definition:
Lean supply is a process for removing all unnecessary costs at each junction in the supply chain.

Interfaces between companies are artificial. Therefore, recognition of the costs associated with any departure from the perfect execution of tasks is necessary in providing long-term customer satisfaction. The effects of any inefficiency are not limited to a specific employer.

In theory, effective supply flow is an absolute. In practice, companies just have to keep applying continuous improvement to be leaner than the competition. Adopting an approach in which the supplier and customer are joint guardians of the value in transit is vital. Examination of the value in transit demands that both the supplier and customer open their 'books' and facilitate two-way assessment in order to optimize performance. There should be no blame and no excuses.

Lean supply practice also lends itself to sharing some costs critical to mutual success.

Lean supply practice also lends itself to sharing some costs critical to mutual success. Joint research and development, joint merchandizing, integrated logistics and electronic data interchange (EDI) are just a few examples of the opportunities available for making things happen better, cheaper and faster.

Process refinement

Companies must be flexible, not just to raise customer satisfaction but to avoid waste and loss.

The technological revolution of the 1980s resulted in flexible manufacturing, logistics control systems and business process redesign. Company activities have shifted away from producing predefined products or services towards having the capability to produce creative solutions for customer requirements. Companies must be flexible, not just to raise customer satisfaction but to avoid waste and loss.

It has been claimed that EDI alone can reduce transaction costs between a selling company and their buying companies by 90 per cent. However, efficiency is not enough.

The prerequisite for process redesign is access to information across organizational boundaries. Without that exchange of information, no streamlining can be achieved. Buyer–seller partners are increasingly sharing common databases. The obvious example is stock management. If point of sale data is transferred to commonly held databases of stock information, the suppliers of logistics services and goods can make sure that retail outlets are always fully stocked with the fastest moving lines. That way everybody makes more money through the consumers obtaining what they want when they want it. This correlation between heightened quality perceptions and boosted profits is depicted in Figure 1.1.

If companies in the supply chain do not learn how to share information, it could result in the reconfiguration of the chain or its fragmentation, as manufacturers and primary service providers try to reach consumers directly and consumers have access to them via their home personal computers. As companies move into implementing 'intranet' services to ensure that all employees have ready access to the right quality and quantity of information, suppliers and customers can also be linked in.

Moving on from the sharing of information, buyers and sellers need to examine their current activities together in order to explore and optimize processes. In establishing opportunities for process efficiencies, it is helpful to use computer-based modelling tools for simulating the flows of goods, information and value. These tools enable 'what if' situations and large quantities of potential variables to be evaluated quickly.

Concept modelling rather than structural modelling provides a flexible, cross-boundary technique. Concept modelling can facilitate the consideration of radical options. It animates, manipulates and abstracts entities in the supply chain and removes organizational constraints. This

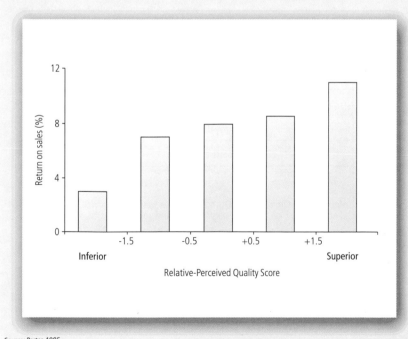

Source: Porter, 1985

Figure 1.1
Quality perceptions
boost profit

diagnostic technique is still being developed and automated by information systems specialists.

The output of process redesign (or re-engineering) should be enhanced customer value. Customers want quality through attention to detail: they want suppliers to solve their 'soft management issues'. However, quality is not just about traceability and accountability. Some selling companies have hundreds of quality indicators, including the time taken to answer the telephone. Any customer wanting to initiate new quality indicators with a supplier is more likely to do so if there is a strong element of trust and partnership. The closeness of customer relationships can be greatly enhanced through collaboration, both across and between organizations. Joint planning initiatives and coordinated working practices can be used to create mutual understanding, benefit and commitment.

There is an underlying assumption in process orientation that the internal value chain of a commercial organization needs to change from a linear, functional design to a 'holistic' design. This is diagrammatically expressed in Figures 1.2 and 1.3.

Within this holistic model, companies will train purchasing, logistics and marketing professionals together, ensuring a consistent and integrated approach to the development of value. Job swaps within the company and across the blurred, overlapped boundaries with other companies in the supply chain will be encouraged.

In years to come, both purchasing and marketing professionals may well be working together within companies as well as across them, looking at the entire flow from raw materials to the end consumer and how it can be optimized. Professor Martin Christopher of Cranfield School of Management has already stated that it is supply chains which

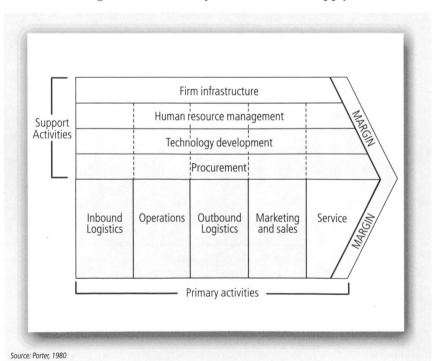

Figure 1.2
The value chain

Source: Porter, 1980

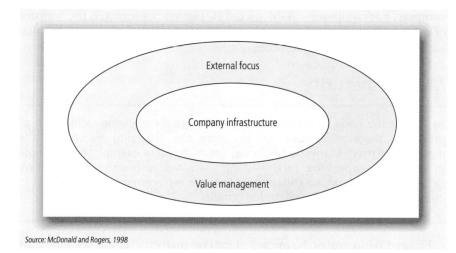

Source: McDonald and Rogers, 1998

Figure 1.3
The internal value
'cake' of the future

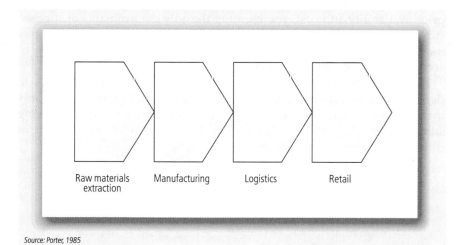

Source: Porter, 1985

Figure 1.4
The linear value
chain

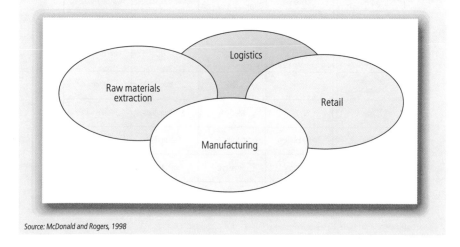

Source: McDonald and Rogers, 1998

Figure 1.5
The integrated
value chain

compete, not companies. As depicted in Figures 1.4 and 1.5, the transfer of value will start to look more like a collection of interlocking circles than a chain of unrelated organizations.

Market maturity

Insight

Definition: ●
A mature market is one in which all potential users of a product or service are using it.

As well as the need to respond to rapid change through the refinement of processes, there is a need to recognize the changing nature of the marketplace itself. Many markets today are mature. For example, most people in Western Europe have cars, washing machines, dishwashers, televisions, calculators and so on, so competitors in these replacement markets need to innovate and to look elsewhere for growth.

There is considerable danger in allowing products and services to degenerate into commodities with price and availability as the only ingredients of success. It is this danger more than any other that is forcing suppliers to pay more attention to key customers as a way of differentiation.

Figure 1.6 illustrates the impact of market maturity on the key elements of business management. The final column clearly illustrates the danger of allowing products and services to degenerate into commodities, with price availability and costs representing the only determinants of success. It is this danger more than any other which is forcing suppliers to pay more attention to key customers' specific requirements as a means of securing effective differentiation.

There is considerable danger in allowing products and services to degenerate into commodities with price and availability as the only ingredients of success. It is this danger more than any other that is forcing suppliers to pay more attention to key customers as a way of differentiation.

Definition: ●
A product/market life cycle is the aggregate sales at a point in time of all goods or services which satisfy the same or similar needs in a market.

Key characteristics	Unique	Product differentiation	Service differentiation	'Commodity'
Marketing message	Explain	Competitive	Brand values	Corporate
Sales	Pioneering	Relative benefits Distribution support	Relationship based	Availability based
Distribution	Direct selling	Exclusive distribution	Mass distribution	80:20
Price	Very high	High	Medium	Low (consumer controlled)
Competitive intensity	None	Few	Many	Many
Costs	Very high	Medium	Medium/low	Medium/low
Profit	Medium/high	High	Medium/high	Medium/high cost
Management style	Visionary	Strategic	Operational	Cost management

Figure 1.6
The product/market life cycle and market characteristics

Source: Based on Wilson, M., Marketing Improvements Group

The fact that most industry-to-industry product/service markets in the developed world are mature has clearly propelled the development of KAM. Suppliers know that they can only grow at the expense of a competitor and the obvious first option is to prise more of existing customers' business away from the opposition by means of account penetration. Highly professional KAM can facilitate the achievement of this objective.

Mini-case 1:

Renishaw's response to market maturity

Renishaw produces high-technology measuring equipment for precision manufacturing. One-third of the company's business is based in Germany and Japan. The slowdown of markets in 1990–3 forced some cost cutting. Competitive pricing was required, but was not a long-term solution. Product innovation was essential as patents deliver price protection. The company also had to invest heavily in relationship building with customers and end-users (McDonald *et al.*, 1994).

When inflation and growth were high in Western economies, companies enjoyed a comfort zone, which masked inefficiency. Now, most economists are advising us to plan for low inflation worldwide. In fact, in many sectors across the world, prices are falling. The combination of increased competition due to globalization, deregulation and economic management by governments has ensured inflation in the 1–3 per cent band.

In such a climate, there is no room for complacency. Business can only be won by being better than competitors and taking market share from them. Product, process and people improvements are imperative. The depth of customer feedback required to achieve continuous improvement is easier within a KAM/partnership framework for reasons described more fully in Chapter 2.

> Business can only be won by being better than competitors and taking market share from them.

Customer power

The change within the business environment which is having the most dramatic impact on the development of KAM is the new-found expertise and power of customers and consumers in exercising choice. Customer empowerment is not just a cultural change emanating from the growing popularity of adopting a customer focus, it is a consequence of mature markets. Nowadays, customers know that they can demand more from suppliers because suppliers must seek to retain customers – not just to maintain profitability, but to stay in business.

> Nowadays, customers know that they can demand more from suppliers because suppliers must seek to retain customers.

Customer power manifests itself in many ways. For example, there is the considerable concentration of industry which has occurred in the 1980s and 1990s, most recently on a transnational scale, which has made big customers even bigger (see Figure 1.7). However, bigger customers do

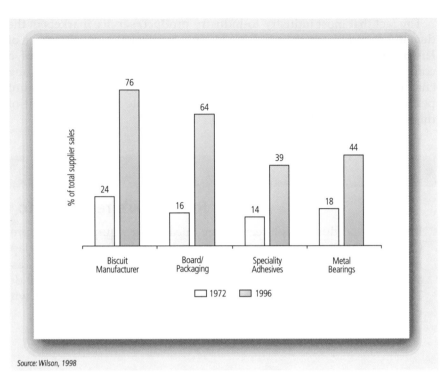

Figure 1.7
Concentration of buying power in industries

Source: Wilson, 1998

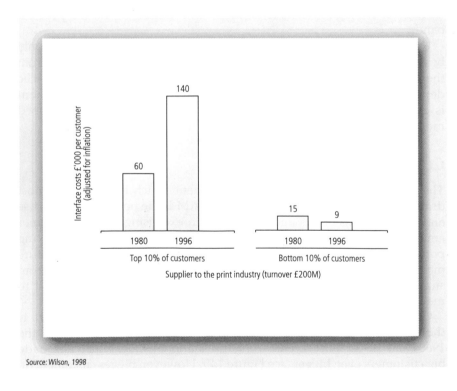

Figure 1.8
Cost of servicing the customer

Source: Wilson, 1998

not necessarily mean more business opportunity. Suppliers who cannot meet the geographical scope and consistent outputs demanded by global customers are rationalized off lists of preferred suppliers. Customers want bespoke, sophisticated solutions which means that winning customer accounts can be very costly. It also means that retaining customers, which requires ongoing investment, is critical in achieving long-term profitability (see Figure 1.8).

> Suppliers who cannot meet the geographical scope and consistent outputs demanded by global customers are rationalized off lists of preferred suppliers.

Mini-case 2:

Electrospeed's response to the danger of commoditization

Electrospeed is a specialist distributor of branded electronic products offering over 20 000 parts. In addition to having to offer a comprehensive range, the company has received industry recognition for innovation and service. It offers extremely rapid delivery, electronic data interchange and will take on the assembly of parts if the customer requires it. In discussions with customers, they place the emphasis on end-to-end value rather than unit price (McDonald *et al.*, 1994).

The customer may have always been hailed as king but, not being a very well-informed monarch, the king was often at the mercy of his 'subjects' (suppliers). The rising power of consumer pressure groups and the popular media have changed all that. They have wrested power from companies and vested it in the ultimate users of their products and services. End customers expect a great deal of respect, which is now often contractually assured in some sort of charter document. The logical extension of this consumer-driven scenario is cooperation between all organizations delivering value in the flow of supply from raw materials to the consumer. The concept of adding value is significant. Consumers will soon leap-frog any links in the supply chain which they feel do not add value.

> Consumers will soon leap-frog any links in the supply chain which they feel do not add value.

Customers need raw materials to be converted into what they can use, taken to where they need them and presented to them for choice. Which company in the supply chain does any of these is irrelevant. Consumer champions are also casting a critical eye over the whole supply chain in the new millennium for ethical and environmental reasons. Trusted brand names have to ensure that their values are passed up the supply chain.

Mini-case 3:

C&A's response to environmental concerns

C&A formalized its ethical trading policy in 1966 when it began trading in the Far East, because of concerns about working conditions. In 1997, the company spent $3 million monitoring its ethical code through its in-house auditing organization, which conducts thousands of supplier audits per annum (Hancock, 1998). Suppliers have to reveal their sources of supply so that they also can be checked. If the auditors find any breaches of the C&A code, such as child labour, the account is closed unless the supplier concerned can come up with a plan for positive change. That will undoubtedly involve considerable investment on their part, such as the provision of a school and switching to employment of adults.

Consumers today know more about supply chains than might ever have interested them ten to twenty years ago.

Consumers today know more about supply chains than might ever have interested them ten to twenty years ago: they see it as relevant to the end-product they obtain. The idea of companies working together with their suppliers in order to deliver more value to the end consumer is an attractive one, a matter of common sense. This is particularly pertinent to businesses which operate across national boundaries where the value chain is exceedingly complex and cultural sensitivities must be respected.

Definition:
The value chain maps the value which is added to goods and services in the route from supplier to user.

Globalization

The globalization of business has had many side-effects. It has led to a greater interdependency between global customers and suppliers who have the capability to meet each other's increasingly complex needs.

The globalization of business has had many side-effects including a greater interdependency between global customers and suppliers who have the capability to meet each other's increasingly complex needs. These suppliers also realize the extent to which they can grow with their key customers if they consistently succeed in meeting their customers' expectations cost-effectively.

The impact of these environmental changes – the imperative of keeping pace with rapid change, the requirement of revising processes, the necessity of redefining the character of the marketplace, the need for satisfying increasingly sophisticated customers/consumers and the obligation of facing the growing scope and scale of competition – has reverberated through the business relationship itself. It has encouraged KAM away from the traditional construct of a single relationship between salesperson and buyer, and towards the concept of strategic customers where key customers command attention on vital statistics measuring more than simply their size.

We see companies starting to build models of account attractiveness, matching their resources to the profit and status potential of any given customer or prospect. We also witness increasing professionalism among purchasers and decision-making units in buying companies as they evaluate the longer-term value offered by suppliers (the quality of products, processes and people) rather than solely the price deal.

However, in the final analysis it has to be people who deliver value to key accounts and, even when some organizations have a sound, value-enhancing proposition, they frequently find themselves losing out to

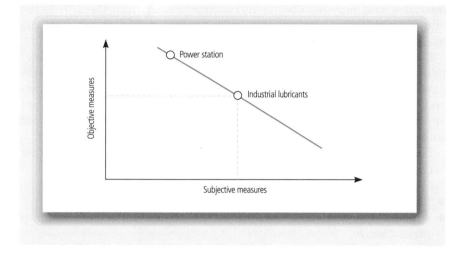

Figure 1.9 Personal relationships and suppliers

suppliers whose people are seen to be more caring. Figure 1.9 illustrates the fact that, when different suppliers make a similar offer, it is the personal side of the business relationship which determines the successful candidate.

Why understanding relationships is important

The relationship between two organizations has an existence beyond the obvious types of interaction, such as product and service adaptation, operational delivery and underlying strategy. All of these contribute to the nature and development of the relationship as well as depending on it (see Figure 1.10). The intercompany relationship is affected by these

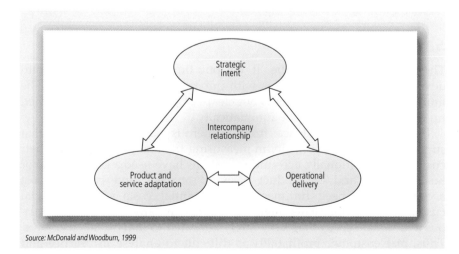

Source: McDonald and Woodburn, 1999

Figure 1.10 The relationship as a medium

interfaces and may also buffer turbulence arising from them. It is the 'glue' which binds companies together more or less closely and the medium through which interactions take place in delivering action.

Clearly, understanding the nature and potential of the customer relationship is critical in assessing opportunities and managing business development. We need to know where we stand now with our customer and what further engagement might entail. We will also need a sound appreciation of their market position, and internal strengths and constraints (see Chapter 5).

Understanding key relationships is both important and challenging because:

- the risks are ambiguous and the stakes are high,
- supplier–buyer interactions are already complex and lie at the heart of major change,
- key relationships operate at different levels which require different behaviour.

Relationship risks

One of the primary reasons for relationship development is risk reduction.

One of the primary reasons for relationship development is risk reduction. There are risks associated with building close relationships with key customers as well as risks with not building them. In theory, there should be less chance of relationship breakdown where there is joint commitment, barriers to exit and mutual understanding and trust (see Chapter 3). However, while these attributes may appear highly desirable, they actually carry risks of their own. For example:

- The risk of being vulnerable to opportunism and not obtaining a satisfactory saving or return on investment in the relationship.
- The risk of committing to one partner at the exclusion of others and 'backing the wrong horse'.
- The risk of misunderstanding the relationship and failing to achieve reciprocal security.

Satisfactory return

The major question must be 'If we put time, effort and money into developing closer relationships with our trading partners, will they be more profitable?' The answer is not clear-cut, though it may be summed up as 'Yes, possibly, but not automatically'.

There is ample evidence from numerous sources indicating that suppliers have great difficulty in measuring the real profitability of their customers. Traditionally, accounting systems have used a geographical or business unit and/or product basis of analysis and customer cost accounting has been rudimentary. Substantial costs such as special customized developments, high-level, intercompany contacts and various additional services are very rarely allocated to individual customers. Thus, real customer profitability is difficult to analyse in practice and these intrinsic difficulties are compounded by inherent challenges to internal vested interests.

Alarmingly, although few suppliers can assess the profitability of individual key accounts accurately, many suspect that, ultimately, they lose money on them. While Chapter 5 explores this problem in greater detail, the issue is introduced here to highlight some fundamental points.

1 Close relationships with key accounts have substantial cost implications.
2 The mismanagement of just a few large accounts can be potentially (disastrously) loss making.
3 Customer relationships should be carefully selected and prioritized for the prudent investment of scarce resources (see Chapter 5).

The costs of building close, sophisticated, groundbreaking, new relationships should not be underestimated. Frequent, multilevel, multi-function communication alone represents a considerable expense. Further, relationship development usually entails investment in initiatives such as joint marketing, new restructuring, electronic commerce, staff retraining and stockholding. All too often the cost of pursuing a closer relationship is not anticipated and properly quantified.

> All too often the cost of pursuing a closer relationship is not anticipated and properly quantified.

Firmness can pay off handsomely: one loss-making company, admittedly with dominant shares in its core markets, implemented 'an aggressively upward pricing policy' with great success and achieved a return to excellent profits within two years.

Insight

Implications of joint commitment

In many cases, the commitment of the buying company is greater than that of the selling company (although the latter would not see it this way). Where it does not make sense to multisource a product or service, the buying company may be obliged to adopt a sole supplier. Meanwhile, the selling company will continue to supply other customers. The buying company must ensure that it has made the right choice, not only in relation to the matter at hand, but also because its decision will be a statement to other suppliers.

Similarly, a selling company's key customers may demand supplier exclusivity, preventing the supplier from broadening its customer base by serving the customers' competitors. The practice of exerting such pressure has generally been accepted by advertising agencies, for example, while other sectors have resisted it. However, the growth in the number of customers of considerable size has meant that this practice is increasingly tolerated.

The range of functions and initiatives involved in the relationship may reach a point where significant company-level backing is required which cannot be satisfied simply by allocating more resources, people and time. At this level of relationship, there may not be any room for parallel relationships, even for the selling company. For example, if two competing companies were developing similar new products at the same time using a shared supplier, the supplier would find it exceedingly difficult to work with both customers in the same way. Confidentiality might be hard to guarantee, as might be the origins of a research breakthrough. If the supplier and each of the buying companies were to approach the marketplace together, the fact that the company is offering products together with two different partners might confuse consumers.

However, by choosing to work with a single business partner, both supplier and buyer are consciously excluding others and declaring that the decision is right for them. Both companies want a partner they can work with and benefit from. 'Backing the right horse' for a strategic-level relationship need not be as much of a gamble as backing a real horse if the pre-existing relationship is well-understood and well-managed.

> 'Backing the right horse' for a strategic-level relationship need not be as much of a gamble as backing a real horse if the pre-existing relationship is well-understood and well-managed.

Misconception and disappointment

There is a common misconception that closer relationships will automatically bring greater profits. The reality is not so simple. The inability of companies to measure profitability accurately or realistically gives cause for confusion. However, it would appear that relationship-stage maturity and business success are linked: closer key relationships are widely considered more successful than relatively distant key relationships according to a range of accepted success and financial indicators. Nevertheless, there is a substantial minority of relationships which do not conform to this 'rule' and it would be a mistake to assume that developing any relationship will automatically bring success or that relationships which are not developed to closer levels are failures. This was clearly demonstrated in a recent Cranfield/Financial Times research report (McDonald and Woodburn, 1999). Figure 1.11 shows the correlation between relationship closeness and relationship success.

> There is a common misconception that closer relationships will automatically bring greater profits.

A proportion of this substantial minority of non-conformists represents successful relationships which are not particularly close for good reasons. For example, if the product or service purchased is not a core item and does not offer opportunities for deriving differential benefit, the customer may naturally decide that a simple purchase with minimal support is adequate. Any extra attention or additional services lavished on the customer might be accepted, but not necessarily valued. From the supplier's perspective, an attempt at forced intimacy would be a mistake in this case and the business should be serviced with efficiency and a positive attitude, but not much more.

Insight

'I do not think suppliers would benefit from getting any closer to us: quite the reverse. We are a very "taking" company and it would not do them any good' (retailer).

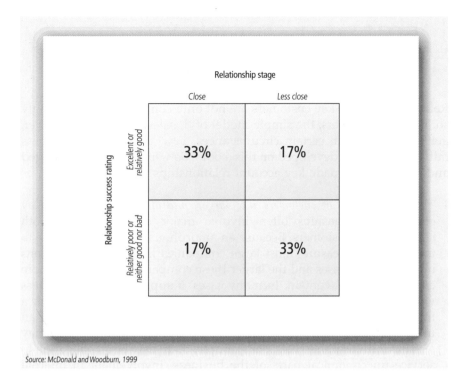

Source: McDonald and Woodburn, 1999

Figure 1.11
Relationship
closeness versus
relationship success

It is not uncommon for some key relationships to be close, but to be considered unsuccessful and/or unprofitable. They may be intransigent situations into which companies have been cornered, perhaps by a determined buyer, optimistic key account manager or poorly written contract.

> The fact that relationships can reach higher levels of intimacy and still prove unsuccessful should make companies wary of selecting the right relationships to develop in the first place as well as managing them extremely carefully (see Chapter 5). Part of that selection process should be an assessment of the relationship's current stage of development and the buyer's and supplier's respective degrees of commitment.

There is yet a further danger: that of sliding imperceptibly, by numerous smaller steps, into a relationship which the company has failed to anticipate, that has implications which they are unprepared for or cannot recognize. Logically, the development of key customer relationships should be a strategic process linked into the design and implementation of overall business strategy. Surprisingly, this critical connection is often overlooked. Customer relationships, be they key accounts or otherwise, should be examined objectively and developed deliberately in line with company aims and capabilities.

Customer
relationships, be they
key accounts or
otherwise, should be
examined objectively
and developed
deliberately in line
with company aims
and capabilities.

Increasing complexity of key account relationships

Relationships with key customers are not only complex, but increasingly so. For top customers, the simple model of 'I, salesman, sell: you, buyer, get' only applies in certain circumstances. Few, if any, major business initiatives are now developed on this axiom. So why have things changed and how has this made key account relationships more complex?

1 *The consolidation of customers into larger, multidivision companies.* Key customer relationships often involve major corporations as both suppliers and customers. Because an amorphous mass is impossible to motivate and measure, most large companies introduce subdivisions into their businesses and the larger these companies become, the more entities they will contain. In many cases, a supplier will do business with more than one entity within the client company. While such a multiple interface offers potential benefits in terms of developing an inside track to new business with other parts of the organization, it may also incur undesirable costs. For example, there may be an obligation to service uneconomical parts of the business, involvement in internal competition, downward price levelling and additional communication costs.

'When we arrived to see our largest customer in Japan, he said, "You were here last week." He meant someone from one of our other divisions, but he did not realize the distinction. We did not know about the visit: no particular reason why we should, but we felt very silly anyway. He was surprised, confused and not impressed' (McDonald and Woodburn, 1999).

Insight

Customers want seamless service, one point of contact and possibly services delivered jointly across divisional boundaries.

At the same time, suppliers may also be large businesses with subdivisions of their own. Customers are generally completely indifferent to suppliers' organizational issues, even when they mirror their own. Customers want seamless service, one point of contact and possibly services delivered jointly across divisional boundaries. They also want to leverage their purchasing power across the whole of their business, regardless of what type of product is purchased or for which business unit. To customers' disgust and despair, delivery on these issues is extraordinarily problematic for many suppliers. Their irritation is understandable; they tend to overlook the complexity of the situation on both sides.

2 *The consolidation of customers leading to the adoption of dual roles: the customer may be 'competitor' as well as 'client'.* As companies consolidate, the situation in which a customer is also a competitor and sometimes a supplier as well arises more frequently. Obviously, this intertwining of relationships and roles complicates behaviour. Takeovers which

juxtapose competitors inappropriately are a common cause of terminated key account relationships. However, some companies struggle on and learn to live with ambivalence, perhaps because industry consolidation leaves them with very little choice of customer or supplier. The potential for internal and external conflict is heightened and management of the relationship becomes evidently more strained.

3 *The development of global businesses which demand global supply.* Global customers requiring global supply and service add additional complexity to the task of managing relationships effectively. Problems which are easily identified but not easily resolved originate from differences in terms of language, culture, time zone and geography, making the servicing of pan-global operations a tough challenge for even the fittest of suppliers. The prevalence of knowledgeable and powerful country managers helps somewhat, but the scope and size of the task remains formidable. In addition, new infrastructure may be required to service markets previously outside the supplier's sphere of activity which now fall within its global contract, meaning more new partners, languages and cultures to assimilate into the relationship.

4 *The accelerating pace of change, particularly as new information technology (IT) reshapes markets.* IT, in particular electronic commerce, is forcing huge changes in the way companies work and how their markets operate. As always, there is a lag between the availability of the new technology which is possessed by the enlightened few and mass uptake with full-scale revision of basic practices and processes. While it is not yet clear what the ultimate impact of IT development will be for business, it is already evident that many companies will have to make huge adjustments very quickly as customers adapt to electronic commerce and demand similar immediacy and intimacy from their existing suppliers.

5 *The emphasis on strategic alliances as a fast and flexible, but less clear-cut, approach to growth.* New needs may be satisfied on both sides of the relationship by the creation of a strategic alliance with another company which has strength in a specific area rather than through the development of existing internal expertise and physical assets. Selling companies may find themselves supplying third-party associates of their customers instead of their customers directly. They may also be supplying customers alongside other suppliers who may have been selected by them or by the customer. As supply chain management reaches further up- and downstream, more complex relationships are be formed involving more participants. Communication is likewise complicated and, because strategic alliances are often forged as a fast and flexible response to market change, opportunities for misunderstanding and confusion abound.

'We deal with our suppliers on product development, marketing and ordering, but our warehouse is managed for us by Tibbett & Britten, so suppliers deal with them on inbound logistics.'

Insight

With today's flattened management structures, cross-functional teams are encouraged to take part in the activities traditionally allocated to lower levels of responsibility, including direct customer contact and decision making. Key customer relationships put more people and more functions in direct contact with the customer or supplier than ever before.

While the internal interactions required to drive the machine which actually delivers the customer promise are discussed later in Chapters 7 and 9, it is already abundantly clear that relationships and, in particular, key account relationships are redoubtably complicated by the increased quantity and variety of contact with the customer.

Summary

The external context in which buyer–seller relationships exist is becoming increasingly extensive and complex. Change drivers include the rapid pace of change, the refinement of processes, market maturity, heightened customer power and the globalization of business. At the same time, the internal, organizational context is also changing, removing traditional delineations of remit and responsibility. Conditions are more conducive to 'partnering' between suppliers and customers and, hence, the nature of marketing has altered. Marketers are moving away from a traditional transaction focus towards a customer focus. Thus, there is a pressing need for finding ways of describing relationships as a basis from which to understand them better and build them stronger – and this has led to the ascendancy of KAM.

References

Hancock, S. (1998). Fair's fair. *Purchasing and Supply Management*, 5 November.

McDonald, M. and Rogers, B. (1998). *Key Account Management – Learning from Supplier and Customer Perspectives*. Butterworth-Heinemann.

McDonald, M. and Woodburn, D. (1999). Key account management – building on supplier and customer perspectives. *Financial Times*, Prentice Hall.

McDonald, M., Millman, A. and Rogers, B. (1996). *Key Account Management – Learning for Supplier and Customer Perspectives*. Cranfield School of Management.

McDonald, M., Ryals, L., Dennison, T., Yallop, R. and Rogers, B. (1994). *Marketing, the Challenge of Change*. Cranfield University.

Porter, M. E. (1980). *Competitive Strategy*. The Free Press.

Porter, M. E. (1985). *Competitive Advantage: Creating and Sustaining Superior Performance*. The Free Press.

Wilson, C. (1998). *Profitable Customers: How to Identify, Develop and Keep Them*, 2nd edn. Kogan Page.

Chapter 2
The origins of key account management

Introduction

This chapter is important in that it puts key account management (KAM) in a historical context and traces its evolution from a sales-push approach to what it is today: a partnership between supplier and customer with the purpose of delivering superior value propositions to the ultimate consumers.

Readers are encouraged to read the whole of this chapter. However, those who wish to go straight to the nitty-gritty of developing key account relationships may turn immediately to Chapter 3.

Historical foundations

KAM has evolved from the principles of customer focus and relationship marketing in business-to-business markets. It is distinguishable from key account selling by its emphasis on long-term, mutually beneficial relationships between selling companies and buying companies which are rooted in the realization of opportunities for profit enhancement for both parties. KAM is a *management* approach adopted by selling companies aimed at building a portfolio of loyal key accounts by offering them, on a continuing basis, a product/service package tailored to their individual needs. Where appropriate, technical, social and process links are built up between supplier and customer.

Defining the appropriate 'KAM' approach and integrating it as a process is a significant challenge for selling companies. It is a challenge not least because different accounts demand different approaches and processes. The success of KAM is largely determined by the key account Key accounts are those customers in a business-to-business market which are identified by selling companies as being strategically important. However, what constitutes strategic importance to the selling company?

> ● Definition:
> KAM is a *management* approach adopted by selling companies aimed at building a portfolio of loyal key accounts by offering them, on a continuing basis, a product/service package tailored to their individual needs.

> ● Definition:
> Key accounts are customers in a business-to-business market identified by selling companies as being of strategic importance.

Revenue and volume are easy to measure, but accounts can be both big and unprofitable. Success also depends on the strategic importance to the customer of the selling company and what it supplies. The degree of receptivity demonstrated by the customer to a partnership approach is also influenced by the skills of the supplier in meeting the customer's needs. Those skills have to be consistently demonstrated not just at the single point of contact represented by the key account manager, but at every point of contact between the two organizations.

Peter Drucker reorganized the importance of customer dynamics in his early works in the 1950s. Specific study of the topic began in the 1960s. 'What the customer thinks he is buying, what he considers "value" is decisive – it determines what a business is, what it produces and whether it will prosper' (Drucker, 1955).

The decision-making unit

The origins of KAM are rooted in the history of industrial marketing. The first theoretical breakthrough in analysis of the relationships between selling companies and buying companies was the concept of the decision-making unit (DMU), which was developed in the 1960s by Robinson, Farris and Wind (1967) of the American Management Association. This notion was valuable because it ensured consideration of the way in which buying decisions are made within buying organizations. It demonstrated that there was more to successful selling than clever negotiations with a purchasing professional. Understanding the motivations and roles of all the people involved in the purchasing decision became a relevant selling skill. It encouraged managers who had been resistant to 'soft' methodologies to recognize the importance of people in the dynamics of trade.

The decision to purchase in a complex organization involves those with purchasing and financial expertise, those with technical expertise and those with hierarchical clout. In some cases, the purchasing department may even be excluded from the purchasing decision. The number of people in the DMU is likely to be a factor of the cost of the purchase, the complexity of the product and the inherent degree of risk (which will be particularly high if the product is new). Thus, if a selling company's product is strategic to the buying company, then it is probable that a significant number of buying company personnel will have an interest in new purchases. However, research at the time suggested that salespeople were heavily reliant on single contacts within buying companies and were not influencing the customer's whole DMU. The direct relationship between company size in terms of the number of employees and DMU size is contrasted in Table 2.1 with the average number of contacts made by salespeople over a defined period.

The point was made that, no matter how persuasive the arguments of the salesperson, identifying and influencing all the people involved in the buying decision was a prerequisite selling activity. Selling required research, the ability to make constructive contacts at senior levels in the customer organization, and tailoring the selling role and selling message to decision makers with differing interests and needs.

Table 2.1 Contrasting the number of buying influences and number of contacts made by salespeople

Number of employees	Average number of buying influences (people in the DMU)	Average number of contacts made by salespeople
under 200	3.42	1.72
201–400	4.85	1.75
401–1000	5.81	1.90
over 1000	6.50	1.65

Source: McGraw-Hill

Despite this progress in recognizing the complexity of purchase decision making, sales management specialists tended to present the human interactions in selling and negotiation as an adversarial interface. Advice to sales professionals was (and often still is) centred on their personal communications and negotiations with the customer, and there was no discussion of the role of the salesperson's colleagues in building and maintaining relationships with customers. The approach of purchasing management specialists was equally flawed by a concentration on adversarial approaches.

As different supply chain relationship opportunities opened up in the late 1980s and early 1990s, the concept of the DMU soon became insufficient in helping selling companies achieve their objectives.

> Sales management specialists tended to present the human interactions in selling and negotiation as an adversarial interface. The approach of purchasing management specialists was equally flawed by a concentration on adversarial approaches.

Relationship marketing

Soon after the theory of the DMU was first promulgated, the Industrial Marketing and Purchasing Group (IMP) advocated the simultaneous analysis of buyer–seller relationships, an 'interactionist' approach. Their model highlighted the interaction process, participants, environment and atmosphere. Relationships were deemed to represent both a valuable resource and an investment, providing an effective information channel and serving to increase economic and technological efficiency and to reduce uncertainty.

The IMP's work was followed by the concept of relationship marketing. As mentioned in Chapter 1, it contrasted traditional approaches to sales and marketing, which became known as the transactional focus, with the relationship focus which seemed more appropriate to the market conditions of the 1990s. Relationship marketing seemed to build on the quality movement in operations management by presenting an ideal based on building customer satisfaction through quality, service and value.

> Relationships were deemed to represent both a valuable resource and an investment: to increase economic and technological efficiency, to serve as an information channel and to reduce uncertainty.

Table 2.2 The different characteristics of transactional and relationship marketing

Transactional focus	Relationship focus
Single sales	Lifetime value of a customer
Product features	Satisfaction of customer needs
Tactical promotional campaigns	Strategic marketing
Short-term reward structure	Varied reward structure
Only in contact with a customer during the sale	Continuous customer contact
Limited points of contact/influence	Contacts and influence from the boardroom to the shopfloor
Salesperson guards his/her access to the customer	Team approach to inter-company communications and activity
Limited commitment	Extensive commitment
Special department for 'after sales service'	After sales service involves the whole team
Quality is policed by Quality Control	Quality involves the whole team

Source: Payne, 1993

The transactional focus concentrated on single sales, product features, tactical campaigns, discontinuous customer contact, limited commitment and a view of customer service and quality as being the concern of specialist departments (Table 2.2). The relationship focus embraced customer retention as a deliberate strategy through continuous customer contact, delivering benefits, a long-term outlook, high commitment and an expectation that all staff would deliver service and quality (Table 2.2). Strategic intent and shared internal values became part of the product and services offered.

Strategic intent and shared internal values became part of the product and services offered.

There has been much debate about what circumstances made relationship marketing appropriate. In 1985, Barbara Jackson (as quoted in Kotler, 1997) argued that the investment was most worthwhile in industries where customers would have long-term horizons and high switching costs, such as buying capital equipment. Customers buying commodities might still be best served by a transactional approach. In 1991, Anderson and Narus presented the idea that it was the nature of the individual customer that should be the deciding factor in relationship approaches as some customers value high service levels, brand values and long-term relationships with suppliers while others do not. When making buying decisions, some customers take into account more than just the price – time and 'hassle' being significant factors as well as a variety of benefits which could loosely be called 'value'.

Definition:
A transactional approach is one which focuses on buyer–seller interactions transaction by transaction.

Some customers value high service levels, brand values and long-term relationships with suppliers, while others do not.

Studies on the relationship between customer retention and lifetime profitability started to suggest that, where at all possible, a long-term approach was likely to deliver significant benefits to the selling company. The cost of attracting a new customer is estimated to be five times the cost of keeping a current customer happy. A study by Bain and Company (Reichheld, 1996) indicated that companies could improve profits anywhere from 25 to 85 per cent by reducing customer defections by 5 per cent (see Figure 2.1).

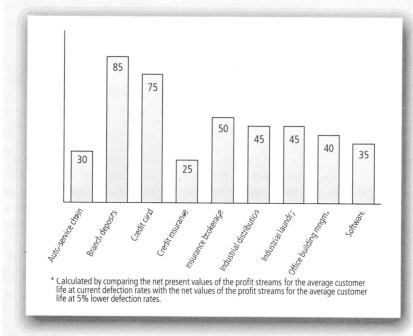

* Calculated by comparing the net present values of the profit streams for the average customer life at current defection rates with the net values of the profit streams for the average customer life at 5% lower defection rates.

Source: Reichheld, 1996

Figure 2.1
Reducing customer defections by 5 per cent boosts profits by 25 per cent to 85 per cent

In the past, companies sought to erect 'exit barriers' to deter customers from switching suppliers. Measures included loss of discounts and refusal to service multisupplier installations. Such negative reinforcement only served to ensure that customers who defected never returned. In contrast, relationship marketing seeks to retain customers by improving their satisfaction. It embraces all that companies do to understand valued customers and to improve their offerings to them. The ultimate aim is to convert prospects and customers to 'advocates' who praise the company and encourage others to buy from it. The relationship marketing ladder of customer loyalty shown in Figure 2.2 emphasizes the two main marketing tasks of attracting new customers and retaining existing customers. The creation of customer advocates involves progressing customers up the loyalty ladder. This is achieved through the successful fulfilment of customer requirements and expectations – which necessitates an in-depth understanding of the customer and their relative importance to the supplier.

The premise for developing customer satisfaction is to realize the customer's lifetime value. A rough guide to calculating customer lifetime

● Definition: Relationship marketing is the practice of transforming repeat business from customers into long-term relationships based on understanding of customer needs and delivery of promises concerning the value elements of the solution required, e.g. quality, service, fair pricing, etc.

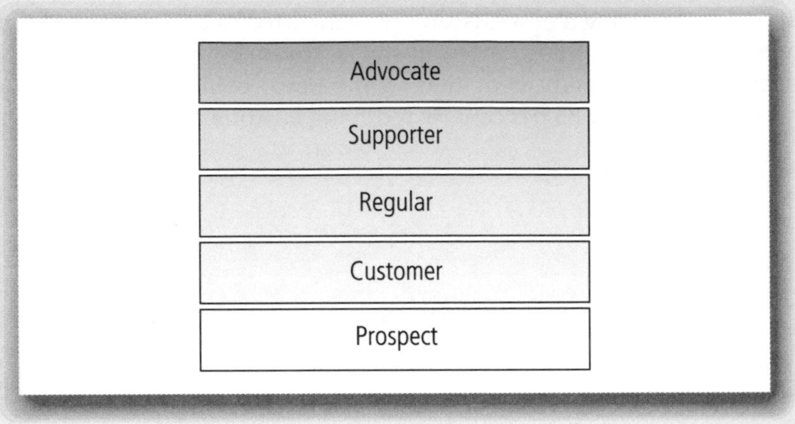

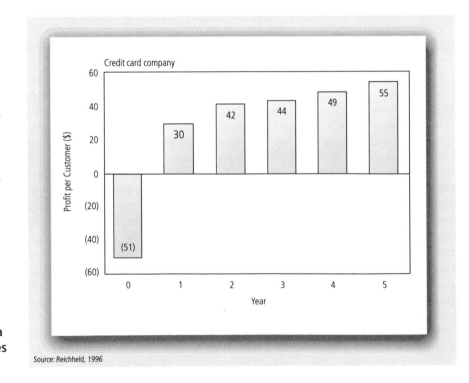

Figure 2.2
Ladder of customer loyalty

Source: Payne, 1993

value is to multiply the annual customer profitability (revenue less the costs to service that customer) by the number of years they are likely to need the product or service being consumed. In fact, customers tend to become increasingly profitable over time. Figure 2.3 demonstrates how customer retention contributed to increased profits in a number of service industries.

Carl Sewell, the owner of a highly successful US car dealership chain, estimates that a typical car buyer represents a potential lifetime value of

Figure 2.3
How much profit a customer generates over time

Source: Reichheld, 1996

over $300 000 in car purchases and servicing. Obviously, to improve customer satisfaction costs money, but the investment can make it easier to realize profits in the long term (Sewell and Brown, 1990).

Berry and Parasuraman (1991) distinguished three approaches to enhancing customer value:

1 Adding financial benefits such as loyalty discounts, better credit terms and financial services.
2 Adding social benefits such as club membership, theatre trips and sports links.
3 Adding structural ties such as special delivery arrangements and electronic data interchange (EDI).

The benefits to be gained from better customer relationships were seen to vary by industry. In industry-to-industry markets where there are fewer and larger customers to be won and lost, the potential for developing partnerships with customers became a new focus of attention.

Thus, in the 1990s, marketing was redefined as building and sustaining customer relationships. Analogies were drawn with courtship and marriage in order to emphasize that a fundamental element of the new concept was ensuring long-term relationships with customers. A correlation between customer retention and profitability was seriously explored for the first time.

Relationship marketing can be clearly identified as a major breakthrough in terms of a marketing-led contribution to company prosperity. However, thirty years of growth markets meant that companies could get away with being production led and technology led. The difficult market conditions of the 1990s were going to force dramatic change.

The rise of key account management

Until recently, KAM was often dismissed or downgraded to key account selling and selling to major or national accounts. 'Account manager' has often been regarded as a euphemistic term for 'salesman'. However, some companies moved beyond sophisticated selling towards customer retention through integrated processes and enhanced value delivery. These 'partnership' arrangements became a benchmark for KAM best practice.

The belief that companies can best satisfy their customers by being tough on suppliers has declined in the last ten years, although it persists in some industries. A few business analysts claim that US and UK business cultures are adversarial and there is not enough trust between organizations and individuals within them to make partnerships work. During the 1980s, the influence of the Japanese 'keiretsu' model of supply chain relationships was being felt, but interdependence between suppliers and customers was still treated with considerable apprehension.

> A correlation between customer retention and profitability was seriously explored for the first time.

> Until recently, KAM was often dismissed or downgraded to key account selling and selling to major or national accounts.

Nevertheless, some Western companies, such as motor parts manufacturers, were beginning to see advantages in the way Japanese car companies conducted their business. Discussions in some manufacturing industries began to address the risks of the adversarial approach.

Later in this chapter we shall discuss whether more sophisticated approaches were driven by exhortations from industry leaders about partnerships or by the practicalities of market conditions. In the 1980s models were developed both by marketing and purchasing academics (Ford, 1980; Dwyer, Schurr and Oh, 1987; Lamming, 1993) in order to explain the way in which relationships between particular buyers and sellers evolve over time. These models indicated that each exchange is not only affected by market considerations of price and the fit of the product/ service to the need, but also by relational and process factors. The relational development model of Millman and Wilson (1994) was explored in Cranfield research (McDonald, Millman and Rogers, 1996). Further quantitative research (McDonald and Woodburn, 1999) modified the concept of an evolution to an analogy with Maslow's (1943) hierarchy

Table 2.3 The risks inherent in the alternative approaches to buyer–seller relationships

Adversarial	Interdependent
Sellers and buyers are constantly jostling for advantage and relationships between companies are inherently unstable.	Sellers' over-dependence on a few customers is mirrored by customer over-dependence on a single source of key products/services.
This can lead to:	*This can lead to:*
Lack of trust resulting in frequent, costly supplier switching/customer churn	Inertia and lack of flexibility
Unequal power relationships are exploited	Unequal power relationships are perpetuated
Sellers and buyers have no chance to learn from each other or 'best practice'	Influence over the way the companies are run is legitimized
Price is the main focus of attention, at the expense of value	Complacency on price
Advances in technology may not be advances in fulfilling customer needs	Technology may stagnate
Waste involved in duplicating technical skills	Loss of independent skills in each company
Purchasing skills cannot evolve	Decline in purchasing expertise
Tailored offerings are rarely available	Dedicated plant cannot be re-used

of needs. The importance of recognizing different stages of relationship development is discussed in Chapter 3.

> The extent to which a relationship between buyer and seller can develop will be dependent on anticipation of mutual benefit.

As early as 1982 and 1986, academics had been working to develop ways of discerning different types of customers and their relative attractiveness to suppliers, and of determining the value of the selling company's capabilities as perceived by customers (Fiocca, 1982; Yorke, 1986). This would mean that 'key' customers could be defined and the relative strategic importance of any particular customer to the selling company could be identified.

Cranfield's 1996 (McDonald, Millman and Rogers, 1996) research discovered that few companies were able to include the relative profitability of their accounts in their attractiveness criteria because most management accounting systems were unable to facilitate the allocation of costs to individual customers. However, the recognition of the need to measure and evaluate the cost of servicing customers is widely accepted. Chapter 6 explores the possibilities for measuring and managing customer profitability.

There is growing evidence that partnership reduces costs. Up to 70 per cent of the costs in a company can be associated with supply chain issues, so there is plenty of opportunity for improvement and a need to focus on smart solutions. From a 1995 survey, Partnership Sourcing Limited (1996) reported that in 75 per cent of buyer–seller partnerships costs had been reduced and in 70 per cent quality had improved.

Mini-case 1:

Partnership from the viewpoint of buyers

In his report 'Constructing the Team', Sir Michael Latham said that it is generally accepted in principle that partnering can deliver significant benefits to customer and supplier. Market research conducted by Galliford plc indicated that 75 per cent of purchasing professionals in the construction industry would agree that partnering is the future. As a response, Galliford developed a system specifically for managing construction projects on a partnership basis. The system incorporates a comprehensive set of performance measures. George March, chief executive of Galliford, commented that partnering had to be more than a philosophy; it had to be tangible, transparent, structured and measurable (*Purchasing and Supply Management*, 1995).

Even after objective considerations of mutual benefit have been established, the potential for a 'partnership' KAM approach is still constrained by other factors. The receptivity of the customer to KAM is obviously paramount. The sophistication of purchasing practices may depend on the degree to which the company has developed the purchasing function, the size of the company, the depth of change in the

> Even after objective considerations of mutual benefit have been established, the potential for a 'partnership' KAM approach is still constrained by other factors.

Many chief executives talk about partnership but in reality are unwilling to take on the investment and culture change it requires.

market and the nature of the company's values. Many chief executives talk about partnership, but in reality they are unwilling to undertake the investment and culture change it requires. Further, the selling company may not be equipped for integrating their processes with those of their customers. The strategic value of the product or service needed has to be taken into account along with the relative power of each party. A supplier may need to reconfigure an offering or the process by which it is delivered in order to improve its value.

Wilson and Croom-Morgan (1993) proposed a problem-centred model in order to assess whether the operational synergy possible at the highest levels of KAM/supplier partnership can be achieved. In addition to the product need, the selling company must address the process need – reducing the hassle factors inherent in incorporating their products/ services into those of the buying company. Solutions such as just-in-time (JIT) delivery, packaging and palleting, consignment stock management, EDI and subassembly have all been used to transform buyer–seller relationships from being transactional to being interdependent. Wilson and Croom-Morgan (1993) also discussed ways in which the selling company can meet the 'facilitation need' of the buying company by being on-site or accessible by telephone or e-mail to help the customer use the product or service. In the Cranfield research (McDonald, Millman and Rogers, 1996) buying decision makers expressed strong preferences for 'suppliers who are easy to do business with'.

Buying decision makers expressed strong preferences for 'suppliers who are easy to do business with'.

Closer relationships between buying and selling companies require a broader range of skills from those who are responsible for managing the value interchange. Consequently, sales representatives graduate to consultative selling to general business management. The origins of KAM may have been in sales, but many companies have key account managers reporting directly to general managers. The purchasing profession has also graduated from price negotiation to value delivery to strategic management. Each profession now has the opportunity of managing a variety of approaches to supply chain relationships and the risks inherent in them. However, the determination for achieving the benefits from that must be driven from the top of the organization and be reflected in the firm's systems, including reward and career development structures. If there is an association in the sales or purchasing professional's mind between achieving short-term gain and career progression, win–lose scenarios will dominate their thinking.

Each profession now has the opportunity of managing a variety of approaches to supply chain relationships and the risks inherent in them.

The wide range of buyer–seller relationships is portrayed in Figure 2.4. At one end of the spectrum, there are big league global buying–selling dyads pursuing the leanest supply and achieving synergy and integration. Where power, risk and trust are in balance between buyer and seller, partnerships of equals can be highly successful. Partnerships between unequals are unlikely, although some larger companies may emulate the Japanese model of 'benevolence through loyalty' in order to develop smaller suppliers.

At the other end of the spectrum, smaller players in smaller economies who may not be highly attractive or 'key' accounts to any of their suppliers are forced to adopt tactical approaches to supply chain issues in order to survive.

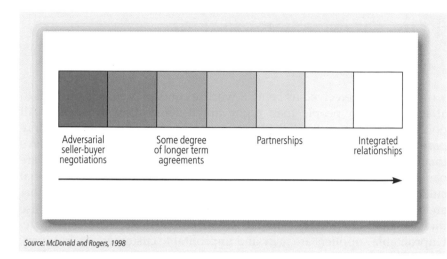

Adversarial seller-buyer negotiations	Some degree of longer term agreements	Partnerships	Integrated relationships

Source: McDonald and Rogers, 1998

Figure 2.4
The spectrum of buyer–seller relationships

In the middle of the relationship range there are moderate degrees of preference, including longer-term contracts accompanied by some nervousness over single sourcing and/or over-reliance on a few customers.

KAM in selling companies and <u>partnership sourcing</u> in buying companies are now well-established approaches to the management of value in the supply chain. They are not universally appropriate, but they have proved to be a considerable leap in progress. However, that progress has not been based solely on recognizing the objective benefits of a more cooperative business philosophy. Those benefits might have been realizable years ago. Instead, it is the way in which markets and economies have changed in the 1990s which has provided the driving forces for change.

As mentioned in Chapter 1, Cranfield produced a report called *Marketing, the Challenge of Change* (McDonald et al., 1994) for the Chartered Institute of Marketing. The research was commissioned in the light of criticism of 'the marketing department' and what it delivered. The researchers identified that problems did indeed exist with the use of marketing as an add-on to selling. Such an approach was proving inadequate. Marketing as 'a philosophy' was the driving force for industry leadership. However, it was not being embraced through altruism or a recognition of the genius of the 'gurus' who recommended it but because the business environment demanded it. The same factors were identified when researching the driving forces behind the trend towards KAM. These change drivers, as discussed in Chapter 1, are:

- rapid change
- process refinement
- market maturity
- customer power
- globalization

Definition: Partnership sourcing is a purchasing approach to strategic suppliers which usually involves single sourcing, long-term agreements and 'added value' solutions.

It is the way in which markets and economies have changed in the 1990s which has provided the driving forces for change.

The preference for partnership

Partnership is perceived as being a worthy concept, which is difficult to attack, although people may argue about what it really means. All political parties in the UK have exhorted businesses to be more partnership oriented. Many politicians and senior civil servants believe that adversarial relationships between buying and selling companies are bad for overall industry competitiveness. For example, the adversarial culture in the UK construction industry between architects, contractors and subcontractors is believed to add 30 per cent to costs. Common sense dictates that the interests of all parties in a project are legitimate. Unprofitable suppliers are risky and unprofitable customers are also very risky. Therefore, KAM and partnership sourcing are encouraged by expert opinion.

Governments have 'done their bit' to encourage responsibility in supply chains by legislation designed to protect employees and customers. Throughout the USA and Western Europe legislation has become increasingly influential in supply chain management (see mini-case 2).

Mini-case 2:

US employment law applies throughout the supply chain

In the USA, buyers have been put under legal as well as moral pressure not to buy from suppliers who violate US labour laws, whether they are based in the USA or other countries such as Latin America or Asia. A fifty-year-old law holds buyers liable for suppliers' illegal labour practices. Recent raids in California revealed Thai refugees in barbed wire encampments producing goods for major department stores. It is not uncommon in the USA for the law to require companies to police their sources of supply, even when those sources are outside US borders (Hancock, 1998).

Quality and traceability have been powerful reasons for partnerships in the manufacturing industry. It is certain that legislation will force the traceability issue wider and wider.

Besides legislative imperatives, the global economy is also a driving force for partnership. Consumers around the world have more choice and lower prices. In industry-to-industry markets the opportunities for buying from anywhere for anywhere are almost universal. Providing a consistent level of service worldwide to key accounts is a task selling companies have to work very hard to fulfil. In the 1970s, most multinational companies operated in a way which resulted in the only commonality between their geographical operations being the company logo (and sometimes even that was altered). Opening up the boundaries of business has helped suppliers to realize the extent to which they can grow with their key customers if they are able to meet the challenges presented successfully. Going global may also, in the long term, be an opportunity for spreading risk.

Mini-case 3:

Rentokil goes global with a consistent service formula

Rentokil has successfully exported its service formula and plans to run its business in virtually the same 'best practice' way in every country, although local organizations also enjoy considerable empowerment. The company has had to acquire local knowledge in new markets by acquiring the local companies with the best reputations and then gradually rebranding as Rentokil over a short period. Rentokil's international business overshadowed its UK operations within less than ten years (McDonald et al., 1994).

In the past few years, different leagues of supply chain activity have been identified and these are outlined in Table 2.4. Companies with global scope want to deal with other companies with global scope and local companies tend to deal with others who know their cultural markets.

Table 2.4 Leagues of supply chain activity

League	Operational level
Premier League	Global
First Division	Regional
Second Division	National
Third Division	Local/Niche

We know that global businesses represent approximately one-third of the private sector worldwide. The concentration of global buying companies seeking global selling companies in order to ensure consistency of supply worldwide means that it will be increasingly difficult for geographically restricted players to move up to the 'premier league' except via the minor element of 'benevolence through loyalty' in the system. That minor element could be critical to companies vying for promotion. The cost reductions which can be achieved through partnership will make the company more competitive and, therefore, better equipped for expanding to a larger geographical scale. An alternative route to league promotion for ambitious small companies will be the creation of alliances with more influential players in their supply chain.

End consumers still perceive variety and choice in the economy and most are still highly dependent on local companies and the public sector

> The cost reductions which can be achieved through partnership will make the company more competitive and, therefore, better equipped for expanding to a larger geographical scale.

for a high proportion of their weekly spend. Global economies of scale are attractive in many industry segments, but global firms do not dominate every segment.

In the global premier league, an increasing number of opinion leaders come from the Far East. These new giants are mostly manufacturing companies whose distinctive competence is making things smaller, cheaper, faster and more reliable. Partnerships between buying companies and selling companies are perceived to be part of the business culture of the Far East. Japanese companies have influenced best practice around the world. Many award-winning US and European companies have adopted partnership sourcing. It is therefore easy to conclude that partnership will become a mainstream concept in global business and demand KAM responses. Companies operating on a global scale need to transcend geographically narrow definitions of business culture and adopt best practice.

> Partnership is an enduring theme of best practice and KAM complements it. The challenge for selling companies is to keep 'raising the bar' of account management achievement in order to realize business growth in the future.

Enduring strategies for selling companies

Flagship selling companies have the following topics on their KAM agenda.

Monitoring and measurement of relationships

Research by Kearney and UMIST (in Nolan, 1996) has indicated that the foundation stone of improving performance in relationships with customers is monitoring and measurement. Each relationship must be measured at the transactional and process level and at the strategic level. Attention to detail is a quality attitude which is universally welcomed by customers and it helps in establishing an aura of integrity and professionalism.

Continuous and proactive improvement of products/services

Related to this is continuous improvement of the product or service on which the company's identity is based. The best of professional relationships will not be able to survive a deterioration in the competitive position of the selling company's core offering. In addition to continuous improvement, it is helpful to be the initiator of dramatic breakthroughs in technology or service delivery. Buying companies like to see their chosen suppliers acquire prestige alongside discovering better ways of fulfilling their needs.

Training and development of employees

The pioneering selling company must also invest in the training and development of the whole customer-focused team, not just the key account manager. Assigning multiple levels and functions of staff with objectives related to particular customers' needs will weave the philosophy of KAM into the whole fabric of the company.

● Definition: To coordinate interaction with each key account, suppliers form dedicated teams led by a key account manager. These are known as key account teams.

Integration of processes and systems through collaborative associations with customers and other suppliers

One of the technical specialisms that the selling company needs to acquire is an understanding of processes, whole supply chains and transfer of value. All selling companies should consider how they might expand their scope of activities with customers. The customer may also require a supplier to work together with other key suppliers to solve a particular problem such as systems integration (see mini-case 4). Proactively presenting new, integrated solutions to customers would be even more attractive to them. Apart from anything else, it reduces the fear of monopoly associated with single sourcing if the single source is, in effect, a variety of consortia (perhaps but not necessarily with a common leadership).

Mini-case 4:

Systems integration in the computer industry

Computer companies in the late 1980s/early 1990s had to migrate from promoting their proprietary systems in isolation to providing complete solutions for customers. This meant that they had to work together with other suppliers of information systems and services on what were usually called systems integration projects. In the first instance, they had to establish tactical alliances with companies who might in other circumstances be competitors in order to gain mutual benefit from fulfilling a customer need. In some cases, these relationships developed into strategic alliances.

The future of key account management – integrated value management

As discussed in Chapter 1, the future of relationships between companies in the same supply chains will depend on their mutuality in terms of understanding, interest, investment and commitment. They will be in

Definition: ●
Integrated value management is long-term cooperative relationships between three or more companies in a supply chain with the aim of mutual benefit and benefit for the end consumer.

competition with other supply chains. The simplistic concept of buying and selling as being the buyer–seller transaction will be considered 'history' and KAM and partnership sourcing will be seen as stepping-stones towards integrated value management

Summary

The concept of KAM has evolved from academic exploration of the DMU and relationship marketing. As a profession, KAM has become distinct from key account selling, encompassing the management of integrated processes with customers in order to deliver enhanced value. As KAM has developed, so has the purchasing profession. Partnership sourcing is a complementary mirror-image concept to KAM. From mutual benefit between two partners in a buyer–seller dyad, the future of KAM is destined to evolve into value management of several companies in the supply chain.

References

Anderson, J. C. and Narus, J. A. (1991). Partnering as a focused market strategy. *California Management Review.* Spring, 95–113.

Berry, L. L. and Parasuraman, A. (1991) *Marketing Services: Competing Through Quality.* Free Press.

Drucker, P. F. (1955). *The Practice of Management.* Heron Books.

Dwyer, F. R., Schurr, P. H. and Oh, S. (1987) Developing buyer–seller relations. *J. Marketing,* 5, 11–27.

Fiocca, R. (1982). Account portfolio analysis for strategy development. *Industrial Marketing Management,* April, 53–6.

Ford, D. (1980). The development of buyer–seller relationships in industrial markets. *Eur. J. Marketing,* 14(5/6), 339–53.

Hancock, S. (1998). Fair's fair. *Purchasing and Supply Management,* 5 November.

Kotler, P. (1997) *Marketing Management.* Prentice-Hall.

Lamming, R. (1993). *Beyond Partnership: Strategies for Innovation and Lean Supply.* Prentice-Hall.

Maslow, A. H. (1943). A theory of human motivation. *Psychol. Rev.,* 50(4), 370–96.

McDonald, M. and Rogers, B. (1998). *Key Account Management – Learning from Supplier and Customer Perspectives.* Butterworth-Heinemann.

McDonald, M. and Woodburn, D. (1999). Key account management – building on supplier and customer perspectives. *Financial Times,* Prentice-Hall.

McDonald, M., Ryals, L., Dennison, T., Yallop, R. and Rogers, B. (1994). *Marketing, the Challenge of Change*. Cranfield University.

McDonald, M., Millman, A. and Rogers, B. (1996). *Key Account Management – Learning from Supplier and Customer Perspectives*. Cranfield School of Management.

Millman, A. F. and Wilson, K. J. (1994). From key account selling to key account management. In *Tenth Annual Conference on Industrial Marketing and Purchasing*.

Nolan, A. (1996). Purchasing failure costs £2.4 bn. *Supply Management*, 14 March.

Partnership Sourcing Limited (1996) Can David and Goliath patch things up? *Purchasing*, February.

Payne, A. F. T. (1993). *The Essence of Services Marketing*. Prentice-Hall.

Purchasing and Supply Management (1995). Galliford puts partnering into practice. *Purchasing and Supply Management*, October.

Reichheld, F. R. (1996). *The Loyalty Effect*. Harvard Business Press.

Robinson, P. J., Farris, C. W. and Wind, Y. (1967). *Industrial Buying and Creative Marketing*. Allyn & Bacon.

Sewell, C. and Brown, P. (1990). *Customers for Life*. Pocket Books

Wilson, K. J. and Croom-Morgan, S. R. (1993). A problem-centred approach to buyer–seller interaction. In *Conference on Industrial Marketing and Purchasing (IMP)*.

Yorke, D. (1986). The application of customer portfolio theory to business markets – a review. In *Third Annual Conference on Industrial Marketing and Purchasing*.

Further reading

Axelrod, R. (1984). *The Evolution of Co-operation*. Basic Books.

Axelsson, B. and Easton, G. (eds) (1992). *Industrial Networks: A New View of Reality*. Routledge.

Barnett, H., Hibbert, R., Curtiss, A. and Sculthorpe-Pike, M. (1995). The Japanese system of sub-contracting. *Purchasing and Supply Management.*, December.

Barrett, J. (1986). Why major account selling works. *Indust. Marketing Manage.*, 15, 63–73.

Bonoma, T. V. and Johnston, W. J. (1978). The social psychology of industrial buying and selling. *Indust. Marketing Manage.*, 17, 213–24.

Campbell, N. and Cunningham, M. (1983) Customer analysis for strategy development in industrial markets. *Strategic Manage. J.*, 4.

Christopher, M. G., Payne, A. F. T. and Ballantyne, D. F. (1991). *Relationship Marketing: Bringing Quality, Customer Service and Marketing Together*. Butterworth-Heinemann.

Cyert, R. M. and March, J. G. (1963). *A Behavioural Theory of the Firm*. Prentice-Hall

De Monthoux, P. B. L. G. (1975) Organizational mating and industrial marketing conservatism – some reasons why industrial marketing managers resist marketing theory. *Indust. Marketing Manage.*, 4, 25–36.

Easton, G. and Araujo, L. (1986). Networks, bonding and relationships in industrial markets. *Indust. Marketing Purchasing*, 1(1), 8–25.

Forsgren, M. and Johanson, J. (eds) (1992). *Managing Networks in International Business*. Gordon and Breach.

Frazier, G. L., Spekman, R. E. and O'Neil, C. R. (1988) Just in time exchange relationships in industrial markets. *J. Marketing*, XXIII, 261–70.

Freeman R. E. (1984), *Strategic Management: A Stakeholder Approach;* Pitman.

Gadde, L. E. and Hakansson, H. (1993). *Professional Purchasing*. Routledge.

Grabher, G. (ed.) (1993). *The Embedded Firm: On the Socio-economics of Industrial Networks*. Routledge.

Grashof, J. F. and Thomas, J. P. (1976). Industrial buying center responsibilities: self versus other member valuations of importance. *Proc. Am. Marketing Assoc.*, 344–9.

Gummesson, E. (1987). The new marketing: developing long term interactive relationships. *Long Range Planning*, 20, 10–20.

Hakansson, H. (ed.) (1982). *International Marketing and Purchasing of Industrial Goods: An Interactive Approach*. John Wiley & Sons.

Hakansson, H. (1987). *Industrial Technological Development: A Network Approach*. John Wiley & Sons.

Hakansson, H. (1989). *Corporate Technological Behaviour: Co-operation and Networks*. Routledge.

Hakansson, H. and Henders, B. (1992). International co-operative relationships in technological development. In *Managing Networks in International Business* (M. Forsgren and J. Johanson, eds), pp. 32–46, Gordon and Breach.

Hanan, M. (1982). *Key Account Selling*. American Marketing Association.

Henderson, J. C. (1990). Plugging into strategic partnerships: the critical IS connection. *Sloan Manage. Rev.*, Spring.

Hutt, M. D. and Speh, T. W. (1985). *Business Marketing Management: A Strategic View of Industrial and Organizational Markets*. The Dryden Press.

Hutt, M., Johnston, W. and Ronchetto, J. (1985). Selling centres and buying centres: formulating strategic exchange patterns. *J. Personal Selling Sales Manage.*, 5, 33–40.

Jackson, B. B. (1985). *Winning and Keeping Industrial Customers: The Dynamics of Customer Relationships*. Lexington Books.

Johnston, W. and Bonoma, T. (1981). The buying centre: structure and interaction patterns. *J. Marketing*, 45, 143–56.

Lyons, T. F., Krachenberg, A. R. and Henke, J. W. (1990). Mixed motive marriages: what's next for buyer–seller relations? *Sloan Manage. Rev.*, Spring.

McKenna, R. (1992). *Relationship Marketing*. Century Business.

McWilliams, R. D., Naumann, E. and Scott, S. (1992). Determining buying centre size. *Indust. Marketing Manage.*, 21, 43–92.

MaCall, M. (1966). Courtship as social exchange, some historical relationships. In *Kinship and Family Organisation* (B. Fraber ed.), John Wiley & Sons.

Melkman, A. (1979). *How to Handle Major Accounts Profitably.* Gower Press.

Miller, R. B., Heiman, S. E. and Tuleja, T. (1988). *Strategic Selling: Secrets of the Complex Sale.* Kogan Page.

Millman, A. F. (1993) The emerging concept of relationship marketing. In *Ninth Annual Conference on Industrial Marketing and Purchasing.*

Millman, A. F. (1994). Relational aspects of key account management. In *Fourth Seminar of the European Research Network for Project Marketing and Systems Selling.*

Mitroff, I. I. (1983). *Stakeholders of the Organizational Mind.* Jossey-Bass.

Payne, A. F. T. (ed.) (1995). *Advances in Relationship Marketing.* Kogan Page.

Powers, T. L. (1991). *Modern Business Marketing: A Strategic Planning Approach to Business and Industrial Markets.* West Publishing Company.

Rackham, N. and Ruff, R. (1991). *The Management of Major Sales.* Gower Press.

Shapiro, B. P. and Wyman, J. (1981). New ways to reach your customers. *Harvard Business Rev.*, July–August, 103–10.

Sheth, J. N. (1973). A model of industrial buyer behaviour. *J. Marketing*, 37(4), 50–6.

Spekman, R. L. and Johnston, W. J. (1986). Relationship management: managing the selling and the buying interface. *J. Business Studies*, 14, 519–31

Thompson, G., Frances, J., Levacic, R. and Mitchell, J. (eds) (1991). *Markets, Hierarchies and Networks.* Sage Publications.

Turnbull, P. W. and Valla, J.-P. (eds) (1985). *Strategies for International Industrial Marketing.* Croom Helm.

Unger, H. G. (1995). Foreign sweatshops may cost US buyers dearly. *Purchasing Supply Management*, December.

Walker, O. C., Churchill, G. A. and Ford, N. M. (1975). Organizational determinants of the industrial salesman's role conflict and ambiguity. *J. Marketing*, 39, 32–9.

Webster, F. E. and Wind, Y. (1972a). A general model for understanding organizational buying behaviour. *J. Marketing*, 36(2), 12–19.

Webster, F. E. and Wind, Y. (1972b) *Organizational Behaviour.* Prentice Hall.

Wilson, D. T. (1978). Dyadic interactions: some conceptualisations. In *Organizational Buying Behaviour* (T. V. Bonoma and G. Zaltman eds), pp 31–48, American Marketing Association.

Wilson, D. T. and Mummalaneni, V. (1986) Bonding and commitment in buyer–seller relationships: a preliminary conceptualisation. *Indust. Marketing Purchasing*, 1(3), 44–59.

Wind, Y. (1978). The boundaries of buying decision centres. *J. Purchasing Materials Manage.*, 14, 23–9.

Yorke, D. A. and Droussiotis, G. (1993). The use of customer portfolio theory – an empirical survey. In *Ninth Annual Conference on Industrial Marketing and Purchasing.*

Chapter 3
Key relationship development

Introduction

Very often, when companies win new business with blue-chip customers the occasion is greeted with great joy, although little attention has been given to analysing the future implications. Quite naturally, it is deemed pointless spending valuable time considering the development of the business until it is known whether the account has been won.

Later on, however, the picture becomes more complicated. The supplier may discover it 'has a tiger by the tail'. Losing the new account would be very painful for the company and for key people in it, but retaining the customer now involves greater investment and higher risk. Clearly, for the supplying company at least, managing the relationship effectively must be a key priority.

This chapter discusses the nature of key relationships in terms of the interaction between two companies and how it develops. This insight into relationship development provides valuable knowledge with proven practical application. Clearly, practitioners who can establish their current position and realistically identify the potential for improving it are able to plan how to move forward better than those who do not have a vision of the future or even an accurate grasp of the present.

Cranfield School of Management undertook a quantitative research study into the nature of supplier–customer relationships (McDonald and Woodburn, 1999). Some of these findings are represented in the figures given in this chapter.

Key relationship development

Definition:
A key relationship is the connection established between two trading companies which are of fundamental importance to each other, which consists of mutual knowledge and commitment to the exchange of goods and services, money, time and information.

A business relationship is clearly different from a personal relationship. In the buyer–seller context, a relationship is formed by the exchange of money and goods or services. A key relationship extends beyond this basic transaction, at least to repetition, and it often features a degree of mutual trust and dependency which is reflected in relationship continuity or longevity. It does not necessarily involve the parties liking one another, although the relationship will work much better if the people involved get on well together.

The formation and development of business relationships is more a matter of involvement than of attitude (Gadde and Snehota, 1999)

Even in personal relationships, simply liking each other does not constitute a relationship. A mutual attraction between two parties requires some kind of joint activity, such as the sharing of time and interests, to become a recognizable relationship. Because business relationships do not depend on personal liking, focusing on the attitudes of the parties to the relationship can be very misleading. The formation and development of business relationships is more a matter of involvement than of attitude (Gadde and Snehota, 1999). Figure 3.1 shows the relationship as divided into three layers of involvement of which people bonds is only one. All of them are likely to exist in a key account relationship and all will grow as the relationship develops. The different layers arise largely from the pursuit of different objectives and they deliver different benefits within the relationship.

A desire for greater coordination will most often be pursued through *activity links*. For example, the adoption of a new procedure or process will involve a blueprint for task execution in which both sides elect to carry out the elements for which they are best suited. In the final process design, the activities of both sides will be interwoven and the companies will rely on each other for implementation of the process. When the set-up is complete, the companies will be bound together more closely by the

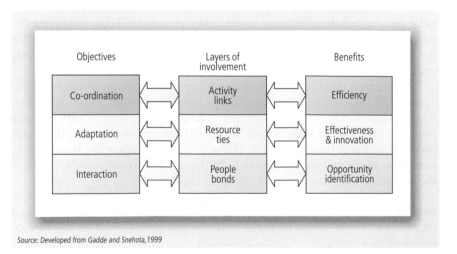

Figure 3.1
Layers of relationship involvement

Source: Developed from Gadde and Snehota, 1999

convenience of the procedure and the way it is stitched into each of their systems. They will also gain a better understanding of each other based on the exchange of all kinds of information about the underlying situation and the procedure itself. The selling company will probably have made new contacts with customer staff and collected more ideas on how to be useful to the buying company, and the buying company will have gained new insight into the competencies of the supplier.

The achievement of customizations and other adaptations from current practice are likely to require a commitment of *resources*, quite possibly from both sides, but particularly from the selling company. Although the kind of unique development which the customer really values necessitates investment, it can also deliver major growth in the business. This layer of linkage can be characterized as the one which delivers innovative and effective propositions. The overall effect of committing resources to specific relationships is the creation of mutual dependence as each side becomes involved with the other in a unique way.

Clearly, *people bonds* are important as well. The relationship may fail if there is a real personality clash between key people and good 'chemistry' certainly makes doing business together easier. A change of key account manager or buyer is often cited as the reason for relationship breakdown, although this suggests that the relationship is rather fragile anyway. It is more likely to happen when selling companies have not penetrated the account at a sufficiently high level and they should therefore nurture bonds with people at both strategic and operational levels.

The crucial component of close relationships is trust, as discussed later in this chapter and in Chapter 4. Without trust, the development of relationships is capped at a level which does not yield much benefit to either side. While the organizations might be seen as responsible for the activity and resources dedicated to the relationship, the responsibility for building and maintaining a reputation of integrity and trustworthiness is likely to rest with the individuals most closely concerned. Perception of trustworthiness, which is all-important to the buying side in particular, therefore resides within the people bonds layer of relationship involvement.

> Key relationships are based on real substance rather than predilection. They are built on a web of interactions between people, interlinked processes, promotional programmes, joint projects, committed costs, shared facilities and other factors. In other words, the relationship consists of the actions and commitments which underpin the business the two companies do together, not just how they feel about each other.

Time does not appear to play the role commonly expected of it. Although it might be assumed that relationships grow closer and better with time, research has shown that older relationships are not automatically the most satisfactory (McDonald and Woodburn, 1999). On average, they appear to be considered no more or less successful than younger relationships.

There are many potential reasons why time does not guarantee greater intimacy and a higher level of regard for the benefits of a relationship. For instance, it may be inappropriate to seek further relationship development (see Chapter 6), although quite often one of the parties is unable to recognize this situation and to accept the intrinsic limitations of the business. Some relationships just cease to develop and become stuck in a rut of suboptimal benefit to either or both parties. Where the customer is disappointed, it may be that familiarity has led to a sense of being taken for granted or an impression of being less exciting to the supplier than other, newer business. If the selling company is disenchanted, it may be because, over the years, the customer has accumulated punitive prices and a huge raft of services which eat into the supplier's profit margin. The supplier may realize that the customer generates very little profit for the amount of investment and risk undertaken or that the account is actually loss making.

> *The supplier may realize that the customer generates very little profit for the amount of investment and risk undertaken or that the account is actually loss making.*

Relationship development does not necessarily always proceed in the same direction or at an even pace. Buyer–seller relationships can take a variety of routes and development to greater intimacy is only one of them. Relationships may remain at a given level which suits either or both parties indefinitely or they may regress or even self-destruct. Companies tend to assume that closer, more sophisticated relationships are automatically better than simple ones. The reality is that they may be better or they may be worse, particularly in terms of profitability. Concern should not focus on the age, momentum or sophistication of key relationships, but on their appropriateness at any given time.

We can illustrate this point using relationships in our personal lives. We know a lot of people as passing acquaintances and for them the relationship does not extend much beyond a nod and a greeting. At the other end of the scale are our close family and friends with whom the relationship is warm and intimate. If we reversed our behaviour with these two groups, they would see us as quite mad. From our point of view, we would not want to have the same type of intense relationship, the kind we have with our best friends, with everyone we meet. Not only would it be inappropriate, but we would not have the emotional strength to do it.

> *Organizations have a limited capacity for intimacy.*

In the same way, organizations have a limited capacity for intimacy. They do not have the resources to maintain all of their key account relationships at the most intimate and engaged level, even if their customers wanted it. Like people, organizations will have a spread of relationships and they can decide which they want to intensify, maintain or cool off. Organizational relationship decisions, in contrast to personal relationship decisions, should be guided by strategic considerations about the business potential to be gained for an investment of time, people and resources.

The hierarchy of key relationships

Several groups of researchers have demonstrated that the focus of relationships of the lowest order is on transactions between companies (Scott and Westbrook, 1991; Dunn and Thomas, 1994; Millman and Wilson, 1996), that is to say, a fairly straightforward, operational approach to delivering the goods or services desired, with communication designed to do little more than facilitate those processes. Different stages of relationship development exhibit different degrees of collaboration. Where the focus shifts towards a highly collaborative approach to the relationship, the companies will concentrate on combining their strengths in order to develop new, joint business initiatives which challenge existing boundaries, and the buyer–seller divide may disappear altogether.

Two major milestones in relationship development can be identified:

1 A significant level of *trust*, where both companies are generally prepared to believe that the other company will not indulge in opportunism and take advantage of a privileged position or sensitive information (Morgan and Hunt, 1994) (see Chapter 4).
2 A recognition of *mutual dependency*, which equates to an acknowledgement that a commitment exists and that, in some way, the parties are linked together, though not indissolubly.

Figure 3.2 portrays the hierarchy of key relationships as a pyramid with the most detached, arms-length type of relationship being located at the base and the closest, most intimate type of relationship positioned at the apex.

Portrayal of the relationship stages as a pyramid is reminiscent of Maslow's (1943) hierarchy of human needs. Stated very simply, Maslow suggested that the needs of an individual could be positioned in a hierarchy according to the order in which they must be satisfied. At the lowest level, the individual has 'physiological' requirements, such as food, water and warmth and unless these are adequately fulfilled, the individual will not respond to other needs which are less imperative.

At a slightly higher level, people have a need for safety and freedom from threat. If they are preoccupied with protecting themselves, then they are unlikely to be motivated by more esoteric issues, such as self-image for example. At a yet higher level, people have a need for relationships which give them love and esteem from their fellows and, if this requirement is satisfied, they can proceed to develop themselves to their fullest and most creative potential. In other words, the motivation of individuals towards achievement at the higher levels of their capabilities requires underpinning by the satisfaction of certain types of more basic need.

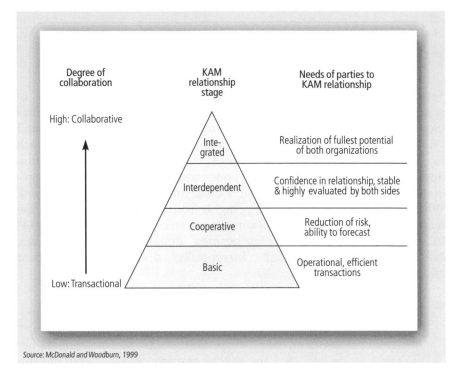

Figure 3.2
Hierarchy of key relationships

Source: McDonald and Woodburn, 1999

The development of key account relationships can usefully be viewed as a parallel to Maslow's approach. At the lowest level, compared with the individual's 'physiological' needs, the relationship requires as a minimum the fulfilment of the basics of sustainable trading, that is the efficient handling of transactions (orders, deliveries, payments and so on). This is appropriately termed the *basic* relationship stage. A supplier who cannot manage transactions adequately will have little success in introducing new products and services and in developing the business further.

At the next stage, which is equivalent to Maslow's need for safety, the relationship has reached a point where the parties are not in constant fear of losing the relationship. The parties are cooperative rather than suspicious of or threatening towards each other and, thus, this is called the *cooperative* stage. As the companies get to know each other better, they can begin to understand each other's *modus operandi* and, at the least, can predict the short-term future. It becomes possible to discuss forecasts of demand.

The *interdependent* stage equates to Maslow's need for love and esteem. The companies recognize that they have an ongoing relationship and this is reflected in their confidence and high regard for each other. Since neither company anticipates or considers termination of the relationship, both can adopt long-term business behaviour.

At the highest or *integrated* level, the relationship becomes a single entity without internal barriers. The companies trust each other and do not maintain protective measures against opportunism. The relationship can now be at its most creative, using the potential of both partners to develop mould-breaking strategies.

This representation of key account relationships as a pyramid suggests that, as the relationship develops to a higher level, it still depends on the sustained satisfaction of the needs at the lower levels and does not leave those elements behind. Indeed, this seems to be the case from our discussions with companies. For example, a buying company, however closely involved with its supplier at a strategic level, still expects that transactions will be carried out efficiently.

Relationships do not always start at the bottom of the pyramid and work their way up. Some will begin at a higher level, although it is hard to imagine companies entering an *integrated* relationship without prior experience of each other. A fairly sophisticated relationship may be required from the outset if the product/service is very complex or customized or particularly important to the buying company. Such relationships may well spend longer at the pre-trading or *exploratory* stage.

The number of relationships at each stage decreases as the level of collaboration increases, even among the elite group of customers already selected by companies as 'key' accounts. Notably, *integrated* relationships are relatively rare. Logically, there is a limit to the number of close relationships which any company can sustain. Such relationships require the adaptation of standard offers and services, and the investment of time, money and people, particularly people with sufficient seniority. The supply of all of these is constrained.

Key relationship stages

The development of key relationships is a continuum more than a series of step changes. However, the scope of relationships can be described in terms of characteristic stages which are significantly different from each other (McDonald, Millman and Rogers, 1996) and progress can be charted against these stages. Let us consider each stage in turn, starting with the earliest stage of relationship development.

Exploratory key account management

The *exploratory* stage actually precedes recognized key account management (KAM): it could be described as a 'scanning and attraction' stage. Like bats in the mating season, both buyer and seller are sending out signals and exchanging messages prior to the decision to get together.

● Definition: *Exploratory* relationships are at a 'scanning and attraction' stage.

It is very important to make a distinction between the handling of any new lead or business prospect and those where the potential importance of the relationship will qualify the buying company as a key account if business is secured. Failure to recognize and segregate the two will result in too much resource being thrown at poor prospects and too little at the really big opportunities.

A mediocre, standardized, arms-length approach will not win a potential key account. On the other hand, as major openings are few and infrequent, giving promising prospects the right treatment from the start is essential. *Exploratory* KAM should be reserved for customers selected as key by the methods described in Chapter 5. Needless to say, as existing key accounts can be lost as well as new ones won, the recruitment of replacements is critical.

The *exploratory* KAM relationship is represented diagrammatically in Figure 3.3. The key account manager and the purchasing manager must be able to interact on a regular basis, possibly over a long period of time, in order to bring the two organizations closer together. Both individuals will want to keep the process highly focused and to limit the amount of interaction with others in their organizations until a decision to work together has been reached. Typically, all communication will go through these two people so that they can monitor and control the content of each exchange.

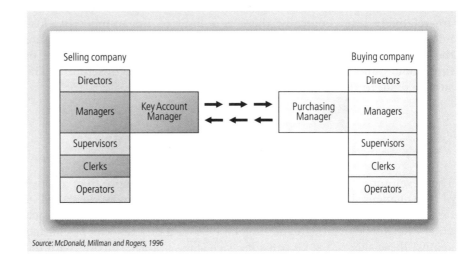

Figure 3.3
Exploratory KAM relationship

Source: McDonald, Millman and Rogers, 1996

At this initial stage of the relationship, the selling company will be courting the buying company and obtaining a general feel for the organization and exploring its particular needs and aspirations. The supplier needs to determine the requirements it will be expected to fulfil and the size and scope of the opportunity. At this stage, commercial issues such as product quality and organizational capability are more important than establishing social bonds. Selling skills are paramount. It will also be important for the key account manager to gain an understanding of how the decision on supplier selection will be made, who will influence the decision and in what way, their *modus operandi* and their personalities.

At the same time, the buying company with an unfulfilled need will be exploring the supplier's offer, capabilities and credentials and quite possibly doing so with more than one supplier simultaneously. It is unlikely that either party will disclose truly confidential information at this stage, for trust is a slow-growing and fragile seedling which must be cultivated with care.

Most commonly, both parties are interested in reducing costs. The supplier's strategy is to look for customers who have a high standing in their respective markets, indicating a likelihood of high-volume sales over a lengthy period. Uncertainty will be diminished and the supplier can look forward to covering fixed costs or better. Prospecting costs are reduced and, with experience of the business, savings in efficiency may be expected. For its part, the buying company will be looking to safeguard its supplies in terms of availability, quantity and quality and to secure efficiency savings from stability of supply. Both parties instinctively recognize that any form of lasting commitment will be superior to ad hoc, tentative arrangements.

In addition to cost minimization, companies which are seeking to enable implementation of a particular strategy often look for relevant and complementary expertise in their opposite numbers. For example, if the supplier's aim is to enter a new market segment, then it may target a well-regarded participant in the sector or, failing that, one which operates in a sector with similar issues in order to tap into their knowledge of tackling those issues. The supplier is attracted by the opportunity of learning from leading-edge customers. Trading with a prestigious partner also gives an incoming supplier good credentials, which often draws more customers from the same segment. Similarly, for buying companies, working with a strong supplier offers parallel spin-offs: sharing the supplier's knowledge, competence and reputation.

After Intel established itself as a strong consumer brand, several manufacturers promoted their products using the slogan 'Intel inside'.

Insight

The key account manager and the purchasing manager have to manage a difficult balancing act between investing enough to secure the business and using up too many resources speculatively. At this investigative stage, the major share of investment comes from the selling company as the buyer asks for inspection visits, evidence of organizational capability, samples made to their specifications, costings and other information which may not be readily available. All too often, the key account manager's requests for assistance in complying with these demands are seen by colleagues as an irritation and a secondary priority. Rather than being aligned supportively behind the key account manager, colleagues are busy pursuing other objectives, as Figure 3.3 implies. The ideal would be a situation approaching that shown for *basic* KAM relationships in Figure 3.4, where the two companies are separated but aligned directly behind their representatives, but this seems to be rare.

> At this investigative stage, the major share of investment comes from the selling company.

Insight

In one case, production-quality samples promised to the prospective customer were late: more than one deadline was missed and, when the delivery eventually arrived, the supporting data was absent. The supplier's production manager saw his priority as hitting targets for a high-volume output and low reject rate. He saw no good reason to compromise his targets by developing samples for people who were not even customers yet. The prospective customer was sceptical about promises that real orders would be treated differently and went elsewhere.

At the *exploratory* stage, the companies have very little history of interaction or experience of each other. Both will make judgements objectively based on the information they are given and, more subjectively, on signals generated directly by the other company and on any indirect feedback about the other's reputation. Reputations and signals are examined very carefully and the impact of any event, communication or rumour is magnified, sometimes disproportionately so.

On both sides, managing the signals transmitted and their implications needs to be a deliberate, conscious process and one supported by the whole of the organization. If the key account manager claims that his or her organization is flexible and responsive, then the purchasing manager will look for signs to support the truth of that assertion. Naturally, the claim will be discounted if, instead of the tailored version promised, a standard service specification arrives with a few suggestions as to how it can and cannot be changed to meet the specification. For example, if a buyer hints at huge volumes of purchases and then lays off significant numbers of workers, the selling company will draw its own conclusions.

The ability of the key account manager to influence his or her own company to change its behaviour towards a genuine customer focus is one of the greatest organizational problems encountered. In order to overcome lack of cooperation from other managers, the key account manager must have high-level status and/or top-level backing. The implications of KAM must be made blatantly clear throughout the supplying organization as the stakes are too high to risk unnecessary gaffes and avoidable mishaps.

> On both sides, managing the signals transmitted and their implications needs to be a deliberate, conscious process and one supported by the whole of the organization.

> The ability of the key account manager to influence his or her own company to change its behaviour towards a genuine customer focus is one of the greatest organizational problems encountered.

Characteristics of *exploratory* key account management

- Pre-trading.
- Customer must potentially qualify as a key account.
- Both sides are exploring.
- Signalling is important.
- Reputation is critical.
- Seller needs to be patient and prepared to invest.

Basic key account management

The *basic* KAM stage implies a relationship with a pronounced transactional emphasis. If it is a new relationship, then it may be effectively a trial time during which the selling company has to prove its ability to deliver its offer in an efficient manner. Buyers will obviously prefer to develop business with suppliers who have demonstrated that they can live up to minimum operational requirements (however, trial experience of each other may not always be possible, as in the case of major one-off contracts). The buying company may also use other suppliers of the same product/service in order to continue market testing on price and checking for value for money.

The key account manager's focus shifts to identifying opportunities for account penetration while continuing to monitor the efficient delivery of the business already won. In order to decide how the account should be developed and what objectives it should have, a greater understanding of the customer and the markets in which it competes will need to be gained.

Broadly speaking, two types of *basic* KAM situations exist (excluding exit situations): those which are targeted at relationship development and those where continuation at the transactional level of the relationship is appropriate (see Chapter 6). Even if the relationship is successful at this level, it may not be possible or advisable to develop it further, for a number of good reasons:

- The length of life of the relationship may be limited by changes pending in the environment in terms of legislation, technology, market, company ownership and so on.
- The buying company may be low-price focused and unresponsive to added value.
- The buying company may be known for supplier-switching behaviour.
- In summary, the overall lifetime value of the relationship is not expected to repay the investment in terms of time, resources, customization and so forth.

Figure 3.4 shows the subtle organizational change which has occurred in reaching the *basic* KAM stage. The key account manager and purchasing manager are now in contact and their organizations are aligned behind them. However, this will generally be a standard arrangement which both companies normally adopt and nothing unusual has been arranged. The key account manager and the purchasing manager still expect all communication and exchanges to be channelled exclusively through them, so as yet no one else on either side has developed a relationship with their opposite number.

Channelling interaction through a single point of contact is, at the least, likely to be efficient. The responsibilities are normally clear and communication and control simple. Overhead costs should be contained because the constriction of interaction between the two companies

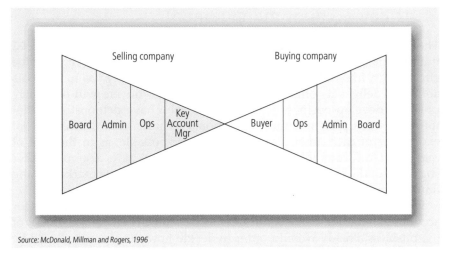

Figure 3.4
Basic KAM
relationship

Source: McDonald, Millman and Rogers, 1996

naturally limits the amount of management time that each party can take up.

Because this arrangement is potentially efficient (though not necessarily the most effective approach), a *basic* type of relationship is indicated for large accounts which are aggressive price fighters without any interest in added value. Some companies adopt this stance in all their purchases while others, who do not take this approach for their core inputs, will still do so if the product is not critical to them.

> However important the customer may be to the supplier, a genuinely closer relationship will not develop with a customer who is not prepared to reciprocate.

In such circumstances, there is a ceiling to the level of relationship which can be attained and any attempts to take it beyond this point are doomed to fail (see Chapter 4). Suppliers are wise to recognize this fact and avoid the fruitless investment of time, money and 'free gifts' in terms of extra services. The customer may happily accept an enhanced offer, but remain uncommitted, buying on price as usual.

However, a *basic* relationship has limitations. It may deliver goods and services, but it is not robust, nor is it likely to create new opportunities in the marketplace or find major cost savings through process re-engineering. The supplier should develop the relationship further provided that the customer meets the criteria for targeting, including a propensity to reciprocate. The key account manager's job then changes from having an operational focus to having a relationship development focus. If suppliers are to progress key customer relationships successfully, then they must make sure their key account managers are fully empowered with sufficient authority, appropriate resources and adequate corporate support in order to get things done.

At this stage, neither party feels particularly committed to the relationship. The perception is that the barriers to exit are low, particularly on the buyer's side, and the key account manager is well aware of this. The business is based on a stripped-down, simple exchange of money for goods and services which is not surrounded by extra systems and services valued by the customer, which it would be awkward and inconvenient to surrender. After all, the buyer is probably simultaneously sourcing from a competitor, so switching is not a big problem. Price is a (if not the) major driver of the business at the *basic* stage, featuring heavily in discussions, negotiations and measurements of success.

Customers are well aware of another important driver: the key account manager's remuneration plan. Managing directors and sales directors of selling companies and their sales forces are accustomed to having a significant proportion of earnings based on short-term sales targets and are reluctant to give up this type of reward structure. However, short-term targets shape short-term behaviour. Key account managers who are paid on immediate results are unlikely to invest much of their time in building longer term relationships if they do not receive any immediate benefit or do not expect to stay in their post long enough to gain from it.

> Short-term targets shape short-term behaviour.

There is not a great deal of information shared in a *basic* relationship, partly because the emphasis on transactions limits the number of topics the two companies talk about and partly because a foundation of trust between the two companies has not been established. The level of exchanges is likely to be low generally, in terms of both quantity and quality. In some cases, however, the volume of communication on operational subjects may be misleadingly high, obscuring the fact that discussion on more important issues is not happening. If neither side is sufficiently well-informed to be more proactive, then both parties will behave reactively, simply responding to situations as and when they arise.

> A high volume of communication can exist at an operational level, obscuring the fact that discussion on more important issues is not happening.

The danger of missing valuable opportunities is outweighed by the ever-present danger of losing the account. In a *basic* relationship the most immediate problem is the vulnerability created by having only a single point of contact which may be opened up easily by the competition. It is a fairly superficial business relationship, devoid of any deeper commitment which might persuade a buyer to be tolerant of a mistake or to warn of impending threats. Even if there were some kind of personal chemistry between the key account manager and the purchasing manager, should either person leave his or her job, that bonding will be lost and their successor might not be able or willing to continue the relationship. Indeed, turnover of these key staff is often cited as the reason for relationship breakdown.

> Accepting the fact that, in some circumstances, a *basic* relationship is most appropriate, there is little chance of growing the business (and a significant chance of losing it) unless the selling company mounts a strategically directed and concentrated campaign to improve the relationship.

Characteristics of *basic* key account management

- Transactional/operational: emphasis on efficiency.
- Can be stable state or trial stage.
- If stable state, often low common interest: not core.
- Buyer is probably multisourcing.
- Easy to exit.
- Driven by price and success measured by price.
- Very little information sharing.
- Single point of contact.
- Reactive rather than proactive.
- Business relationship only.
- Reward structure of key account managers paramount.
- Standard organization, which suits selling company.
- Small chance of growing business.

Cooperative key account management

Definition:
A *cooperative* relationship is positive on both sides. It is less defensive and more open than a *basic* relationship, but the supplier is not really trusted.

A stage beyond the *basic* relationship, the *cooperative* relationship has a positive feel and is less defensive and more open. Nevertheless, the supplier is not really trusted by the customer and so some reserve remains; doors are opened, but not flung wide. More useful information is made available, but this does not include sensitive material.

A *cooperative* relationship may be reached through a period at the *basic* level where the buying company has satisfied itself about the selling company's competence and attitude through direct experience. If performance is acceptable, the selling company may then be allowed to work more closely with the buying company and develop the relationship. If the customer uses a list of preferred suppliers, the selling company will be on it, but the buyer may still not be prepared to put all of its eggs in one basket.

A supplier of chemicals to a food company was considered a preferred supplier; indeed the buying decision maker was very enthusiastic about the supplier's competence and 'likeability'. When asked why he did not single source from them, the buyer said that he believed competition was good for industry and that occasional purchases from an alternative supplier kept his preferred supplier 'on its toes'.

However, for some kinds of purchases, such as large infrastructure projects or capital equipment, this kind of 'getting to know each other' through trial and progression does not work, and the relationship may pass directly from *exploratory* to *cooperative* or even to the *interdependent* level. Even in the absence of actual trading, the discussions and joint development work involved in a prolonged *exploratory* stage may give both companies a reasonable degree of confidence in their ability to deliver their commitments.

The *cooperative* relationship has evolved to something akin to a network, albeit a fairly loose one, as shown in Figure 3.5. Intercompany contact involves a wider range of people and a wider range of interaction than before. Although the relationship begins to draw in more people and harness more resources, it is not a highly organized state so there are many things that can go badly wrong.

> *Cooperative* KAM can be a difficult stage, having lost the efficiency and control of *basic* KAM, but not having gained the benefits of openness and joint activity of *interdependent* KAM.

The key account manager and the purchasing manager now work more closely together. In fact, the people in the front line of transaction handling, that is to say, order processing and customer services, are

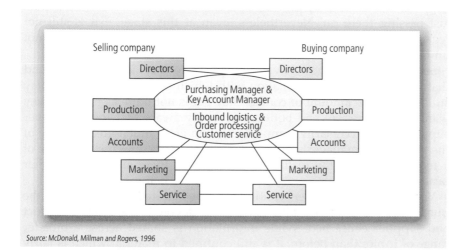

Source: McDonald, Millman and Rogers, 1996

Figure 3.5
Cooperative KAM relationship

generally in much more frequent contact with their counterparts than is the key account manager with the purchasing manager. Although they may not have met face to face, staff from the two companies become familiar with each other through regular dialogue, sharing ongoing jokes by phone and e-mail, and helping each other out in small ways.

As Figure 3.5 shows, other multifunction links have been established as well, though they may not be regular or frequent. The growing web of involvement means that the relationship is better protected against the departure of the key account manager or the purchasing manager. More people have an understanding and appreciation of the business than in *basic* KAM so continuity is more likely. However, the major thread of the relationship still runs between the original two key players.

A social context begins to appear, often fostered by the selling company through organized events such as golf days and trips to sports fixtures or through smaller events such as dinner parties. In the beginning, some of the most valuable gatherings are the more casual lunches or after-work get-togethers where people get to know each other in a more relaxed setting, having set work aside for a short period. This network arrangement brings new strength to the relationship. The participants become driven by a desire not to let personal contacts down, which is a far more effective motivation than formal statements of intent or customer charters.

The underlying shape of the organization does not change. The customer is still handled within the existing structure and no significant organizational adaptations are normally made. However, other adaptations do begin to appear at this stage, such as the tailoring of goods and services, the addition of extra non-core services, the customized provision of information and the adjustment of logistics to suit customer requirements.

In a *cooperative* relationship, opportunities to add value for the customer are suggested by the supplier and the buyer adopts a positive and communicative attitude towards the supplier. The buyer may identify further opportunities of doing business together or help the supplier in solving operational problems which arise, rather than just passing them on. Nevertheless, even at this stage, exit is still not regarded as particularly difficult: inconvenient possibly, but certainly not unthinkable.

Selling companies now have more access to their key customers and that gives them more information with which to work. Either side may still feel that the amount of contact they get is not quite as much as they want (see Figure 3.6) and both are probably aware that there are other suppliers (not necessarily competitors) who get a much greater share of the purchasing manager's time. Like a climber reaching the first peak of a mountain range, the realization dawns that there are further, higher peaks to climb which were simply not visible before.

Visits to the customer continue to be limited by the time the purchasing manager is willing and able to devote to the type of product and supplier concerned. While information is shared across a broader range of topics than before, it is still confined to material which is fairly

---

The growing web of involvement means that the relationship is better protected against the departure of the key account manager or the purchasing manager.

Exit is still not regarded as particularly difficult: inconvenient possibly, but certainly not unthinkable.

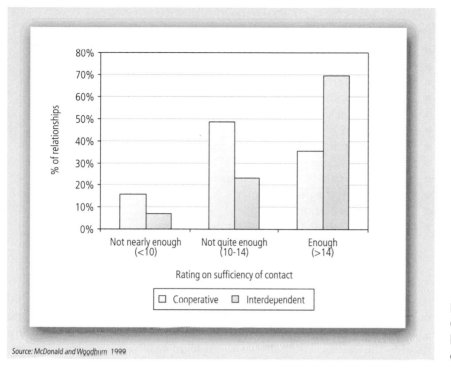

Source: McDonald and Woodburn 1999

Figure 3.6
Contact between buying and selling companies

readily available. The supplier is not sufficiently trusted for the buyer to volunteer highly confidential information and the key account manager remains somewhat 'out in the cold' and 'kept in the dark'. Joint strategic planning is not really possible and does not develop much beyond simple forecasts of price and volume. However, even forecasting constitutes useful progress compared with *basic* KAM, which may not offer demand visibility, never mind demand security.

The business is still very vulnerable to competitors. The selling company has not achieved sole supplier status and the buyer continues to scan the competitive landscape actively to make sure it is getting best value for money. Furthermore, another supplier with the inside track in an adjacent area of business might, for example, gain advance information on new customer sites or new strategic directions which is denied to a selling company at only a *cooperative* stage of relationship development. A competing supplier who has inside knowledge can work out an interesting and innovative proposition long before the latter obtains the same information.

It is often at this stage that the real potential to progress the relationship is grasped, or not grasped, by the supplying company. It is still an uphill task to break out of the cycle of limited information and limited capability to make better and more exciting offers to the customer.

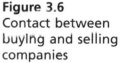

The key account manager remains somewhat 'out in the cold' and 'kept in the dark'.

It is still an uphill task to break out of the cycle of limited information and limited capability to make better and more exciting offers to the customer.

Characteristics of *cooperative* key account management

- Not necessarily preceded by a *basic* relationship.
- Based on the assumption or experience of performance.
- May be preferred supplier.
- Relationship still mainly with buyer.
- Multifunction contacts.
- Organization mainly standard.
- Selling company adds value to the relationship.
- Exit not particularly difficult.
- Not wholly trusted by the customer.
- Limited visits to the customer.
- Limited information sharing.
- Forecasting rather than joint strategic planning.

Interdependent key account management

Definition:
At the *interdependent* stage, both buyer and seller acknowledge the importance of each to the other.

At the *interdependent* stage, both buyer and seller acknowledge the importance of each to the other. The selling company has become the sole or at least first-option supplier and the buying company now regards the selling company as a strategic external resource. The two will be actively sharing sensitive information and engaging in joint problem solving.

The companies are locked in to each other, though not inextricably. If the relationship were to end, retreat would be difficult and inconvenient. They may have set up various initiatives together, such as common working practices, shared product specifications and joint marketing activity, which would take considerable time and effort to unravel. So, while strategic suitability holds the partners together, inertia probably plays a part as well.

Such is the level of maturity and understanding of both parties that each will allow the other to profit from the relationship. Consequently, pricing will be long-term and stable, perhaps even fixed or varied to a formula, which allows both sides to plan and removes the need for constant haggling/negotiating.

Insight

A major company won a ten-year contract to provide services to a large organization and they set up a unit together to deliver the contract. However, the key players in the relationship struggled to deliver the spirit of the contract because a traditional focus on enforcement to the letter of the contract persisted, making it difficult to provide the best solution for the customer.

There is also a tacit understanding that experience and skills will be shared. The expertise of either or both companies may be directed towards product improvement, quality control procedures or administrative systems which underpin commercial transactions. A current focus will be the deployment of new electronic commerce systems in order to streamline processes.

The organizations will collaborate across a range of functions. Interactions will be orchestrated by – rather than administered by or channelled through – the key account manager and the purchasing manager, whose roles are now to oversee the interfaces and ensure that nothing occurs which will discredit the partnership. Figure 3.7 shows how the two companies have become closely aligned, with direct function-to-function communication at all levels.

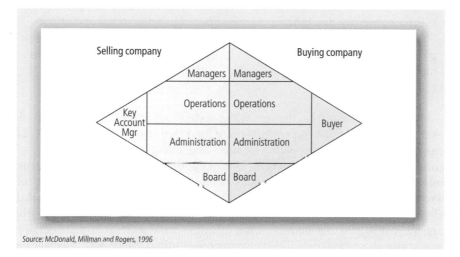

Source: McDonald, Millman and Rogers, 1996

Figure 3.7
Interdependent
KAM relationship

A fixed period agreement may exist, extending from two or three years up to ten years in certain sectors, though not necessarily. Some companies may choose instead to work together on an ongoing basis. However, it is important that each party understands the scope of the agreement, be it formal or informal. Suppliers could be disappointed to discover that they are barred from access to interesting business extensions within the buying company. Similarly, buying companies may expect the selling company to service areas of unprofitable business as well as core, profit-making areas. Setting the expectations of both sides clearly and realistically at the outset is key to the building of successful relationships.

> Buying companies may expect the selling company to service areas of unprofitable business as well as core, profit-making areas.

A different attitude towards the relationship now exists. Senior managers have more confidence in the relationship's sustainability and value. They should look more favourably on requests for investment into the development of the business and are prepared to wait longer for the payback. Normally, financial managers demand a quick return on investment into customer accounts because they are less comfortable about investing in a situation where they have little control over the use of funds, compared with investing in their own people, plant or equipment. (Key account managers need to understand this reluctance and to formulate proposals which address issues of concern to the finance constituency. Unfortunately, many key account managers lack these skills.)

Insight

One company reckoned it took a year to assemble and agree a proposal for investment with a customer. It took another year to deploy the money, making it at least two years before any return would appear. In the initial stages of the KAM programme, it had been hard work gaining approval for investment but, after several successful projects, the company accepted such proposals more readily.

> The volume, quality and scope of information exchange increases considerably in an *interdependent* relationship as more people in the selling company are talking to more people in the buying company. Strategic and sensitive material will be added to the information previously shared, which would have been more transactional and tactical in a *cooperative* relationship and just transactional in a *basic* relationship.

Figure 3.8 illustrates the growing extent to which information is exchanged at the *interdependent* stage of relationship development as compared with the *cooperative* stage. The effect of this new level of communication and interaction is a key driver at this stage of the relationship. The two companies develop a better understanding of each other in a business and organizational sense and individuals build closer social relationships with people in the other company. As people are intrinsically social beings, some affinities may start to appear earlier, but while trust between the companies is limited there will always be

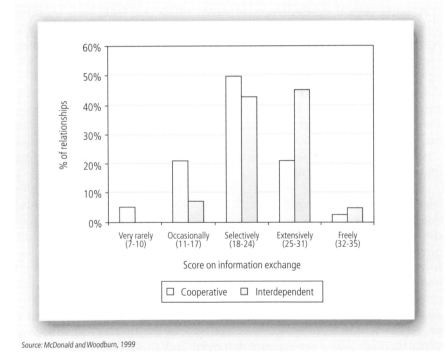

Figure 3.8
Extent of information exchange between buying and selling companies

Source: McDonald and Woodburn, 1999

the need to maintain some distance. When a foundation of inter-organizational trust has been established, individuals can be more comfortable about actually developing friendships with their opposite numbers.

The whole web of interaction and communication draws the two companies even closer together, like a positive gravitational pull. The two companies are reaching further into each other's internal environments and touching more points in the value chain, as depicted in Figure 3.9. Team members from both companies often work together to lobby or gain senior management approval for a project. A selling company in an *interdependent* relationship is 'inside the magic circle', in contrast to the 'out in the cold' position those in *cooperative* relationships have to accept.

> The whole web of interaction and communication draws the two companies even closer together, like a positive gravitational pull.

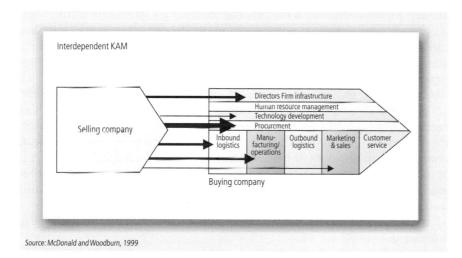

Source: McDonald and Woodburn, 1999

Figure 3.9
Reach and weight of contact in *interdependent* relationships mapped on Porter's (1985) value chain

As a result of this activity mutual trust begins to develop, provided of course that each company has proved itself trustworthy. The key account manager and the purchasing manager must watch out for any opportunistic behaviour on the part of anyone in their own companies which might breach that trust.

> It is critical that all those involved with the relationship in any respect are aware of the way in which the particular customer should be treated in order to ensure that any action or decision will build and not undermine the position of trust achieved. Care must be taken to avoid acting inappropriately inadvertently as well as deliberately.

For example, if the selling company gains a raw material cost reduction, the production manager or product manager may decide to maintain prices to improve the profitability of the line, at least until the competition appears to be reducing their prices. That may be fine for the bulk of customers, but if key customers in an *interdependent* relationship are not informed of the cost reduction, they would see exclusion from sharing in the cost savings as opportunism on the part of the selling company, and react adversely.

It is at this stage that what is arguably the most important benefit of excellent relationships with key accounts emerges: the opportunity for mutual cost reductions. Costs may arise from all kinds of activities which would be unnecessary if companies genuinely trusted each other to stick closely to agreements. For example, counting deliveries, quality checking goods on arrival, keeping buffer stocks, monitoring prices, dual sourcing, covering bad debts, waiting for purchase orders, over trading and many others are all delaying, time-consuming, cost-adding activities.

At previous stages of relationship development the major opportunity for the selling company has been business development, but now, in addition, genuine cost savings also become available to both sides. In an *interdependent* relationship the companies are sufficiently well-informed and familiar with each other to be able work together closely together in order to achieve those savings. Hence, the emphasis on seriously nurturing a relationship which has reached the *interdependent* stage.

Companies in an *interdependent* relationship can focus on the medium- and long-term future, rather than just the present and short term and can adopt a more proactive than reactive approach to business development. Jointly conducted strategic planning begins to appear, though not in all cases. Where strategic planning is not collaborative, it is often due to the fact that the individual companies are still rather poor at strategic planning anyway, most often in pushing it out below board level. Lack of joint strategic planning is then more a characteristic of the individual companies than representative of the relationship itself.

Characteristics of *interdependent* key account management

- Both acknowledge importance to each other.
- Principal or sole supplier.
- Exit more difficult.
- High level of information exchange, some sensitive.
- Wider range of joint and innovative activity.
- Larger number of multifunctional contacts.
- Streamlined processes.
- Prepared to invest in relationship.
- High volume of dialogue.
- Better understanding of customer.
- Developing social relationships.
- Development of trust.
- Cost savings.
- Proactive rather than reactive.
- Joint strategic planning and focus on the future.
- Opportunity to grow business.

It is at this stage that what is arguably the most important benefit of excellent relationships with key accounts emerges: the opportunity for mutual cost reductions.

Companies in an interdependent relationship can focus on the medium- and long-term future rather than just the present and short term.

Integrated key account management

In a few cases, it may be possible for the buyer–seller relationship to advance beyond a separated, albeit interdependent, partnership. In an *integrated* relationship the two parties come together to operate as a single entity, while maintaining their separate identities, in order to create value over and above what either could achieve individually. External boundaries as well as internal boundaries now fall away as the two companies realize that together they can accomplish feats previously unimaginable to either.

Integrated KAM involves working together in cross-boundary functional or project teams, as depicted in Figure 3.10. By this means the organizations become so intertwined that individuals may feel more affinity with their focus team than with their official employer. The borders between buyer and seller have become blurred. The teams, rather than either organization, run the business, making decisions about their interactions with other teams according to the strategy they are implementing. Staff may even be based at the partner's premises, though not necessarily. If it came, exit would be traumatic at both personal and organizational levels.

● Definition:
In an *integrated* relationship the two parties come together to operate as a single entity, while maintaining their separate identities, in order to create value over and above what either could achieve individually.

The two companies realize that together they can accomplish feats previously unimaginable to either.

Hogg Robinson operates on-site travel offices for its key customers. This arrangement benefits the customers because they do not have to employ and train staff in competencies which are not central to their businesses, and they can cut their cost of transactions by paying one invoice at the end of the month. The arrangement is so convenient that staff use the Hogg Robinson office for all their business travel purchases.

Insight

The focus teams may be functional, issue based or project based or they may just serve a motivational purpose. They will meet regularly or have their own communications networks if meeting is difficult as in global relationships. Data systems will be integrated, information flow

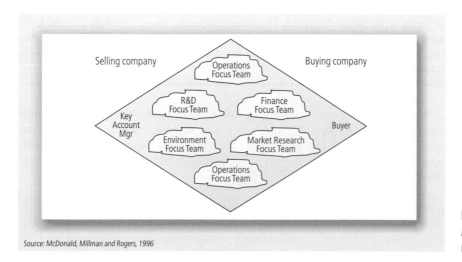

Source: McDonald, Millman and Rogers, 1996

Figure 3.10
Integrated KAM relationship

streamlined and barriers removed. A single business plan can now be produced, linking back into the planning processes of the two organizations.

The roles of the key account manager and the purchasing manager have fundamentally changed. The appearance of competent teams for handling day-to-day processes and developing specified projects enables these two people to assume a more strategic role, ensuring that the whole business is moving in a profitable and sustainable direction. Trouble-shooting should have become a very minor part of their activity.

> Each *integrated* relationship requires the dedication of considerable resources from both sides, and the number of customers with whom a company can have this kind of relationship must therefore be limited. In fact, the number of companies who have even one *integrated* relationship appears to be small.

It will be difficult in most cases to operate two such relationships in parallel within the same market area. In fast-moving consumer goods in particular, advertising agencies work closely with their major clients, often for a very long time, but they can only work with one such client in each sector. Top clients are unwilling to trust an agency which is working with a competitor, however much it claims to operate sealed cells inside its business.

More of the benefits which start to flow from an *interdependent* relationship can be realized now. There is greater confidence in the trustworthiness and commitment of both parties, which allows further disclosures such as transparent costing and openness on even the most sensitive subjects. The feeling shared by both companies that 'we are in this together' transcends normally defensive business behaviour.

Insight

Fashion is a fast-moving and fickle industry which lives or dies by its latest collection. In order to concentrate on designing and manufacturing new items, one manufacturer decided to focus its own people and resources on the supply side and to outsource the management of its warehouse and delivery logistics to another company. The two companies keep very few secrets from each other and the service is run on an open-book basis. The logistics manager, who is actually employed by the supplier, is treated as if he were head of one of the manufacturer's own departments.

Mutually transparent costing in this kind of relationship should not be mistaken for the approach used in some sectors, such as retail and car manufacturing, where powerful buyers have demanded open-book accounting from suppliers in a weak position, in return for continuing to do business at all.

> A liaison between unequals, in which certain aspects of a relationship are dictated by the more powerful partner, should not be confused with a genuinely open and collaborative relationship with a key account.

Since both parties work so closely together in an *integrated* relationship, any opportunistic behaviour would be spotted very quickly. In fact, as the relationship will have established itself within both companies and its value will be generally accepted, the chances of anyone taking inappropriate decisions should be much less than at a lower level of relationship development.

> Overall, it is through an *integrated* relationship that companies have the best chance of maximizing opportunities for cutting costs, developing a broader business base, enhancing their expertise, making creative and innovative approaches to the market and securing their long-term future. As relationships at the *integrated* stage cannot be numerous, they should be particularly well-chosen and well-managed.

Characteristics of *integrated* key account management

- Real partnership: complementary and mutually dependent.
- Dedicated, cross-boundary, functional/project teams.
- Individual organizations subsidiary to team socially.
- High exit barriers and exit is traumatic.
- Few in number.
- Open information sharing on sensitive subjects.
- Sole supplier, possibly handling secondary suppliers.
- Transparent costing systems.
- Assumption of mutual trustworthiness at all levels.
- Abstention from opportunistic behaviour.
- Lowered protection against opportunism.
- Joint long-term strategic planning.
- Better profits for both.

Disintegrating key account management

At any time and at any stage of development, the relationship can fall apart. Breakdown may occur for one or more of a number reasons, including a takeover of either company, a change of key people, the switch to a new supplier offering better products, performance or price or the introduction of new technology.

Disintegration can be sudden and exit complete, or it may be prolonged through a return to a lower level of relationship where the companies continue to do business together, but on different terms. In any case, *disintegrating* KAM is not a stable state, as any of the other stages can be. It is a purely transitional stage where the relationship prepares to settle down into another stage or disintegrate completely. Given the complexity of some relationships and the variety of links involved, disengagement may take some time, so *disintegrating* KAM may last for quite a long while.

● Definition:
A *disintegrating* relationship is in a state of transition to another more detached stage or to terminal breakdown.

The business developer who was ideal at the growth stage is unlikely to be the right person to manage a *disintegrating* relationship.

The key account manager's role may change to one of damage limitation. The business developer who was ideal at the growth stage is unlikely to be the right person to manage a *disintegrating* relationship.

Characteristics and causes of *disintegrating* key account management

- Occurs at any level.
- Rarely caused by price problems.
- Often change in key personnel.
- Key account manager's approach or lack of skills.
- Failure to forge multilevel links.
- Breach of trust.
- Prolonged poor performance against agreed programme.
- Changing market positions.
- Changing culture, organization, ownership or role.
- Complacency.
- Financial disappointment.

Quick relationship check

Ideally, you will be able to recognize the relationships you have with each of your key customers from reading the foregoing descriptions of the typical stages of relationship development. However, as a preliminary check you might try the following test, particularly if you have many key accounts. (If you do have a large number of key accounts, you should be thinking of differentiating between them and focusing on the select few which are really going to move your business forward.)

Read each statement and decide to what extent it applies to the customer you have in mind. Put a score in the box as follows.

Rating	Score
Strongly agree	4
Agree	3
Disagree	2
Strongly disagree	1

Does this statement apply to your relationship with your key customer?	Score
If our relationship ended, both companies would find it difficult and complicated	
There is a real spirit of partnership and trust between our two companies	
Together we have produced long-term strategic plans for the development of our relationship and business together	
Any information at all relevant to our business together is passed straight on to our customer	
People at all levels in both organizations are in constant communication with each other	
We have realized substantial cost savings through working with this customer.	
Total score	

Score	Relationship stage
6–9	*Basic*
10–15	*Cooperative*
16–21	*Interdependent*
22–24	*Integrated*

Selling companies beware: there is a clear tendency for suppliers to be overoptimistic in their assessment of the relationship, probably by one relationship stage (McDonald and Woodburn, 1999): buyers do not rate relationships in quite such a positive light. A relationship cannot in reality have developed beyond the stage perceived by the least positive party (see Chapter 4). Therefore, if you are a selling company, you may be over-rating the stage you have reached.

Summary

Understanding the nature of key relationships and the behaviour of the companies involved in them is crucial to the profitable management of the business they represent. Without it, companies can easily attempt inappropriate strategies which are unlikely to succeed. Failure may be expensive, both in terms of actual expenditure and lost opportunity.

Five stages of key supplier–customer relationships have been identified. To characterize the nature of the relationship from the point of view of either party, they are described as *exploratory* (precedes actual trading), *basic, cooperative, interdependent* and *integrated*. Relationships may develop progressively through each stage in turn, or they may not. They can also start at a fairly mature stage in certain circumstances, for example where multisourcing is inappropriate, or they can remain at any given stage indefinitely.

Disintegration may occur at any stage for a large number of reasons. More distant, less-sophisticated relationships (*basic* and *cooperative*) are more vulnerable than closer relationships (*interdependent* and *integrated*) and, therefore, suppliers in particular are often keen to develop them further. However, companies have a limited capacity for intimacy, partly because of the potentially heavy costs associated with key relationships, and they should choose the partners with whom they wish to develop close ties very carefully.

Suppliers at a lower stage of relationship development have to work hard to overcome the self-perpetuating cycle of being kept 'in the dark' and 'out in the cold'. Recognition of their current relationship position should at least help them to identify what action to take in order to break the pattern.

Table 3.1 Summary of development stage characteristics

Relationship feature	Exploratory	Basic	Cooperative	Interdependent	Integrated
Relationship emphasis	Research, reputation	Transactional and price	Mainly transactional but positive	Mutual and developmental	Open and strategically-focused
Supplier status	One of several/many	May be one of several	Preferred	Principal or sole, possibly primary managing secondary suppliers	Sole, possibly primary
Ease of exit	Easy: not started trading	Easy	Not difficult, slight inconvenience	Difficult	High exit barriers, separation traumatic
Information sharing	Careful, as necessary	Very little, based around transactions	Limited	High volume, some sensitive	Open, even on sensitive subjects
Contact	Channelled through individual KAMgr	Channelled through KAMgr and Buyer	Close: KAMgr and Buyer, Logistics and Order Processing Occasional: others	Close: all functions as necessary	Intimate: focus groups and teams
Access to customer	Customer request only	Limited	More, but not quite enough	Much more, enough	Constant, both sides
Adaptation of organization and processes	Supplier proposes standard, buyer may accept or reject	Standard	Mainly standard	Streamlining of processes, some organizational adaptation	Joint processes, new organization
Relationship costs	May be small or large. Speculative investment	Limited	Increasing for selling company, few savings if any	Major running costs and investment, possibly offset by savings and increased business	As for *interdependent*: probably larger sums but easier to identify
Level of trust	Exploring reputation and 'signals'	Neither trusted nor mistrusted	Not wholly trusted	Real trust developing, protective barriers lowered	Trustworthiness assumed at all levels
Planning	Variable	Little or none, probably only short-term forecasts if any	Forecasting rather than planning	Joint strategic planning, though not all cases	Joint strategic, long-term planning
Relationship potential	Important, to qualify as key account	Limited	Could be good, but not easy to win from here	Very good	Very good/excellent in revenue and profits

References

Dunn, D.T. and Thomas, C.A. (1994). Partnering with customers. *J. Business Indust. Marketing*, 9(1), 34–40.

Gadde, L.-E. and Snehota, I. (1999). *Proceedings of the Ninth Biennial World Marketing Congress*. Sage Publications Inc., Thousand Oaks.

McDonald, M. and Woodburn, D. (1999). Key account management – building on supplier and customer perspectives. *Financial Times*, Prentice Hall.

McDonald, M., Millman, A. and Rogers, B. (1996). *Key Account Management – Learning from Supplier and Customer Perspectives*. Cranfield School of Management.

Maslow, A. H. (1943). A theory of human motivation. *Psychol. Rev.*, 50(4), 370–96.

Millman, A. and Wilson, K. (1996). Developing key account management competences. *J. Marketing Practice Appl. Marketing Sci.*, 2(2), 7–22.

Morgan, R. M. and Hunt, S. D. (1994). The commitment–trust theory of relationship marketing. *J. Marketing*, 58, 20–38.

Scott, C. and Westbrook, R. (1991). New strategic tools for supply chain management. *Int. J. Phys. Distribut. Logistics Manage.*, 21(1), 23–33.

Chapter 4
The buyer perspective

Introduction

Books on selling and account management, and suppliers as well, often make the mistake of assuming that the customer is bound to fall in with a well-developed, well-presented plan. This is, of course, quite untrue. Customers have their own agendas, their own strategies and their own priorities. If, and only if, the selling company's plans fit the customer's plan, are they likely to succeed.

It follows that understanding the customer is fundamental to the selling company in adopting the right strategy and making acceptable offers. Yet suppliers generally devote remarkably little time and effort to gaining this crucial knowledge about their customers. In order to understand the customer's perspective fully, this chapter considers the buyer's standpoint and looks at the world and the supplier through the buyer's eyes, rather than viewing the customer from the supplier's standpoint.

We will look at the circumstances which provide fertile ground for close, cooperative relationships and the circumstances which suggest that attempts at greater intimacy will fall on stony ground. However, even if intimacy is not an option, being very good at what you do still is.

The purchasing context

The companies in a modern supply chain are more closely connected together than ever before. The market environment of one becomes a factor in the market environment of the next. Pressures felt by one are passed on to the next. To understand its own business, each company needs to understand the business of the others to a far greater extent than it has in the past.

Within companies too, the aim is now cross-functional integration. Traditionally, buyers were quite remote from their own company's customer strategy and therefore operated to a different agenda. Suppliers responded to that agenda and sold on specification and price. Now that buyers are generally much more in tune with the concerns of their whole company, the key account manager can make more creative offers and business propositions to them. That kind of applied creativity can only come from a deeper and more extensive knowledge of the customer's business.

Even when a supplier is working with a deep understanding of the customer, this is still only one side of the equation: the receptiveness of the customer is also critical in achieving relationship success. Key account relationships do not genuinely exist at the higher levels discussed in Chapter 3 unless they are reciprocated. Selling companies are liable to delude themselves about the favourability of their position with the customer. In fact, close business relationships are constructed of two-way linkages wrought by frequent operational interactions, dedicated resources, shared assets, joint planning and other business-based bonds between buying and selling companies. Such linkages will not exist unless the buying company as well as the selling company chooses to participate actively in the relationship (McDonald and Woodburn, 1999).

There is a tendency for selling companies to view their relationships with buying companies in isolation as if buyers do not have relationships with other suppliers or with other kinds of organization. This is obviously not the case, and understanding the network of relationships within which the buying company operates can be very illuminating as a way of

> Applied creativity can only come from a deeper and more extensive knowledge of the customer's business.

> Such linkages will not exist unless the buying company as well as the selling company chooses to participate actively in the relationship (McDonald and Woodburn, 1999).

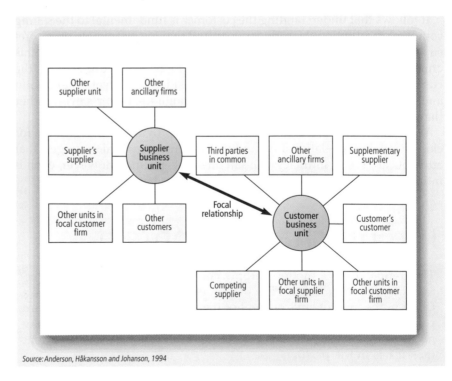

Figure 4.1
Business relationship network

Source: Anderson, Håkansson and Johanson, 1994

identifying what drives buyers to behave one way and not another. Figure 4.1 illustrates the different types of organization with which any company might have a relationship. As the buyer and the supplier and, indeed, every other body represented in Figure 4.1 will each belong to a similar network, the business reality is exceedingly complex.

For suppliers competing in increasingly challenging business environments, understanding the purchasing context can provide valuable insight into buyer behaviour. Knowing, for example, what are the buyer's resources, motivations, pressures and sources of information can provide a supplier with a lucrative competitive edge. An intelligent supplier realizes that the best route to the achievement of its own objectives is by helping customers to achieve their objectives. In summary, it is a simple three-step process:

1 Acquire an in-depth understanding of the customer environment and the customer drivers.
2 Discover or deduce the customer's objectives and strategic response in relation to suppliers.
3 Develop solutions to match the customer's strategy and needs.

Let us next examine the common customer drivers and the strategies customers adopt in relation to their suppliers. The actual processes by which companies deliver solutions are described later in Chapter 10.

Customer drivers

Often, the information held by a supplier about a buyer is either rudimentary and confined to contact details, purchase history with the company and sometimes wider purchasing activity, or it is more extensive but diffused around the company. However, the data does not attempt to identify the forces which are really driving the customer's business. These underlying influences are a combination of factors exclusive to the buying company, its business, its relationship network and its environment. Figure 4.2 shows some of the major forces which affect customers and, therefore, influence customer purchasing behaviour.

Arguably, the business world is changing faster now than it ever has before: certainly it is more interconnected across the globe than ever before. Companies of every kind are fighting to deal with new forces in order to manage this new *speed of change*. Managing and exploiting this escalating rate of change requires new creativity and competencies. Businesses need additional *flexibility* in order to respond in the time frames available and they are seeking resources and allies to help them. Speed is of the essence in maximizing opportunities. Nimble competitors catch up very quickly, so 'windows' of profit-making, competitive advantage are getting smaller all the time.

In the past, buying companies were reasonably confident about anticipating the future and were prepared to commit to assets which could be expected to provide a good return in the longer term.

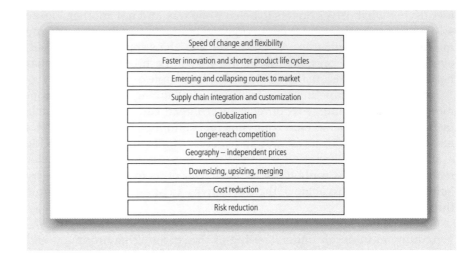

Figure 4.2
Customer drivers with supplier impact

Nowadays, buying companies are less confident of the shape of the future, and so they prefer to secure their needs through supplier partners, rather than through wholly owned assets.

Nowadays, buying companies are less confident of the shape of the future, and so they prefer to secure their needs through supplier partners, rather than through wholly owned assets. Buyers are willing to trade off some of the margin they might have made themselves in order to maintain their flexibility and speed of response.

One of the most important components of the rapid pace of change is *faster innovation*, which leads to faster product obsolescence and, hence, *shorter product life cycles*. As a result, companies which have developed a product or service innovation must capitalize on their lead very quickly before it is overtaken by the next development. This means that they need to get to market quickly, achieve wide penetration quickly and amortize the costs quickly. Traditional trial, production and launch processes do not work well enough at high speed, so companies are trying out all kinds of new formulas, such as concurrent engineering, modular design, electronic commerce and strategic alliances for every stage of the value chain. Suppliers who do not keep up with their customers will very soon be left behind.

Turmoil at the product end is now amplified by upheaval in the marketing and distribution channel.

This turmoil at the product end is now amplified by upheaval in the marketing and distribution channel. Not very long ago, companies could concentrate on the development of new products and concepts and then simply release them through the supply chain via well-understood processes. Today, with the arrival of electronic commerce, *new routes to market* are emerging while traditional routes are collapsing. Companies are no longer able to make standard assumptions about the most effective way of reaching their markets. They will be trialling new routes to market at the same time as they launch new products. Until electronic commerce has ceased to be a revolutionary force and a different pattern of doing business has established itself, and this will take some time, businesses will be multiplying their risk because they are venturing into the relatively unknown on two fronts simultaneously.

Some customers are making a late start on *supply chain integration*. Others are well-advanced and have achieved smooth-running, robust processes, while others are only now discovering the pitfalls along with the benefits. Selling companies need to engage with the integration process and to work with the buying company in order to achieve the goals of the supply chain as a whole. Those who simply supply what they are asked for are likely to find themselves divorced from their original customer and managed by a primary supplier. However, closer collaboration is bound to demand *customization* rather than the provision of standardized offers, and suppliers need to be geared up to respond appropriately.

Many blue-chip companies, and some smaller ones as well, now operate as global suppliers and/or in global markets. Nevertheless, almost all suppliers struggle to match the needs of customers who are involved in global markets. In fact, *globalization* is probably not as genuinely ubiquitous as many pundits suggest. It is a dominant factor in some markets, such as computer software and high-technology business-to-business products, which are driven by short product life cycles and a need to maximize sales in the least possible time. In other markets, particularly where services are consumed as they are produced, it is generally not so important.

Advances in information technology and telecommunications, which have culminated in the arrival of electronic commerce technology, have enabled customers to extend their reach to encompass the globe. Equally, *competitors* are lengthening their reach and are moving into yet more markets. Competitors who were previously confined to serving home markets by the costs of attracting customers overseas are joining the global arena, now that they can market from their base country and no longer need an expensive marketing infrastructure. This lowering of entry barriers opens the field to smaller companies as well, so that customers are not only facing an incursion of good competitors from elsewhere in the world, they are also facing an explosion in the range of size and quality of competitors. As long as these new competitors can deliver, or hold out a reasonable expectation of delivery, prices will inevitably come under pressure.

In some markets the Internet acts as a 360° periscope on pricing. Buyers can surf the web looking for best prices. Although they may then return to the supplier they know, it will be with new targets for price decreases. Where the products they seek are made by well-known brands with global guarantees, the premium they will pay for using a familiar distributor will be minimal. Now that internal constraints have been removed, many selling companies inside the European Union are fighting a rearguard action on *geography-independent pricing* and will not succeed in maintaining differentials. Thus, suppliers and customers operating in high-cost areas such as Western Europe will have to work much better in order to maintain margins. The pressure will be felt all the way up the supply chain. Buying companies will seek to work with suppliers whose objective is to maintain margins on an equitable basis, while suppliers who are focused on maintaining their prices are likely to be abandoned.

Inevitably, the current turbulence will affect organizational structure. The rate of *downsizing, upsizing and merging* taking place has reached new

Selling companies need to engage with the integration process and to work with the buying company in order to achieve the goals of the supply chain as a whole.

Suppliers who are focused on maintaining their prices are likely to be abandoned.

highs as companies jostle to reposition themselves in growth markets and to escape from mature and declining markets. Second-tier companies are generally no longer viable and many have been subsumed into larger or more resourceful companies. The big and the bold are getting bigger and bolder still. This turbulence contains a mix of dangers and opportunities. Companies operating in the expectation of a takeover or acquisition are obviously limited in the commitments they can make and this presents difficulties for buyers as well as suppliers. A buyer in such a transitional situation needs a 'safe pair of hands', flexibility and understanding from its suppliers as it undergoes radical change. In the meantime, a supplier will want to check the robustness of its buyer contact base in case some of its key contacts become casualties. Threats may appear from competitors who supply the other company in a takeover, while outsourcing opportunities may emerge from downsized companies. In short, uncertainty is increasing.

Insight

A public sector organization was merging several buying functions from very different parts of the organization. The buyers would have to move locations, deal with cultural issues, understand their new role and develop strategies to match. Meanwhile, if services to current users were not maintained, they would get off to a bad start with their customers. The supplier could have stood back until the situation became more settled. Instead, it aimed to increase support during the transition to gain commitment from the newly integrated buying function when it emerged from this period.

> Underlying all these customer drivers are the two most enduring ones: *cost reduction* and *risk reduction*. As the pressure to reduce costs features so strongly in customer purchasing behaviour, it is imperative that suppliers appreciate why customers pursue cost savings and what cost savings are potentially available. Suppliers also need to understand how customers perceive the risk in their relationship and how it might best be managed.

Cost reduction

While suppliers concentrate on customer value and profitability, the priority for buying companies is often cost reduction. This section examines the financial aspects of key account relationship management in terms of cost savings, which are not necessarily limited to the buying company. Figure 4.3 lists some of the cost savings which are potentially available to companies when two links in the supply chain work closely together.

Undoubtedly, this list is not complete, nor will all of these savings be available in a single trading relationship. How much cost saving is available will clearly depend on the nature of the product or service and

Better information and reduced uncertainty
Reduction of protective measures
Elimination of duplicated processes
Better flow of supplies
Routinized transactions
Tighter quality control
Improved supply chain efficiency
Reduced production costs
Better, more cost effective design of new products
Cost sharing on research and development
Lower sourcing/business development costs

Figure 4.3
Cost savings available with trusted trading partners

the environment in which it is used. It will also depend on how well the two parties know and trust each other. In a *basic* relationship (see Chapter 3) the parties may well enjoy a degree of familiarity, but very little trust and, therefore, standard processes should be employed wherever possible. Efficiency is characteristic of a *basic* relationship.

The level and nature of cost savings in *cooperative* relationships will vary. If the relationship has been singled out by the selling company as appropriate for development, then the selling company should be expecting to invest in it. The two companies will decide together how that investment can be used to deliver mutual cost savings and enhanced customer value. If, on the other hand, the selling company's strategy is only to maintain its business and competitive position (see Chapter 5), then the opportunities for reducing or saving costs will be limited, which will place constraints on enabling investment and underlying trust.

In an *interdependent* relationship, however, much more becomes possible. Buyer and seller will identify the cost elements most important to them and both parties will have the commitment and confidence in each other to make major changes in order to achieve savings in those costs. Where a high proportion of the cost savings listed in Figure 4.3 are achieved, this may signal arrival at the *integrated* stage of relationship development.

Better information and reduced uncertainty can save costs for buyers and sellers alike in all kinds of ways. Whether this is achieved through a better understanding of the market or through making commitments, accurate demand forecasting can save substantial costs. Finance, staffing, use of plant and premises and marketing resources can all be optimized if requirements can be accurately predicted. Inputs can be bought at good rates rather than high, emergency prices. Strategies can be more useful, more effective and more likely to succeed. Shareholder expectations and share prices can be managed better. On both sides of the relationship, an openness and willingness to share information is important, both in itself and as an indicator of the closeness of the relationship.

Openness and willingness to share information is important, both in itself and as an indicator of the closeness of the relationship.

When companies do not trust each other, they will install protective measures in order to prevent their trading partners from damaging their business. Vertical integration is one example of how buying companies protect themselves against unreliable or opportunistic suppliers. Upstream integration is designed to secure continuity of supplies of a key input to core processes (Ellram, 1991). For example, oil and chemical companies own mining operations which feed their refineries and plants. In fact, they may not always be the most efficient producers and they may be able to buy in at lower prices than the cost of their own production. However, since the companies must run their plant continuously in order to achieve competitive costs, they could not surrender their own sources of raw materials unless they had cast-iron and entirely credible guarantees from their suppliers that deliveries will be made on time.

Although vertical integration is clearly appropriate in certain sets of circumstances (Williamson, 1985), companies are now more inclined to question whether their funds are invested in strategically valuable assets or outmoded supply formats. There are many other examples of expensive protective measures for buying companies, including large buffer stockholdings, advance payment for shipments, legal fees and contract policing, quality checks on goods inwards, constant competitor monitoring and 'mystery shopping'. While buying companies may not be prepared to dismantle all barriers, substantial savings can be made even through partial reductions in protective measures.

> Substantial savings can be made even through partial reductions in protective measures.

The elimination of duplicated processes is an obvious candidate for cost savings. For example, the selling company counts goods out as they leave the factory and the supplier counts them in to confirm delivery in full. Quality is also checked by the producer and again by the receiver. Accounts departments in both companies are engaged endlessly in the reconciliation of purchase orders, delivery notes, invoices and payments. These procedures cost money and cause delays, so many companies have gone part of the way to reducing the costs incurred in checking everything by operating spot checks. Some companies have gone one step further and reconfigured the whole process on the assumption that a check conducted by either party will be acceptable to the other.

Insight

The buying function of a major international company now only involves itself and its warehouses in purchases where it can add value to the process. Office supplies have been taken out of the goods received–store–internal requisition order sequence. Users manage their own budgets and order direct, and their materials are delivered to their desks. The buying function sets up the supplier contract, receives a single monthly report which is automatically generated, and pays one monthly invoice for everything received. Substantial time and effort is saved by the buying company, while the supplier's costs balance out and prices remain competitive.

This case is a good example of how the better flow of supplies and *routinized transactions* can affect efficiency and cost savings. Here, users receive their supplies the following day, whereas previously, availability varied from immediate delivery for a select few items to two to three days for most items. A transaction procedure was established, specifically tailored to the buying company's specification. It operated to a very regular and efficient routine because it was slimmed down exactly to the services required and omitted any 'frills'. Cutting out superfluous handling is one way of improving the flow of supplies. Other ways of streamlining processes include combined process engineering, joint forecasting and improved management gained from a better understanding of requirements, which is achieved through greater information sharing.

A multinational components company has developed a systematic approach to price negotiations with customers. Discussions focus on a matrix based around Michael Porter's 1985 value chain, which identifies sources of cost. Together, the parties concerned identify which elements are valuable to the customer, and which are not, and derive an appropriate price from this resulting menu of tailored and standard elements.

Insight

Waste of material as reject product and waste of time in services are both regularly targeted sources of cost. However, reject product is a relatively minor part of the real cost of poor quality and, hence, the constant attention to *tighter quality control* is driven by the wider implications. For example, substantial amounts of time and money can be absorbed in handling and remedying complaints if a customer receives poor service or a defective product. Further, losing customers to the competition as a result of poor quality can result in substantial loss of earnings, with further repercussions if disappointed customers spread their disenchantment by word of mouth.

Today, after more than a decade of concentration on quality and the adoption of Japanese methods, quality standards have reached new highs: some companies are even committed to zero-defect production. However, quality is not cheap for suppliers. In addition, buying companies are always seeking to achieve tighter quality control at lower cost. In order to concentrate on the quality of their own processes, buyers want to be able to assume the quality of inputs. Suppliers who can meet buyers' stringent standards are saving costs for the buying companies, but they must equally control the costs for themselves.

These last three elements are major contributors to the *improvement in supply chain efficiency* overall, where the aim is the creation of a lean, mean, low-cost supply 'machine'. Efficiency has been defined as 'doing things right' and effectiveness as 'doing the right things'. In fact, by working closely with a supplier, a buyer can significantly improve supply chain effectiveness as well as efficiency. Improvement of effectiveness in supply chain terms will mean identifying the critical pathways on both sides and ensuring that these processes in particular are seamless and robust.

Traditionally, suppliers would encourage customers to buy as much as possible from them and, if customers were using more of the product than was really necessary, so much the better. However, this kind of opportunistic behaviour generally meets with disapproval from buyers. Buyers expect trusted suppliers to point out over-specified products, unnecessary wastage or inefficient usage and to *reduce production costs*, even if it means lower revenue for the supplier. High production costs will make the buying company uncompetitive in the marketplace and, ultimately, the supplier will lose out as well. Suppliers (not necessarily the key account manager) should therefore have a high degree of technical understanding of their own products and be able to offer their expertise in order to support the customer's production function in various ways, including reducing the consumption of other inputs. To make gains beyond the normal levels, the buying company may have to give the supplier access to closely guarded production secrets, in the confidence that such critical information will not reach competitors.

However, information from the European Institute of Purchasing and Supply shows that, in many cases, as much as 90 per cent of the final unit cost of a product is determined before it reaches full production, most of which is committed in the design stage (see Figure 4.4). Thus, the major opportunity of achieving low unit costs for the manufacturer lies in the design stage. Research at Cranfield has shown a large difference between *cooperative* relationships and *interdependent* relationships on this point (see Figure 4.5): a substantial proportion of suppliers in *interdependent* relationships are admitted to the buying company's development process and can therefore contribute to *better, more cost-effective design of new products*, while suppliers in *cooperative* relationships are largely excluded from product development activity.

If the buying company trusts the selling company and involves it in new product development activities, this can potentially lead to the creation of a role for the supplier in the buyer's long-term research and development (R&D) effort. Participation may mean contributing expertise and/or project funding. Much mutual benefit can be gained from such collaboration, including *cost sharing on R&D*, particularly where programmes are long-running and expensive. Further, pooling resources in

> Buyers expect trusted suppliers to point out over-specified products, unnecessary wastage or inefficient usage.

> The major opportunity for achieving low unit costs for the manufacturer lies in the design stage.

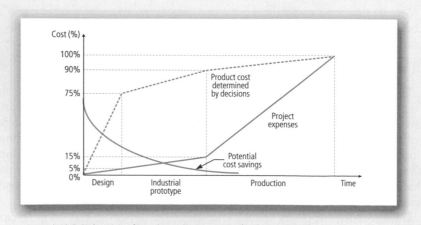

Figure 4.4
Progress of product development compared with commitment of final unit cost

Source: Reprinted with the kind permission of Bernard Gracia, European Institute of Purchasing and Supply

order to secure the input of experts who may be scarce and costly can help to avoid the pitfalls of entering into projects with insufficient vision and directional guidance. Figure 4.5. depicts the degree of information exchange on product development compared with other subjects.

Buyers can also achieve *lower sourcing costs* and suppliers will benefit from *lower business development costs* through involving trusted trading partners in development activity. They can work together in helping develop specifications and sourcing criteria and, if the supplier can then fulfil the need, the buying company may decide to look no further. If the buyer believes that the selling company is a good source for the product required and will not make opportunistic profits, then the working processes and widespread familiarity which already exist represent a real bonus: the buyer can avoid the effort, delays and costs involved in evaluating alternatives.

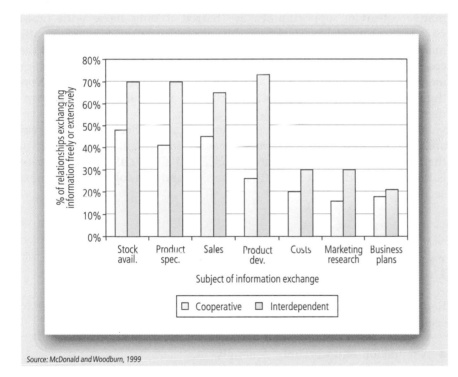

Source: McDonald and Woodburn, 1999

Figure 4.5
Topics for information exchange in KAM relationships

The public sector seems reluctant to take this pragmatic approach and generally insists on compulsory competitive tendering, which not only incurs huge bid costs for suppliers, but also means that buyers ultimately carry the costs of implementing the process through higher prices. In the private sector the supplier's unique expertise and competence may prove so invaluable to the buyer that, even where the selling company itself may not represent an attractive source for the product or service required, the partnership may grow to the point where the supplier takes on the sourcing and ongoing management of the supply as a primary contractor managing smaller, secondary contractors. This arrangement is increasingly common as buying companies seek to reduce their supplier base.

Clearly, close relationships between buying and selling companies have the potential for saving a substantial amount of cost for both sides. However, both sides will have to invest significantly in order to secure these cost savings, in relationship building, communication and committing time to joint projects, and also in new facilities, equipment, staff or whatever is needed for implementation. Expenditure on the less tangible activities, such as relationship building, is as real as expenditure on tangibles, though often the systems applied to accounting for it are very poor or non-existent.

It is important for business success that expectations are set correctly and that the timescales used for evaluation are of a suitable length. In *basic* or *cooperative* relationships, both sides realize that exit is quite easy and either company will look for a quick return on any investment it makes because it cannot be sure that the relationship will last. Obviously, many cost-saving opportunities are barred if only those with rapid payback are acceptable. Therefore, the value of cost savings which can be made at these relationship stages is limited and may not even exceed the costs of running the relationship. In contrast, in *interdependent* or *integrated* relationships there is an expectation of durability and trustworthiness which lowers the perceived risk and allows longer-term investments to be considered.

In effect, reducing risks leads to lower costs and, indeed, risks and costs are closely linked. Sensible companies and, in particular, companies in their buying capacity are extremely concerned about risk. Risk reduction is therefore worthy of a separate discussion and this follows in the next section.

> Both sides will have to invest significantly in order to secure these cost savings.

> Many cost-saving opportunities are barred if only those with rapid payback are acceptable.

Risk reduction

Reduction of risk is one of the major drivers which cause companies to seek closer relationships and encompasses the following:

- A reduction of uncertainty generally.
- Protection against pressures from the business environment.
- Protection against opportunism by powerful trading partners.
- Protection against losing the business altogether.

If buyers or sellers were to articulate the main reason why they labour so hard in making closer relationships work, it would be because they seek the security of retaining trading partners who will be critical to their long-term business future.

The value of risk reduction to both parties can easily be overlooked in the day-to-day management of the relationship. It is therefore a worthwhile exercise for companies to understand what risks their partner perceives and to deconstruct them to see how they might be diminished

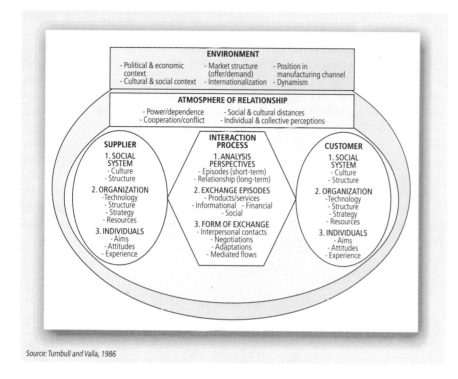

Source: Turnbull and Valla, 1986

Figure 4.6
The IMP model

and/or be seen to be diminished. The model developed by the International Marketing and Purchasing (IMP) Group (see Figure 4.6) provides a useful framework from which to view sources of risk.

Business risks derive from two dimensions: external to the relationship (environment in the IMP model) and internal to the relationship (atmosphere of relationship in the IMP model). External risks originate in the marketplace or the wider environment, but have an impact on the market, for example government legislation. A wide range of external factors potentially have implications for both parties, such as new technology (for example, substituting for current products), economic recession (downturn in demand), competitor activity (downturn in demand and pressure on prices) and many more.

Buyers perceive plenty of internal risks as well. The buying company's first concern is always opportunism on the part of selling companies (Williamson, 1985). Will suppliers pass on any lower costs to the buyer? Will they hold the buyer to ransom for higher prices if they have the advantage? Will they respect confidential information? Will they provide continuity of supply? Buying companies can and do protect themselves against such behaviour in all sorts of ways, such as broadening their supplier base, playing one supplier off against another and insisting on contracts being fully specified to every last detail. However, these 'protective' measures cost buyers money and flexibility, and tend to reduce their leverage with suppliers. Nor do buying companies which carry such 'sandbags' stand up well today against leaner competitors who have taken calculated risks in order to work

'Protective' measures cost buyers money and flexibility.

with suppliers and who have opted for speed and adaptability rather than security and safety.

Assuming the supplier is indeed ethical, honest, committed and currently competent, the buyer's second concern is the long-term orientation and capability of the selling company. Does the supplier represent the best available partner? After all, an honest fool is not necessarily more valuable as an ally than a talented knave. The buying company is likely to be looking for a partner who is at the leading edge of current products and practice and looks certain to stay there. If they have to make investments in assets dedicated to a particular supplier's products or systems, buyers want to be sure that they are making prudent purchases. They do not want to be obliged to write off the costs of such equipment and systems in the event that they need to change their supplier in order to stay ahead. Figure 4.7 shows some examples of risks and the ways in which they can be tackled.

The buyer's second concern is the long-term orientation and capability of the selling company.

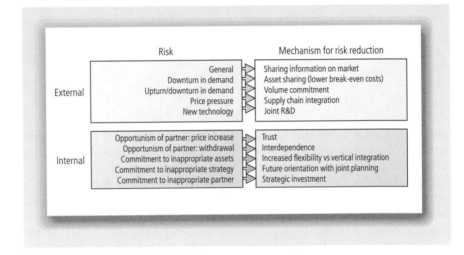

Figure 4.7
Risks and risk reduction mechanisms

There will be people inside the buying company, particularly those who are not normally in contact with the selling company, who are uncomfortable about lowering their protective barriers against suppliers. Unfortunately, they may well be people who can maintain the barriers and effectively prevent the desired development of the relationship. The structure in Figure 4.7 can be used to expose the kinds of risks which are of real concern from their point of view. The mechanisms which could address those specific areas can then be identified. An audit of the relationship's current exchanges and structure will show whether new action is required in order to reduce the risk itself or whether the need is really for internal communication in order to show more clearly how risk is already being managed.

Key account managers need to 'get inside the skin' of their customers in order to piece together the concerns which kindle further commitment to the relationship, as well as the underlying strategies which together determine the buying company's behaviour. In fact, many selling companies list 'a desire to partner' (with acceptance of the risks involved) and 'strategic fit' as two of the most important criteria in selecting key accounts and developing close relationships with them. They believe that compatibility of strategies is necessary to the fulfilment of their own corporate objectives and, indeed, to the development of an intimate relationship.

> Selling companies believe that compatibility of strategies is necessary to the fulfilment of their own corporate objectives and, indeed, to the development of an intimate relationship.

Buying company strategies
Strategy independence

It should come as no surprise to learn that buyers operate strategies for working with suppliers which run parallel to those which selling companies use. The most successful buying companies and particularly those focused on achieving drastic reductions in their supplier base develop specific strategies for their key suppliers individually. However, many buying companies take a more generic approach and work to simple strategies such as 'cut supplier numbers', 'reduce prices by 10 per cent all round' or 'use ISO 9000 suppliers only'. Even if these generic strategies are not entirely and explicitly exposed to suppliers, they are very real and suppliers need to understand them.

Selling companies are rarely good at acknowledging and responding to the customer's strategy. At one level, selling companies know that their customers have some kind of strategy and yet, at another, they are capable of ignoring it completely and developing their own strategy to be applied to the key account, quite independently of the customer's strategy. Not surprisingly, customer buy-in is poor and the exercise tends to get swept to one side.

> Selling companies are rarely good at acknowledging and responding to the customer's strategy.

'Last January they came in here in their droves, with their PowerPoint presentations and their flip-charts – I think they had all been on the same course – but it was just the same as usual. It was all about how much more we were going to buy from them. They did not bother with what we wanted. So we just ignored it' (major retailer).

Insight

When selling companies do not understand what causes their customers to respond to them in the way that they do, they have little chance of developing an appropriate strategy, in other words one which is likely to succeed. Ideally, strategic planning should be carried out jointly, but research has shown that this is still not the norm (McDonald and Woodburn, 1999). Joint strategic planning was found in only approximately one-third of even the most important relationships (the top two or three in each case) and it is presumably even more rare at the next level down.

> An appropriate strategy is one which is likely to succeed.

Strategy direction matrix

If the selling company's relationship with the customer is not close enough for joint planning, then the next best approach is to carry out a strategic analysis from the customer's point of view and to deduce an appropriate strategy on the basis of the findings. To do this, selling companies may find it helpful to employ the strategy direction tool commonly used by buyers in determining how they should manage their suppliers (see Figure 4.8). This is the equivalent of the selling company strategic direction matrix shown later in Figure 5.9.

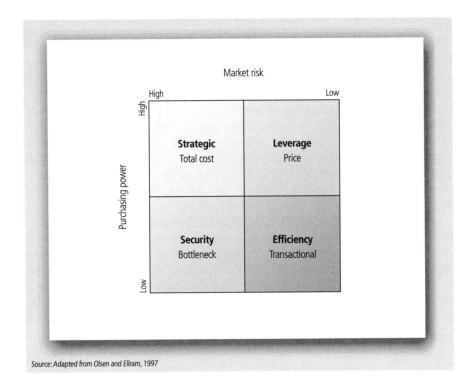

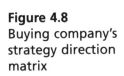

Figure 4.8
Buying company's strategy direction matrix

Source: Adapted from Olsen and Ellram, 1997

The vertical axis 'purchasing power' is self-explanatory. The quantity purchased will obviously be the most important factor, but others may also be taken into account, such as stability of demand, product quality and competitive position in the marketplace. The horizontal axis 'market risk' refers to the supply position. Market risk will include factors such as the number and quality of suppliers, capacity to cope with demand, market turbulence and price stability. Stability and plenty of choice for the buying company will give a low market risk assessment. Unpredictable fluctuations and few suppliers to choose from will result in a high market risk assessment. Each buying company will define the criteria by which it wants to measure its purchasing power and the market risk for itself, largely depending on the sector in which it operates.

If the buying company has low purchasing power in a low-risk market situation (bottom right box), then it will simply seek efficiency and a transactional relationship. The purchase will not be deemed sufficiently important to warrant further engagement with the supplier and the buyer will not be in a strong bargaining position anyway. If, on the other hand, the product market is high risk, then there is chance that supplies could be interrupted ('bottleneck', bottom left box). The buying company is not in a strong enough position to apply leverage and protect itself. Buyers in this situation may react by increasing buffer stocks, seeking a substitute product or finding a more reliable source.

In situations of high purchasing power and a low-risk market (top right box), the buying company can use its muscle to play one competitor off against another in order to secure a better price or some kind of additional value. However, in a high-risk market, where buyers purchase large quantities and, thus, have high purchasing power (top left box) and where the product is important to them, they may seek a strategic relationship with their supplier in order to reduce risk and uncertainty. Here the buying company is more likely to look at value or the total cost of acquisition rather than just the price.

Of these four options, only in the latter is a high-involvement relationship with the supplier likely to take root. Buying companies, like selling companies, have a limited capacity for intimacy and they cannot squander it on situations and suppliers which are not important. It therefore follows that, if the supplier's product/service falls into one of the other boxes of the matrix, however important that customer is to the supplier, the selling company is unlikely to succeed in developing a close relationship.

> Buying companies, like selling companies, have a limited capacity for intimacy.

This conclusion suggests that the selling company should not waste its resources on such a relationship. Investment would be better employed in becoming super-efficient in order to operate effectively in either of the two boxes on the right or in developing a different offer which is designed to fall into the top left box of the matrix. If the matrix indicates a need for strategic product development, it should not be mistaken for a need for relationship development. Key account management (KAM) will not compensate for an inadequate offer and misapplication will only result in misdirected, wasted resources.

> A need for strategic product development should not be mistaken for a need for relationship development.

Supply chain integration

Supply chain management and integration strategies, which are often accompanied by supplier base reduction, have had a major impact on many selling companies in recent years. New electronic commerce capabilities will drive this trend forward and few companies are likely to be unaffected. Figure 4.9 shows the development of supply chain management from the baseline of traditional management to current advanced practice in which companies are operating cross-boundary integration.

Figure 4.9 charts the change from a traditional manufacturing approach, which keeps the supplier on the doorstep, to one in which the supplier has become part of an extended enterprise. The boundary between one company and the next in the chain is breached and may even be dissolved. Processes and strategies must be integrated. As the organizations are so

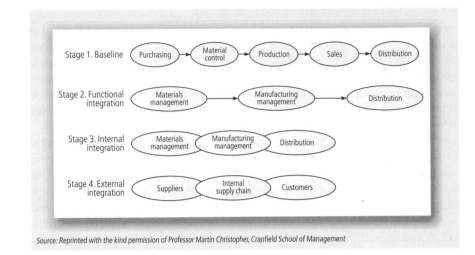

Figure 4.9
Development of
supply chain
management

Source: Reprinted with the kind permission of Professor Martin Christopher, Cranfield School of Management

Determination of
strategy should be a
collective process.

closely linked, they cannot operate to different strategies successfully and, therefore, determination of strategy should be a collective process, not a process owned by an individual member of the chain.

The roles played by the supplier, its customer and other members of the extended enterprise are clearly different from the role played in the other configurations. Some companies are very uncomfortable with the loss of distinction between 'us' and 'them'. Other companies, such as Amazon, the Internet store which launched as a bookseller, can operate the model with equanimity. It is undoubtedly easier to start a company in a new mode than convert one which has innumerable functions and processes orientated in a different way. However, the arrival of electronic business in force, which we are now witnessing, will oblige many companies to adapt to cross-boundary activity. The contrast between single-company, boundary-confined thinking and extended-enterprise, cross-boundary thinking is shown in Figure 4.10.

The arrival of
electronic business in
force will oblige
many companies to
adapt to cross-
boundary activity.

Single company thinking	Extended enterprise thinking
• Focus on the customer	• Focus on the ultimate consumer
• Increase own profits	• Increase profits for all
• Consider own costs only	• Consider total costs
• Spread the business around	• Team with the best
• Guard ideas, information and resources	• Share ideas, information and resources
• Improve internal process efficiency	• Improve joint process efficiency

Figure 4.10
Single company
thinking versus
extended enterprise
thinking

Source: A.T. Kearney

Supply chain integration is probably the strategic development which is most critical for suppliers. A selling company which is not selected as a dependable ally in a newly integrated core supply chain is likely to end up as a secondary supplier, dealing with the original customer through an intermediary. Being separated from the customer limits the supplier's access to information and restricts its ability to demonstrate added value. The supplier becomes much more vulnerable to the agenda of the intermediary.

Most opportunities for cost reduction and value enhancement are currently seen to lie at the interface between members of the supply chain. Much has therefore been written about this subject and it cannot be adequately covered here. Clearly though, understanding the position and strategy of neighbouring members in its supply chain is fundamental to the buying company's strategy and the management of the relationship between itself and its upstream suppliers and its own downstream customers.

> A selling company which is not selected as a dependable ally in a newly integrated core supply chain is likely to end up as a secondary supplier.

Matching strategies

The climate and culture of purchasing has changed in recent years and supply chain partnerships have become more acceptable and, indeed, popular. Even so, in many cases suppliers have found the new partnering philosophy to be little more than skin deep. Customers have promised a partnership approach with a focus on added value and mutual benefit and then have forced prices to the floor anyway, resulting in the sorry state of customer profitability described in Chapter 7.

> In many cases suppliers have found the new partnering philosophy to be little more than skin deep.

Of course, buying companies are not absolutely bound by the strategic direction indicators discussed here: they can choose to adopt different approaches and behaviour. However, buyers will readily revert to type if that strategy is not founded on sound logic and sense, so selling companies should beware of a customer promising a strategy which is out of line with that indicated by analysis.

Companies naturally seek to work with other companies whose strategies and goals match theirs. If the selling company has adopted a strategy of developing high-involvement partnerships with key customers, then it will look for buying companies whose strategies mirror its own and who will reciprocate. The customer's propensity to partner must be a criterion for admission to a supplier's KAM programme. Some companies have managed to be fairly ruthless in wielding that criterion and have excluded any customer who, however huge, operates a price-fighter strategy and plays competitors off against one another. Key account managers are often horrified at the thought of excluding this type of customer but, of course, there is no obligation to tell the customer of the decision.

> The customer's propensity to partner must be a criterion for admission to a supplier's KAM programme.

KAM programmes restricted to customers who offer genuine opportunities for mutual and committed relationships have shown excellent growth in reserves and margins, even astronomical in some cases. Pressure from key account managers and buyers to include other types of large customer is often considerable, but the temptation should be resisted. As emphasized elsewhere in this book, a company's capacity for close business relationships is limited and expansion of the customer base will inevitably detract from the focus on the most important customers. Inclusion of other, less-suitable customers will add plenty of cost and probably not much growth. Of course, these customers are still very important to the selling company. They probably represent a large part of its current cash income, but they should be managed in a different way, with a focus on efficient transactions.

Insight

Hewlett Packard started their global account programme in 1993 with twenty-six global key accounts. By 1996 it had grown tenfold to 250. The following year, Hewlett Packard cut the number back to ninety-five.

Supplier delusions

| Only the reciprocated elements of a relationship are relevant and real.

A relationship is intrinsically reciprocal: you cannot be married to someone unless they are married to you. Only the reciprocated elements of a relationship are relevant and real. If there is a mismatch of perceptions, the relationship is defined only by the elements which are matched. Figure 4.11 illustrates this point: the genuine extent of the relationship is represented by a square, which defines an equal and shared perception. Anything outside the square is delusion.

Determining what stage of development a relationship has reached depends on the views of both of the parties involved. Research has shown, perhaps not surprisingly, that key account managers tend to overestimate the stage of relationship by approximately one development stage (McDonald and Woodburn, 1999). From the buyer's perspective, the two parties are not as close as the supplier probably imagines. Selling companies need to be aware of this phenomenon if they are to avoid engaging in inappropriate behaviour and embarking on premature strategies.

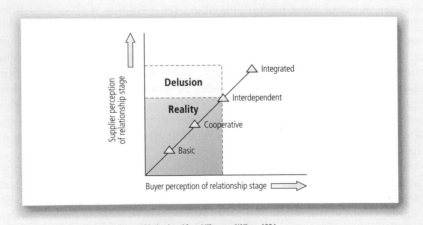

Figure 4.11
Buyer and supplier perceptions of relationships

Source: Leppard in McDonald and Woodburn, 1999, developed from Millman and Wilson, 1994

Trust

Trust, or confidence in a partner's reliability and integrity, is one of the most important elements in high-involvement relationships. A significant body of research supports the notion that trust plays a major role in buyer behaviour. Buying companies rated 'integrity/honesty' as one of the two most important attributes of a good key account manager (equal with 'product knowledge') (McDonald, Millman and Rogers, 1996). Interestingly, when selling companies were similarly questioned, they selected completely different attributes and scarcely rated integrity at all. This difference in opinion suggests that selling companies might be wise to re-evaluate their priorities if they want to align themselves more closely with their customers.

Trust can be regarded as a mediator through which many of the interactions between buyer and seller pass. Interactions potentially increase the level of trust but, as in a game of snakes and ladders, they also have the potential to damage it. Suppliers would do well to manage interactions with a view to how the buyer might perceive them and whether they build or destroy trust. Activities such as improving performance, sharing more information, improving communications and even admitting mistakes should all help to build trust if they are handled sensitively. In addition, trust will, according to the degree to which it pre-exists, either add to or detract from the perceived value of these activities.

Achieving a high degree of trust has numerous positive outcomes. There will be more readily offered cooperation between the two sides, less uncertainty because sensitive information is shared, more commitment to the relationship and a lower probability that one or other will exit. Trust can also bridge a patch in the relationship where something is going wrong. However, if the problem persists for too long, then it will eat away at the 'reserves' of trust and, eventually, relationship breakdown will occur. In effect, a dynamic balance exists in the relationship between past experience of performance and behaviour and current perception of performance and behaviour, which is buffered by trust.

Trust is certainly more than an abstract concept in buyer–seller relationships. Lack of trust has significant cost implications for buying and selling companies at both the strategic and tactical levels. At the strategic level, there are many initiatives which a customer could undertake jointly with a supplier to their mutual benefit. However, if the supplier is not trusted sufficiently, the customer may pursue the opportunity alone or with a more appropriate and trusted partner.

At a tactical level, the existence of trust can open up a range of processes for the examination of cost-cutting opportunities. For example, a selling company undertakes an internal environmental audit. Meanwhile, a buying company looking to do business with the selling company requires assurance that the supplier complies with certain environmental standards and proceeds to conduct its own audit of the supplier. Obviously, this duplicate auditing adds extra cost. Much of the cost could be avoided if the buying company trusted the selling company to carry out the audit objectively and if the selling company trusted the buying company to respond sensibly to the audit's results.

> Trust plays a major role in buyer behaviour and can be regarded as a mediator.

Insight

A retailer formalizes the degree of trust it places in its numerous suppliers. On the arrival of deliveries, the retailer may quality check 100 per cent, 10 per cent or 1 per cent of the goods. Suppliers are effectively penalized for being 'untrustworthy' by being charged for the cost of checking deliveries at the level deemed appropriate. In a very few cases of trusted suppliers, 0 per cent of the goods are checked (saves handling costs) and the retailer invoices itself (saves paperwork).

It is not by accident, of course, that these costs are widely incurred. Naturally, many companies feel a need to guard themselves against the opportunism of other companies. Indeed, in innumerable cases companies have been shown to be right in dealing cautiously with other profit-seeking entities. So, although there has been a cultural shift over the last five years towards closer relationships with trading partners, the shift has not been universal. Many companies have not bought into the idea and, even where they have in theory, they may not have done so in practice.

In contrast, where trust exists between two companies, a considerable range of cost savings become available, as shown in Figure 4.3. As a further incentive, greater profits may be achieved through tackling opportunities together.

Companies should therefore adopt a policy of scepticism, but stop short of cynicism. Treating all-comers with universal suspicion is, ultimately, rather limiting. Trustworthy partners do exist, either because they have enshrined ethical principles or because they see it as being in their long-term interest to behave in a trustworthy manner. It is important that companies first choose their strategic trading partners carefully and then work concertedly to develop a productive, mutually beneficial relationship with them. They can continue to work with other companies more cautiously.

Companies should therefore adopt a policy of scepticism, but stop short of cynicism.

Insight

Customer managers in a commercial banking organization were asked to predict whether their key customer relationships would survive another two years at least. The results were analysed against a number of relationship parameters. The research concluded that holding a favourable 'balance of power' or the previous 'duration of the relationship' did not affect expectations of the continuation of relations, whereas 'trust' was strongly linked to expected relationship life (Perrien, Ricard and Landry, 1999).

Balance of power

It is abundantly clear to practitioners of KAM that, although the balance of power between a supplier and a customer might not affect the duration of a relationship, it certainly makes a huge difference to its nature. However, to date, little academic attention has been given to studying the role of control and influence in trading relationships, perhaps because it is not an easy subject to research.

Power is obviously linked to the perceived degree of dependency on the partner. In fact, the one is the reverse of the other. Dependency increases as the size of the business with the trading partner increases and as its share of the company's turnover grows. Dependency also increases if loss of the business would damage either company's reputation and trigger the defection of other partners, or if finding a substitute would be difficult. For a selling company with high fixed costs, the consequences of losing a major customer can be devastating, but where most costs are variable the effects are more manageable.

Figure 4.12 outlines the sources of power in a buyer–seller relationship as identified by a group of practitioners from blue-chip companies. Whether the company is buying or selling, most of the sources of power are potentially mirror images of each other. What differs is the list of them possessed by each organization in a given relationship at a given point in time. For example, the balance of power may favour a selling company over a small buying company in need of its advanced technological support. On the other hand, the balance of power would be in the customer's favour if that customer takes a major part of the supplier's production and has excellent technological support resources in-house. Suppliers can be just as powerful as buyers, although that is not the everyday perception of their key account managers, who usually feel that buyers have the upper hand.

Power may be thought of in terms of the overall 'quantity' of power, as well as the balance of it in a relationship. The framework shown in Figure 4.12 can be used to audit the power position in a particular

> Power is linked to the perceived degree of dependency on the partner.

Buyers' power		Sellers' power
Sources of power	**Nature of source**	**Sources of power**
Big	Size/importance	Criticality to buyer
Consolidation: bigger		Capacity to meet demand
Globalization: even bigger		Share of purchases
Share of total supplier business		
Supply excess	Competitor options	Supply shortage
Commodity markets		Key differentiation
Globalization: cherry-pick suppliers		Access to innovation
Globalization: pick currency & prices		Patents & monopolies
		Brand/demand pull
		Erect barriers to new competitors
Access to information	Buying/selling skills	Access to information
Leverage market knowledge		Leverage market knowledge
Higher expectations		Easy to work with
Competent buyers		Competent Key Account Managers
Supply chain management	New strategies	Recognized relevant expertise
Supplier rationalization		Track record and reputation
Globalization		Global competence
E-commerce		Flexible
Low cost of switching for customer	Threat of exit	High cost of switching for customer
High cost of switching for supplier		Low cost of switching for supplier
Effect of loss on supplier cost base		Limited availability of alternatives
Within supplier	Leverage of contacts	Within customer
Within markets/ability to damage reputation		Within markets
Within regulatory bodies		Within regulatory bodies

Source: Reprinted with the kind permission of the Cranfield Key Account Management Best Practice Club

Figure 4.12
Sources of power

relationship. First, identify the actual sources of power for each side using Figure 4.12 as a preliminary checklist. Then give each source of power a score which represents its relevance and strength in the relationship and total the scores afterwards. This exercise will help to clarify the nature of the power which may be leveraged. It will also indicate the direction and degree of any imbalance in an objective way.

Regardless of the relative power positions, companies with the balance of power in their favour can still choose how they exercise their advantage. Power can be used constructively or destructively. For example, a buying company in a very powerful position could demand very low prices and stand a good chance of obtaining them. However, the selling company's profits may be depressed to the point where it cannot invest in innovation which would ultimately benefit its customer, or it might go out of business. Alternatively, the customer could decide that its long-term interests lie more in imposing specific strategies or higher standards of practice on the supplier because it would make the supplier a better trading partner, to the benefit of both companies.

So, while the balance of power is clearly important in determining the nature of a relationship, it does not provide sufficient explanation on its own. Linking the balance of power with the concepts of common interest/mutual benefit does however offer further insight into relationships. Common interest may be defined as the compatibility between the goals of the companies which are trading together. Companies which approach the business between them in the same manner and share the same aims and objectives are said to have a high degree of common interest. A good example is to be found where both supplier and buyer are dedicated to the same industry sector and have evolved similar responses to the environmental forces at work in that sector. Figure 4.13 plots the balance of power against the degree of common interest and summarizes the different situations to be found in each of the six sets of circumstances shown.

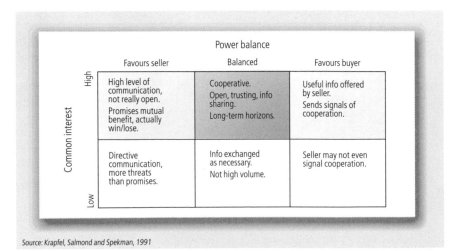

Figure 4.13
Balance of power versus common interest

Source: Krapfel, Salmond and Spekman, 1991

The research behind the development of this matrix showed that, in situations of a low degree of common interest (bottom three boxes), the volume of communication is generally not high, and information is only exchanged as necessary. The volume of communication is much higher where a high degree of common interest exists. However, this volume does not necessarily indicate information sharing: a large part of it may be directive, more like a one-way 'lecture' than a two-way 'conversation'. Chapter 3 highlighted the important roles that communication and information exchange play in key account relationships. Clearly, the quality and nature of each as well as the quantity need to be taken into consideration in understanding the relationship.

The matrix suggests that the only situation in which a collaborative, *cooperative* relationship will exist is where the two parties have the same amount of power and a high degree of common interest. In fact, even where the balance of power lies in favour of one of them, a collaborative relationship could exist if the company with the upper hand chooses to behave in a cooperative manner. Nevertheless, the weaker side should always be wary of the possibility that a policy of cooperation which is not backed up by necessity is liable to change. For example, a selling company might agree to investment in equipment dedicated to a powerful customer, on the understanding that the price of the product will yield a margin sufficient to give a return on the investment in, say, two years. In a relationship based on balanced power and mutual necessity, the agreement might safely be quite flexible and relatively informal. In a relationship based on the benevolence or enlightenment of a powerful partner, a sound contract might be wise protection against the chance of a change in the partner's policy.

> The only situation in which a collaborative, *cooperative* relationship will exist is where the two parties have the same amount of power and a high degree of common interest.

NHS Supplies has divided its contracts into eight major product groups. The organization held meetings with its most important suppliers in each group in order to promote dialogue with them. The organization noticed that, although the meetings had the same agenda and were held in the same kind of environment, each meeting had a very different atmosphere in terms of the suppliers' expressed willingness to participate and cooperate with NHS Supplies. The turnout at some meetings was almost 100 per cent while for others it was relatively low. Afterwards, the organization mapped the balance of power between itself and each group against the evident degree of common interest. The predictions of the matrix in Figure 4.13 matched the actual responsiveness of the suppliers and the degree of cooperation offered.

Insight

Summary

As buying companies seek new routes to competitive advantage and value for their customers, they now look to key suppliers to help them. Naturally, customers are more likely to act according to their own perceptions and aspirations than to any view or objective that selling companies might wish to impose on them. A buying company has its own set of strategic decision support tools to help it select the suppliers who are important to the fulfilment of its aspirations.

First of all, a selling company needs to understand whether it has the opportunity of being a key supplier. The chances are small if it is one of many competitors, or it is in a weak position relative to the customer, or it supplies a product or service which does not contribute to the customer's strategic critical path. If analysis reveals that this is the selling company's situation with this customer, the supplier should look elsewhere for its own key relationships or possibly reposition itself through developing its offer. It should not waste money and effort on trying to develop a relationship which is unlikely to succeed and bear fruit.

At the same time, the supplier should decide what this customer can contribute to its own strategic objectives, using the methods described in the following chapters. These methods require an in-depth understanding of the customer's situation, needs and strategies and, indeed, successful key account managers are those who really know how their customers operate and why.

If and, generally speaking, only if buyer and seller strategies are complementary in terms of products, their approach to business and to the relationship between them, will it be possible to develop the relationship beyond a fairly simple level towards an *interdependent* or *integrated* stage. However, if all these elements are in place and closer involvement is achieved, the flow of benefits to both parties can be very exciting.

At less-developed stages of the relationship the cost of nurturing the relationship can easily outweigh the benefits. The range and extent of cost savings increase on both sides as trust between the two parties grows and barriers are reduced. In some situations, reducing risk by working with a known partner can allow costs to be cut, for example by eliminating duplication of processes. In other situations, reduction of costs may increase risk, for example by moving to just-in-time supply and eliminating buffer stocks. Clearly, reduction of costs and reduction of risks are closely linked and need to be managed jointly from a foundation of a thorough understanding of the partner and its concerns.

Trust is a mediator through which most interactions pass and activities will be interpreted. Care should be taken to manage the partner's perceptions, as reserves of trust may be crucial in carrying a supplier through any difficult patches in performance or in the relationship.

In the end, powerful customers still call the shots

References

Anderson, J. C., Håkansson, H. and Johanson, J. (1994). Dyadic business relationships within a business network context. *J. Marketing*, 58, 1–15.

Ellram, L. E. (1991). Supply chain management. *Int. J. Phys. Distribut. Logistics Manage.*, 21(1), 13–22.

Krapfel, R. E., Salmond, D. and Spekman, R. (1991). A strategic approach to buyer–seller relationships. *Eur. J. Marketing*, 25(9), 22–37.

McDonald, M. and Woodburn, D. (1999). Key account management – building on supplier and customer perspectives. *Financial Times*, Prentice Hall.

McDonald, M., Millman, A. and Rogers, B. (1996). *Key Account Management – Learning from Supplier and Customer Perspectives*. Cranfield School of Management.

Millman, A. F. and Wilson, K. J. (1994) From key account selling to key account management. In *Tenth Annual Conference on Industrial Marketing and Purchasing*.

Olsen, R. F. and Ellram, L. (1997). A portfolio approach to supplier relationships. *Indust. Marketing Manage.*, 26, 101–13.

Perrien, J., Ricard, L. and Landry, C. (1999). *Proceedings of the Ninth Biennial World Marketing Congress*. Sage Publications Inc., Thousand Oaks.

Porter, M. E. (1985) *Competitive Advantage: Creating and Sustaining Superior Performance*. The Free Press

Turnbull, P. W. and Valla, J. P. (1986). *Strategies for International Industrial Marketing*. Croom Helm.

Williamson, O. E. (1985). *The Economic Institution of Capitalism: Firms, Markets, Relational Contracting*. The Free Press.

Chapter 5
Defining and selecting key accounts

Introduction

One of the objectives of this chapter is to place key account management (KAM) in the context of market segmentation for it is creative market segmentation which is universally recognized as the key to sustainable competitive advantage. Another objective is to provide a methodology for identifying and targeting key accounts using account portfolio management.

Market segmentation and key account management

Most organizations' different market segments will contain a number of key accounts. Before proceeding to categorize key accounts, analyse their needs and set objectives and strategies for them, it is necessary to ensure that you have the clearest understanding of how your market works, what the key segments are and where you can exert the most influence on decisions about what is bought and from whom. This is essential knowledge, for it will provide the backcloth against which plans for key accounts are evaluated and eventually controlled. Indeed, it would be fair to say that an appreciation of market segmentation is an essential criterion for effective KAM.

'The good thing about being mediocre is you are always at your best'. Someone once said this to me about corporate life. Imagine getting your sales force up at five every morning to go out and kill for 'We are really mediocre!' The reason no-one has ever heard of Alexander the Mediocre is that he was mediocre and was not Alexander the Great. So what makes any of us think that making mediocre offers to our customers is ever going to have anything but mediocre results?

● Definition:
A market is the aggregation of all products or services which can satisfy a particular need.

● Definition:
Market segmentation is a process for breaking a market into smaller groups in which consumers have the same or similar needs.

Taking this theme a stage further, we can ask ourselves what sort of company would make a commodity out of bread, fertilizer, glass, chlorine, potatoes or mobile phones, for example?

Insight

By way of an answer, ask whether anyone can 'taste' the difference between Castrol GTX or any other manufacturer's oil or between Alfa Laval Steel, SKF Bearings, Intel Microprocessors and so on. Yet these great companies are dealing with low differentiation products in mainly mature markets.

So, what is the secret of success?

A review of the work of a number of gurus, such as Sir Michael Perry, Tom Peters and Phillip Kotler, reveals a striking similarity between what they consider to be the key elements of world-class marketing.

1 A profound understanding of the market.
2 Market segmentation and selection.
3 Powerful differentiation, positioning and branding.
4 Effective marketing planning processes.
5 Long-term integrated marketing strategies.

While this is not the complete list, it is interesting to note the order of the elements listed here. We find it remarkable that, even in 2000, so many companies are messing about with their brands without really understanding their market and how it is segmented or their competitive position. Indeed, 'What shall we do with our brand?' is one of the most recurrent questions and, while it is easy to understand why, branding being the glamorous part of marketing, it is intensely irritating when the questioners know so little about their markets.

It is intensely irritating when the questioners know so little about their markets.

Insight

Let us explain what we mean. We frequently run workshops for the boards of strategic business units. Before we start the workshop, we ask the directors to write a list, in order of priority, of their key target markets. Often they write down their products, such as pensions or main frame computers. Rarely is there any sensible grasp of the meaning of the word 'market'. So, they fail the first test. The second part of the exercise is to write down their sources of differential advantages against each key target market listed. When these senior people fail such an elementary test, it is clear that their organization is either in or heading towards trouble.

We recently came across one insurance company which prided itself on its market segmentation. On questioning, however, its segments turned out to be *sectors*, which explained why it had little or no differentiation and was competing mainly on price. Indeed, this is one of the most commonly observed misconceptions about market segmentation. Everyone knows that a segment is a group of customers with the same or similar needs and that there are many different purchase combinations within and across sectors, yet companies still persist in confusing sectors with segments.

A market segment is a smaller part of a market in which consumers have the same or similar needs.

> Perhaps *the* most frequent mistake however is *a priori* segmentation, which is largely the result of the vast amount of prescriptive literature on the subject of segmentation.

Companies still persist in confusing sectors with segments.

All books state that there are several bases for segmentation, such as demographics, socioeconomics, geography, usage, psychographics, geo-demographics, life style and so on and the literature is replete with proponents of one or more of these. However, this is to miss the point completely, for in any market there is only *one* correct segmentation. One hundred per cent of goods and services are 'made', distributed, influenced and used and the purchase combinations which result are a fact not a figment of someone's imagination. The task is to understand the market structure, how it works and what the actual segments are at different junctions in the market.

In any market there is only *one* correct segmentation.

This brings us to the starting point in market segmentation – market definition and market structure. Correct market definition is crucial for measuring market share and market growth, identifying relevant competitors and, of course, the formulating of marketing strategies in order to deliver differential advantage.

> The general rule for defining a 'market' is that it should be described in terms of a customer need in a way which covers the aggregation of all the alternative products or services which customers regard as being capable of satisfying that same need.

For example, we would regard the in-company caterer as only one option when it comes to satisfying lunchtime hunger. That need could also be satisfied at external restaurants, public houses, fast food outlets and sandwich bars. The emphasis in the definition is therefore clearly on the word 'need'.

Figure 5.1 is an example of a complete 'market map', showing how goods move from originators through to final users, with volumes, values and market shares all adding up in a manner not unlike a balance sheet. However, few companies give sufficient intellectual thought to market definition – witness Gestetner, who thought it was in the duplicator market and IBM, who thought it was in the mainframe market. Hence, few can draw anything approaching an accurate market map and have little chance of doing any kind of sensible segmentation at the key influence points or junctions along the market map.

> At each of these key junctions, segmentation is not only possible, but necessary.

It is here that the process becomes quite complicated, for the trick is to make an exhaustive list of all the different purchase combinations which take place at each junction. This entails listing what is bought (to include applications, features, where, when and how products or services are bought), together with the associated descriptors (who buys what). This will often produce somewhere between thirty and eighty different purchase combinations or what we term *micro segments*. However, the reality is that these micro segments do indeed represent what actually happens in the market.

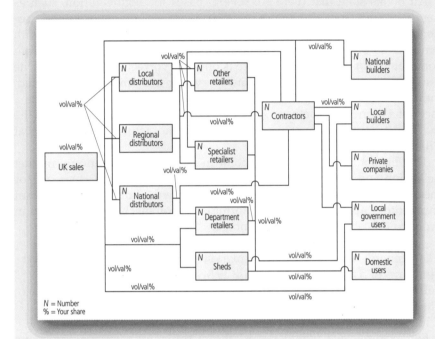

Figure 5.1
Example of a market map including the number of each customer type

NB. Sketch out complex junctions separately. Alternatively, build an outline map, applying details at the junctions to be segmented.

The next step, which is to specify the benefits that each of these micro segments seek by buying what they buy in the way they do, is crucial. It is often here that external market research is necessary.

It is now simply a question of using one of the many software packages available to cluster micro segments with similar requirements. Clusters are given a dimension of size by adding the volumes or values represented by each micro segment. It is our experience that most markets can be broken down into ten or less segments. The only remaining task is to ensure that our offers meet the requirements of each segment and that we, as suppliers, are organized to sell, deliver and support the appropriate value propositions.

Faced with a plethora of options for segmentation, as illustrated in Figure 5.2, it is not difficult to understand why most organizations take an overly simplistic approach to segmentation and end up with little or no differential advantage.

Cooking appliances
Is it a single market or several separate markets?

Volume	(units)
Value	
Domestic/commercial	
Fuels	(gas, electricity, coal, oil, etc.)
Cooking methods	(heat, radiation, convection)
Cooking function	(surface heating, baking, roasting, charcoal, etc.)
Design	(free standing, built-in, combination)
Prices	
Product features	
OEM / replacement	
Geography	
Channels	(direct, shops, wholesalers, mail order)
Why bought	
Others	(promotional response, lifestyle, demographics)
Usage	

Figure 5.2
Determining the presence of market segments

To help overcome the complexity of market segmentation, during the past seven years we have developed a software package which manages the whole complex process of segmentation, starting with market mapping and proceeding right through to forming the final segments. *Market Segment Master* has been market tested and found to be a very successful tool by some of the world's leading companies. (For more information about *Market Segment Master*, please contact Professor Malcolm McDonald at Cranfield School of Management, Cranfield University, Bedford MK43 OAL, UK. Tel: 01234 751122. Fax: 01234 752691. For a full and detailed methodology for segmentation see *Market Segmentation: How to do it; How to Profit from it*, Macmillan, 2nd edition, 1998.)

One thing is abundantly clear from our detailed segmentation work: price is rarely the prime motivator in the way people buy. The following case history will illustrate the point.

> Price is rarely the prime motivator in the way people buy.

Mini-case 1:

How ICI used market segmentation to its advantage

ICI Fertilizers went through a severe loss-making period during the late 1980s as the market matured and foreign competitors entered the market with cheap imports. Prices and margins fell to disastrous levels. However, the company had the perspicacity to go through the segmentation process described here and discovered seven relatively distinct segments of farmers, only one of which was price sensitive. This segment represented only 10 per cent of the market, not 100 per cent, as had been previously thought. One segment was highly technological in its approach, while another was more influenced by the appearance of crops. Yet another was loyal to merchants. Yet another was loyal to brands. Each segment was given a name and the needs of each were researched in depth. Products were developed and offers made to match the precise needs of the individual segments, while the company and its processes were reorganized in order to ensure that the appropriate value could be delivered. ICI Fertilizers became an extremely profitable company in an industry whose own governing body had officially designated fertilizer as a commodity!

Hopefully, this heartening story of creative segmentation leading to sustained profitability in a mature and generally unprofitable industry will encourage readers to rethink their approach to segmentation. The market segmentation process described here is summarized in Figure 5.3.

Why market segmentation is vital in key account planning

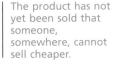

The product has not yet been sold that someone, somewhere, cannot sell cheaper.

In today's highly competitive world, few companies can afford to compete only on price for the product has not yet been sold that someone, somewhere, cannot sell cheaper – apart from which, in many markets it is rarely the cheapest product which succeeds anyway. What this means

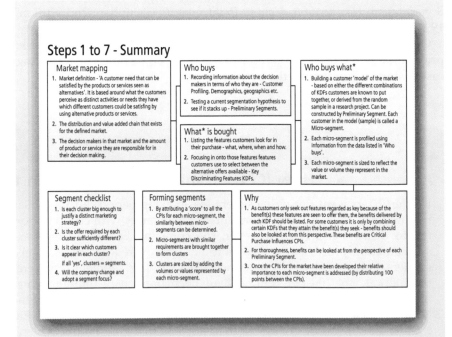

Figure 5.3
Market segmentation process

is that we have to find some way of differentiating ourselves from the competition and the answer lies in market segmentation.

The truth is that very few companies can afford to be 'all things to all people'. The main aim of market segmentation as part of the marketing planning process is to enable a business concern to target its effort at the most promising opportunities. However, what is an opportunity for firm A is not necessarily an opportunity for firm B. So a firm needs to develop a typology of the customer or segment it prefers, for this can be an instrument of great productivity in the marketplace.

The whole point of market segmentation is that a firm must either:

- define its markets broadly enough to ensure that its costs for key activities are competitive or
- define its markets in such a way that it can develop specialized skills in serving them to overcome a relative cost disadvantage.

Both strategies have to be related to a firm's distinctive competence and to that of its competitors.
Correct market definition is crucial for:

- share measurement,
- growth measurement,
- the specification of target customers,
- the recognition of relevant competitors and
- the formulation of marketing objectives and strategies.

To summarize, the objectives of market segmentation are as follows:

- To help determine marketing direction through the analysis and understanding of trends and buyer behaviour.
- To help determine realistic and obtainable marketing and sales objectives.
- To help improve decision making by forcing managers to consider the available options in depth.

A clear and comprehensive understanding of their market, how it works, how it breaks down into natural segments and the specific nature of the unique value sought by each of these segments will obviously give key account managers a significant advantage in building long-term relationships with their customers.

Selecting and targeting market segments

The methodology described here should be read carefully by key account managers because exactly the same methodology (but using different variables) will be used for identifying and targeting key accounts. With a firm grasp of these fundamental principles, the reader will be able to derive full benefit from the detailed, step-by-step methodology set out later in this chapter.

We have seen that a business should define its markets in such a way that it can ensure that its costs for key activities will be competitive. Or, alternatively, it should define the markets it serves in such a way that it can develop specialized skills in servicing those markets and, hence, overcome a relative cost disadvantage. Both, of course, have to be related to a company's distinctive competence.

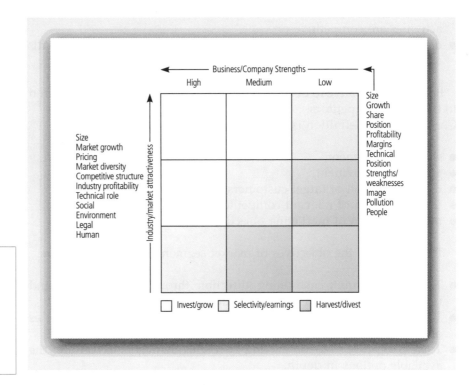

> **Definition:** ●───
> A directional policy matrix (DPM) is a two-dimensional matrix which plots market attractiveness against business strength.

Figure 5.4
A nine-box DPM

However, the approach developed in the late 1960s by the Boston Consulting Group is justly criticized for relying on two single factors, that is to say relative market share and market growth, neither of which explain business success on their own. To overcome this difficulty and to provide a more flexible approach, General Electric and McKinsey jointly developed a multifactor approach employing the same fundamental ideas as the Boston Consulting Group. They used industry attractiveness and business strengths as the two main axes and constructed these dimensions from a number of variables. Using these variables and some scheme for weighting them according to their perceived importance, businesses are classified into one of nine cells in a three by three matrix. Thus, the same purpose is served as in the Boston matrix (comparing investment opportunities among businesses),

> **Definition:** ●───
> A Boston matrix is a two-dimensional matrix which plots relative market share against market growth.

but with the difference that multiple criteria are used. These criteria vary according to circumstances, but often include those shown in Figure 5.4.

However, it is not necessary to use a nine-box matrix and many managers prefer to use a four-box matrix similar to the Boston box. Indeed this is the authors' preferred methodology, as it seems to be more easily understood by and useful to practising managers.

The four-box DPM is given in Figure 5.5. Here, the circles represent sales into a market or segment and, in the same way as in the Boston matrix, each is proportional to that segment's contribution to overall turnover.

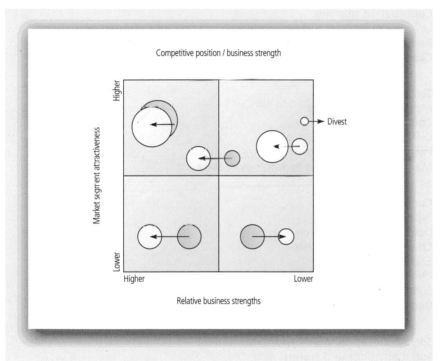

Figure 5.5
A four-box DPM

The difference in this case is that, rather than using only two variables, the criteria which are used for each axis are totally relevant and specific to each company using the matrix. This shows

- markets/segments categorized on a scale of attractiveness to the firm and
- the firm's relative strengths in each of these markets/segments.

The specific criteria to be used should be decided by key executives using the device, but a generalized list for the vertical axis is given in Table 5.1. It is advisable to use no more than five or six factors, otherwise

Table 5.1 Factors contributing to market attractiveness

Market factors
Size (money units or both)
Size of key segments
Growth rate per year: total segments
Diversity of market
Sensitivity to price, service features and external factors
Cyclicality
Seasonality
Bargaining power of upstream suppliers
Bargaining power of downstream suppliers

Financial and economic factors
Contribution margins
Leveraging factors, such as economies of scale and experience
Barriers to entry or exit (both financial and non-financial)
Capacity utilization

Technological factors
Maturity and volatility
Complexity
Differentiation
Patents and copyrights
Manufacturing process technology required

Competition
Types of competitors
Degree of concentration
Changes in type and mix
Entries and exits
Changes in share
Substitution by new technology
Degrees and types of integration

Socio-political factors in your environment
Social attitudes and trends
Laws and government agency regulations
Influence with pressure groups and government representatives
Human factors, such as unionization and community acceptance

the exercise becomes too complex and loses its focus. Read on, however, before selecting these factors, as essential methodological instructions on the construction of a portfolio matrix follow.

An example of a completed matrix is given in Figure 5.6, which shows a portfolio completed for an agrochemical company. It indicates the size and direction of the company's main segments now and in three years' time.

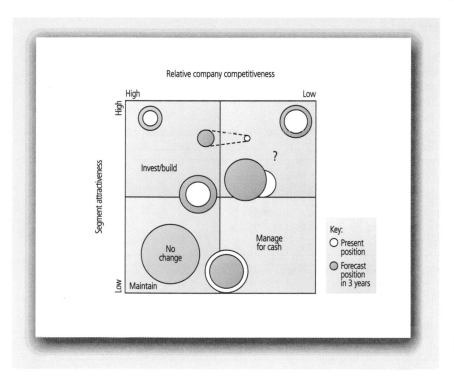

Figure 5.6
Portfolio analysis:
DPM

Setting marketing objectives and strategies

The general marketing procedures which lead to the setting of marketing objectives flow, of course, from the portfolio analysis described above and revolve around the following logical decisions:

1 *Maintain* – this usually refers to the 'cash cow' type of product/market and reflects the desire to maintain competitive positions (bottom left quadrant in Figure 5.6).
2 *Improve* – this usually refers to the 'star' type of product/market and reflects the desire to improve the competitive position in attractive markets (top left quadrant in Figure 5.6).
3 *Harvest* – this usually refers to the 'dog' type of product/market and reflects the desire to relinquish a competitive position in favour of short-term profit and cash flow (bottom right quadrant in Figure 5.6).
4 *Exit* – this also usually refers to the 'dog' type of product/market and sometimes the 'question mark' and reflects a desire to divest because of a weak competitive position or because the cost of staying in it is prohibitive and the risk associated with improving its position is too high.
5 *Enter* – this usually refers to a new business area.

The strategy guidelines suggested by the different positions in a DPM are summarized in Figure 5.7.

● Definition:
A portfolio analysis is the analysis of an organization's strategic position, having plotted the relative attractiveness of its markets against its relative strength in each market.

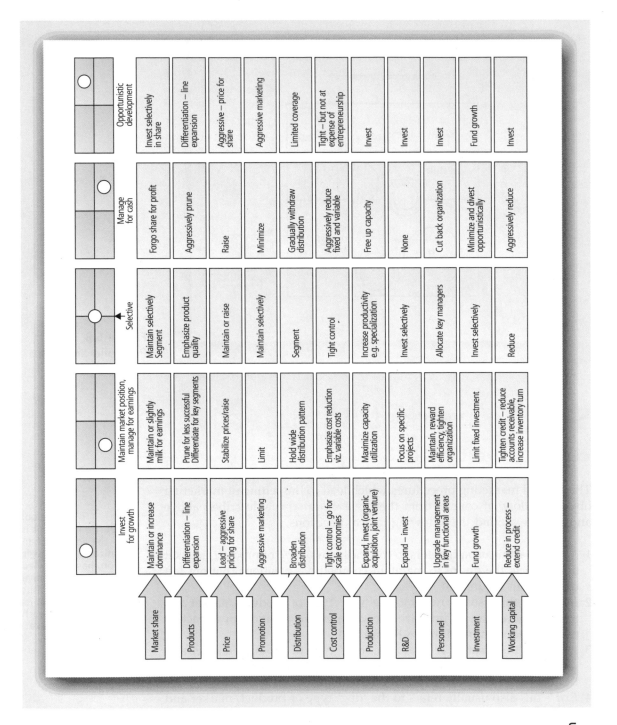

Figure 5.7
Strategy guidelines suggested for different positioning on the DPM

However, great care should be taken not to follow slavishly any set of 'rules' or guidelines related to those suggested here. These guidelines are included more as checklists of questions which should be asked about each major product in each major market before setting marketing objectives and strategies. In addition, the use of pejorative labels such as 'dog', 'cash cow' and so on should be avoided if possible.

It is at this stage in the segmentation process that the circles (representing the segments) in the DPM can be relocated (where applicable) to show their relative size and position in three years' time. You can do this to show, first, where they will be if the company takes no action and, second, where you would ideally prefer them to be. These latter positions will of course become the marketing objectives.

Identifying target key accounts

We have seen in outline the process by which an organization's objectives and strategies can be totally market driven. This is only possible if market segments are first identified and then categorized both according to the potential of each for growth in profit over some designated period of time and according to the organization's competitive capabilities in meeting customer needs.

Inevitably, this means that there will always be part of our market in the 'low-potential/low-strength' quadrant and it is therefore possible that some key accounts within such segments will also fall in this quadrant, as well as in the other three quadrants.

Before carrying out the next phase of analysis, it is worth considering this point very seriously, for clearly it will be the key accounts in the 'high potential/high-strength' segments which we should be targeting for our primary growth focus. We should also bear in mind that key accounts in the 'low-potential/high-strength' quadrant also need targeting as a major activity in order to protect our current business. In addition, we need to consider key accounts in those segments located in the 'high-potential/low-strength' quadrant, for these represent opportunities for future revenue streams. By definition, this means that any key accounts in the 'low-potential/low-strength' quadrant should be the last to command our attention given our scarce resources.

Nonetheless, we still need a methodology for classifying key accounts irrespective of which quadrant they fall in. The next section introduces a method called 'KAM portfolio analysis' and explains in detail how it should be done.

Key account management portfolio analysis

Introduction

Portfolio analysis is simply a means of assessing a number of different key accounts, first according to the potential of each in terms of achieving the organization's objectives and, second, according to the organization's capability for taking advantage of the opportunities identified.

An adapted version of the DPM, portfolio analysis offers a detailed framework which can be used to classify possible competitive environments and their respective strategy requirements. It uses several indicators in measuring the dimensions of 'account attractiveness' on one hand and 'company capabilities' (relative to competitors) on the other. These indicators can be altered by management to suit the operating conditions of particular industrial sectors. The outcome of using portfolio analysis is the diagnosis of an organization's situation and strategy options relative to its position with respect to these two composite dimensions.

The purpose of the following guidelines is to obtain the maximum value out of this methodology.

Definition: KAM portfolio analysis is simply a means of assessing a number of different key accounts, first, according to the potential of each in terms of achieving the organization's objectives and, second, according to the organization's capability for taking advantage of the opportunities identified.

Preparation

Prior to commencing portfolio analysis, the following preparation is advised:

1 Data/information profiles should be available for all key accounts to be scored.
2 Define the time period being scored. A period of three years is recommended.
3 Ensure sufficient data is available to score the factors. (Where no data are available, this is not a problem as long as a sensible approximation can be made for the factors.)
4 Ensure up-to-date sales forecasts are available for all products/services plus any new products/services.

Analysis team

In order to improve the quality of scoring, it is recommended that a group of people from a number of different functions take part, as this encourages the challenging of traditional views through discussion. However, it is suggested that there should be no more than six people involved in the analysis.

Definition: Key account attractiveness is a measure of the *potential* of the key account for yielding growth in sales and profits.

Two key definitions

Key account attractiveness is a measure of the *potential* of the key account for yielding growth in sales and profits. It is important to stress that this should be an objective assessment of key account attractiveness using data *external* to the organization. The criteria themselves will, of course, be determined by the organization carrying out the exercise and will be relevant to the objectives the organization is trying to achieve.

Business strength/position is a measure of an organization's *actual* strengths in each key account, that is to say the degree to which it can take advantage of a key account opportunity. Thus, it is an objective assessment of an organization's ability to satisfy key account needs relative to competitors.

● Definition:
Business strength/
position is a measure of
an organization's *actual*
strengths in each key
account and it will differ
according to each key
account.

Ten steps to producing the key account management portfolio

Step 1 Define the key accounts which are to be used during the analysis.

Step 2 Define the criteria for key account attractiveness and the weight for each.

Step 3 Score the relevant key accounts out of ten on the attractiveness factors.

Step 4 Define the critical success factors (from the customer's point of view) for each key account and the weight for each.

Step 5 Score your organization's performance out of ten on each critical success factor relative to competitors.

Step 6 Produce the position of key accounts in the portfolio.

Step 7 Position the key accounts on the box assuming no change to current policies. That is to say a forecast should be made of the future position of the key accounts (this step is optional).

Step 8 Should redraw the portfolio to position the key accounts where the organization wants them to be in, say, three years time. That is to say the *objectives* they wish to achieve for each key account.

Step 9 Set out the strategies to be implemented to achieve the objectives.

Step 10 Check the financial outcomes resulting from the strategies.

Let us now consider each step in turn.

Step 1: list the population of key accounts which you intend to include in the key account management matrix

The list can include key accounts with which you have no business yet or accounts which are currently small or entrepreneurial, but which have the potential to become big.

To do this, it is suggested that a preliminary categorization be done according to *size* or *potential* size. Thus, if there were, say, one 100 key accounts, the preliminary categorization might resemble Figure 5.8.

It is important *not* to use the methodology which follows on all 100 accounts at once, as the criteria for each group may need to be different. The following methodology should, in the example shown, be carried out as three separate exercises: A, B and C.

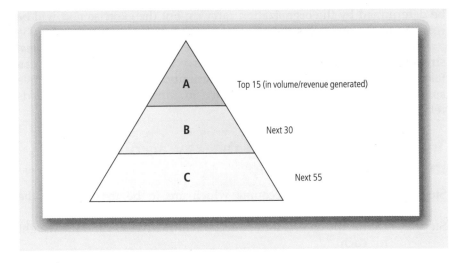

Figure 5.8
Example of an outcome of preliminary categorization

Step 2: define key account attractiveness

Attractiveness definition: this is a combination of a number of factors which can usually be summarized under three headings: growth rate, accessible volume or value and profit potential. Each of these headings will possess a degree of importance to the organization which should be calculated as follows:

Definition:
Growth is the average annual growth rate of revenue spent by that key account (the percentage growth 1998 over 1999 *plus* the percentage growth 1999 over 1998 *plus* the percentage growth 2000 over 1999 divided by three). If preferred, the compound growth rate could be used.

1 Growth – the average annual growth rate of revenue spent by that key account (the percentage growth 1998 over 1999 *plus* the percentage growth 1999 over 1998 *plus* the percentage growth 2000 over 1999 divided by three). If preferred, the compound growth rate could be used.

Definition:
Accessible volume or value is the *total* spend of the key account in t + 3 *less* revenue impossible to access, *regardless of investment made.*

2 Accessible volume or value – an attractive key account is not only large – it can also be accessed. One way of calculating this is to estimate the *total* spend of the key account in t + 3 (year three) *less* revenue impossible to access, *regardless of investment made.* Alternatively, the total spend can be used, which is the most frequent method as it does not involve any managerial judgement to be made which could distort the truth. *The former method is the preferred method.* An accessible volume or value factor score is simply the score multiplied by the weight (20 in example A).

Example A

Factors	Weight
Growth rate	40
Accessible volume or value	20
Profit potential	40
Total	100

Definition:
Profit potential is the margins available to any competitor.

NB. As the profit potential equals the market size multiplied by the margin multiplied by the growth, it would be reasonable to expect a *weighting* against each of these to be at *least* as shown, although an even higher weight on *growth* would be understandable in some circumstances

3 Profit potential – this is much more difficult to deal with and will vary considerably according to industry. One way of assessing the profit potential is to make an estimate of the margins available to any competitor. Another is to use Porter's (1980) five-forces model to estimate the profit potential of a key account, as in example B.

Example B

Factors	10 = Low/Good 1 = High/Bad	X weight*	Weighted Factor Score
1 Intensity of competition		0.50	
2 Threat of substitutes		0.05	
3 Threat of new entrants		0.05	
4 Power of suppliers		0.10	
5 Power of customer		0.30	
	Profit potential factor score	1.00	

*These weights are given as examples and can obviously be altered according to circumstances.

These factors are clearly a proxy for profit potential. Each is weighted according to its importance. The weights add up to 1.00 in order to give a *profit potential factor score* as in Porter's five-forces model used in example B. Please note that, following this calculation, the *profit potential factor* is simply multiplied by the weight (40 in example A).

Attractiveness variation: naturally, growth, size and profit will not encapsulate the requirements of all organizations.

It is then possible to add another heading, such as 'risk' or 'other' to the aforementioned three factors (growth rate, accessible volume or value and profit potential).

The following are the factors most frequently used to determine account attractiveness:

- Regular flow of work – stability.
- Strategy match.
- Prompt payment.
- Customers who see value in a broad product offering.
- Opportunity for cross-selling.
- East of doing business.
- Status/reference value.
- Hub of network/'Focal' company in a network.
- Important to a sister company.
- Requirement for global coverage.
- Time is of the essence.
- Requirement for a single point of total responsibility.
- Requirement for strategic alliances.
- Requirement to manage complex issues (for example, industrial relations and multiworkforces).

- Abdication (customer hands over total responsibility).
- Customer needs financial guarantees.
- Client looking to work with a listed company.
- Requirement to innovate on repetitive type work.
- Blue-chip customer capable of meeting your financial security requirements (top 100 company).

Attractiveness considerations: try to keep the total list of factors to five or less. If you require more, use the method outlined by Porter's (1980) five-forces model as in example B to encapsulate 'risk' or 'other', otherwise the calculations become cumbersome and trivial.

In addition, once agreed, under no circumstances should key account attractiveness factors be changed, otherwise the attractiveness of your key accounts is not being evaluated against common criteria and the matrix becomes meaningless. However, the scores will be specific to each key account.

It is also important to list the key accounts that you intend to apply the criteria to before deciding on the criteria themselves, since the purpose of the vertical axis is to discriminate between more and less attractive key accounts. The criteria themselves must be specific to the population of key accounts and must not be changed for different key accounts in the same population.

Step 3: score each key account

Score each key account on a scale of one to ten against the attractiveness factors and multiply the score by the weight. This will place each key account in the key account attractiveness axis from low to high.

Step 4: define business strength/position

This is a measure of an organization's *actual* strengths in each key account and it will differ according to each key account.

These critical success factors will usually be a combination of an organization's relative strengths versus competitors in connection with *customer-facing* needs, that is to say those things which are required by the customer. They can often be summarized as:

- product requirements,
- price requirements,
- service requirements,
- promotion requirements.

The weightings given to each should be specific to each key account. In the same way that 'profit' can be broken down into subheadings on the market attractiveness axis, so can each of these requirements be broken down further and analysed. Indeed, this is to be strongly recommended. The resulting subfactors should be dealt with in the same way as the subfactors described under key account attractiveness.

A quick way of doing this is to use the key account stages of relationship development outlined in Chapter 3 as a proxy for business strengths.

1 *Exploratory* (you do not currently do business with this account).
2 *Basic* (you have some transactional business with this account).
3 *Cooperative* (you have regular business with this account and may well be a preferred supplier, but you are only one of many suppliers and pricing is still important).
4 *Interdependent* (you have multifunctional, multilevel relationships, but the customer could still exit if necessary).
5 *Integrated* (you have multifunctional, multilevel relationships, your systems are interlinked and exit for both parties would be difficult).

Allocate one of these labels to each key account in your matrix. The labelled list of accounts can include key accounts with which you have no business yet.

Step 5: score critical success factors

Score the organization's *actual* strengths in each key account. An easy way to do this is to decide the actual stage of the relationship, i.e. *basic* to *integrated*, in order to find the position on the horizontal axis.

Step 6: produce the portfolio analysis

The portfolio analysis should produce a matrix which resembles Figure 5.9.

There are likely to be key accounts in all ten boxes. It is advisable to list the names of the accounts, one per line, in order of their position on the vertical and horizontal axes.

Enter two figures next to each account name on each line:

- your current sales and
- the total available sales over three years (to any competitor).

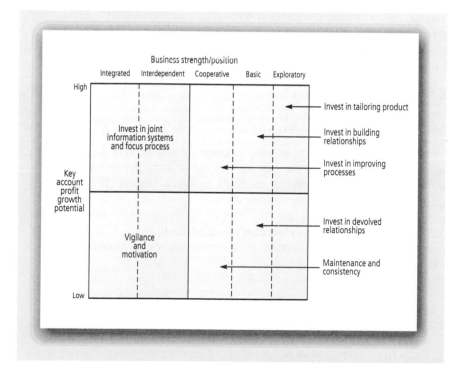

Figure 5.9
Portfolio analysis
matrix

Step 7: produce a forecast matrix (optional)

This analysis should position the key accounts on the horizontal axis where they are projected to be three years from now, *assuming no change to your current policies*.

The key accounts can only move *horizontally*, either to the left or to the right, because you have already taken account of potential future growth on the vertical axis.

Now enter a new figure for your *forecast* sales for each account, assuming no change in your current policies.

The first time you complete this analysis, it is unlikely that the forecast position will be satisfactory.

Step 8: produce a matrix showing the objectives' position

This analysis should position each key account on the horizontal axis showing the *objectives'* position in three years time of each one.

Accounts can either stay in their current box, move to the right or move to the left.

Enter a new figure for your *objectives* sales against each key account. Obviously, the total available sales for each one remains exactly the same.

Step 9: outline the objectives and strategies for each key account for the next three years

Finally, a strategic plan for each key account should be produced. It should outline the objectives and strategies for each one. A methodology for this will also be given in Chapter 6.

Step 10: check the financial outcomes from the strategies

Cost out the actions which comprise the stated strategies.

Summary

Market structure and market segmentation must always precede any kind of key account analysis because some markets and segments will always have a higher priority than others for organizations. Clearly, key accounts in high priority segments are more important than key accounts in lower priority segments.

Once this is done, key accounts should be prioritized according to the relative attractiveness to the organization of each key account and according to its competitive strength in each. This will enable an organization to allocate its scarce resources most effectively to achieve its objectives.

Reference

Porter, M. E. (1980) *Competitive Strategy*. The Free Press.

Chapter 6
Key account analysis

Introduction

We saw the basis on which key accounts should be defined and selected in Chapter 5. This was summarized diagrammatically and is repeated here as Figure 6.1.

The purpose of this chapter is to provide a set of specific and detailed procedures for key account analysis prior to producing a strategic marketing plan for each key account selected as being worthy of focused attention by the key account team.

An overview of the total process, which we have called the business partnership process, is given in Figure 6.2.

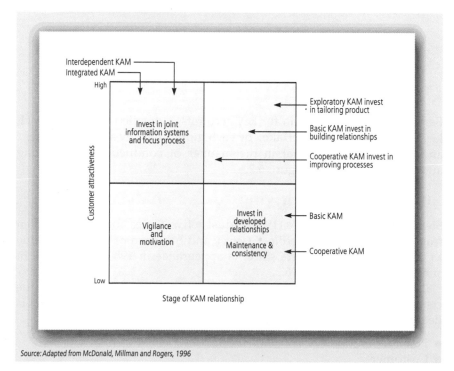

Source: Adapted from McDonald, Millman and Rogers, 1996

Figure 6.1
A four-box directional policy matrix

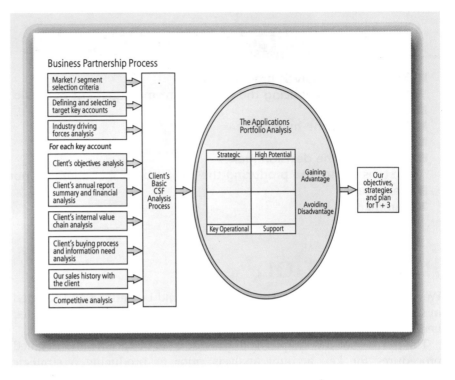

Figure 6.2
Business partnership
process

As steps 1 and 2 were dealt with sufficiently in Chapter 4, it is not necessary to repeat them here. This chapter is devoted to describing each of the remaining steps involved in key account pre-planning, beginning with step 3.

Key account analysis pre-planning

Before it is possible to plan for key accounts, a detailed analysis of each key account must be undertaken by each individual key account manager and their team, somewhat in the manner of conducting a marketing audit. This is step 3 in Figure 6.2.

Step 3: industry driving forces analysis

Step 3 is known as Porter's (1980) industry five-forces analysis. It is taken from Porter's book *Competitive Strategy* and has been of enormous value to generations of managers since its appearance in 1980. It is shown in summary form as Figure 6.3.

Put simply, any industry has a number of competitors (located in the centre of the figure) and the relative performance of these competitors is determined by recognizable forces.

- Potential entrants.
- Customers.

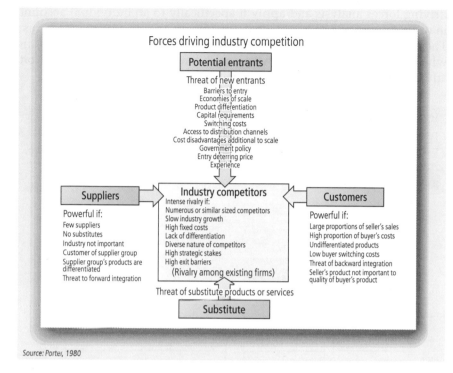

Source: Porter, 1980

Figure 6.3
Forces driving industry competition

- Potential substitute products and services.
- The power of suppliers.

The words in Figure 6.3 aptly describe the implications of each of the four outside forces on the competitors and it is clear that all competitors in a sector or industry will be affected by these driving forces.

> This analysis is obviously best done by someone in central support services, perhaps marketing, as there is little point in a number of key account managers in the same industry all wasting their time conducting the same analysis. If this is not practicable, then the job will indeed have to be done by individual key account managers for their own sectors.

It must be stressed, however, that such an analysis is a prerequisite to the individual account analysis described later, as it provides key account managers with a deep analysis of their customers' industry and how it works and affects their performance.

It should also be stressed here that steps 4–9 are all concerned with the analysis/diagnosis stage which must be completed by each key account manager before preparing a strategic plan for each key account.

Step 4: client's objectives analysis

The exercise given in Figure 6.4 should be completed for each key account being targeted. It can be seen that the intention is to take the industry

It must be stressed, however, that such an analysis is a prerequisite to the individual account analysis described later, as it provides key account managers with a deep analysis of their customers' industry and how it works and affects their performance.

driving forces analysis and apply it specifically to an individual account in order to understand better what advantages and disadvantages it has. The main reason for doing this is to help you to understand ways in which your products or services may enable the client to exploit advantages and minimize disadvantages.

It is not the intention to complete this document as if it were a proforma. Each heading is intended merely to act as a trigger for some powerful conclusions about your client's competitive situation. This information will be used along with the further information to be gathered in steps 5–9.

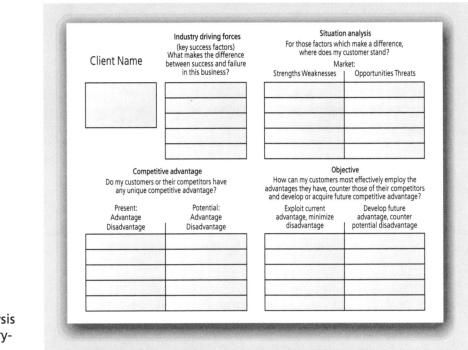

Figure 6.4
Objectives analysis exercise (industry-driving forces)

Step 5: client's annual report summary and financial analysis

Figure 6.5 enables a summary to be made of a careful reading and analysis of a client's published annual report. Even if there is not a formal report published for the shareholders (say, for example, if your client is a subsidiary or division of a larger company), the directors do nonetheless tend to produce internal reports and newsletters which can be used instead.

Such documents can be a major source of information on what your client believes to be the major issues facing them, their achievements and their objectives and strategies – in other words, their hopes for the future.

1. Major achievements	
2. Major problems/issues	
3. Objectives	
4. Strategies	
5. Conclusions/opportunities	

Figure 6.5
Annual report
summary

It is always possible to extract valuable information which can be used in helping you understand how your organization might be of assistance. This information can now be put alongside the information gleaned from the previous objectives analysis summary.

Figure 6.6 focuses on the financial affairs of your client and concerns information which can also be obtained from annual reports and other published sources. At first sight, this might appear to be some way removed from the reality of selling goods and services to a major account. However, a little thought will reveal that most organizations today are acutely aware of their financial performance indicators:

Most organizations today are acutely aware of their financial performance indicators.

- Current ratios.
- Net profit margins.
- Return on assets.
- Debtor control.
- Asset turnover.

The purpose of the analysis contained in Figure 6.6 is to make you acutely aware of the financial issues faced by your client and to encourage you to explore whether any of your products and services could improve any of these ratios.

It will be obvious that any supplier who has taken the trouble to work out what impact its products and services have on the customer's bottom line will be preferred to a potential supplier who focuses only on product features.

Definition: The internal value chain details the flow of goods and services through the organization's processes, from receipt through to aftersales service.

Step 6: client's internal value chain analysis

Figure 6.7 illustrates an organization's internal value chain as popularized by Professor Michael Porter in his book on competitive strategies

Financial ratio indicator	Formula	Source				Company standing	Industry standing	Does it appear as though improvement is needed?		
		Annual report						Yes	No	
Current ratio	Current assets / Current liabilities									
Net profit margin	Net profit / Net sales									
Return on assets	Net profit / Total assets									
Collection period	Debtors less bad debt / Average day's sales									
Stock turnover	Cost of goods sold / Stock									

Description of indicators		
	Current ratio	Measures the liquidity of a company – does it have enough money to pay the bills?
	Net profit margin	Measures the overall profitability of a company by showing the percentage of sales retained as profit after taxes have been paid. If this ratio is acceptable, there probably is no need to calculate the gross profit or operating profit margins
	Return on assets	Evaluates how effectively a company is managed by comparing the profitability of a company and its investments
	Collection period	Measures the activity of debtors. A prolonged collection period means that a company's funds are financing customers and not contributing to the cash flow of the company
	Stock turnover	Evaluates how fast funds are flowing through cost of goods sold to produce profit. If stock turns over faster, it is not in the plant as long before it is saleable as a product

Figure 6.6 Financial analysis

which was published in 1980. It is assumed that readers are familiar with this concept. The value chain is introduced here as an invaluable tool in understanding how a major account actually functions. The bottom level shows bought-in goods or services entering the organization, passing through operations and then moving out to their markets through distribution, marketing and sales and service. Sitting above these core processes are organizational support activities such as human resource management, procurement and so on.

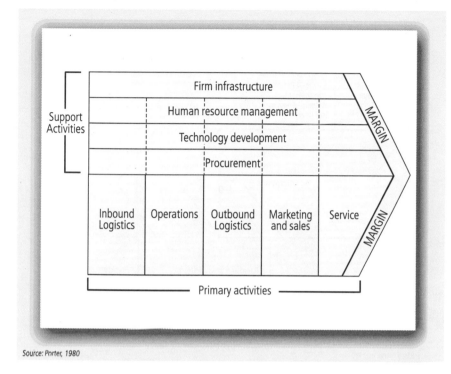

Source: Porter, 1980

Figure 6.7
The value chain

Investigating how a major account actually manages these core activities can be a substantial task for a key account team, involving, as it does, an in-depth understanding of the detailed processes of the customer. This could include, for example, understanding what happens to your goods when they are delivered, where they are stored, how they are handled, how they are moved, how they are unpacked, how they are used and so forth. The purpose of such detailed analysis is to explore what issues and problems are faced by your customer with a view to resolving them through improvements and innovations.

Figure 6.8 is a very simple illustration of some of these issues and how they could be improved, thus representing sources of differentiation in the value chain.

All information emanating from this analysis can be usefully summarized using a format similar to that shown in Figure 6.9. From this, it will be seen that there are four general headings of customer benefits:

1 Possibilities for increased revenue for the customer.
2 Possibilities for cost displacement.
3 Possibilities for cost avoidance.
4 Intangible benefits.

Another way of looking at this is to identify the methods of gaining competitive edge through value in use.

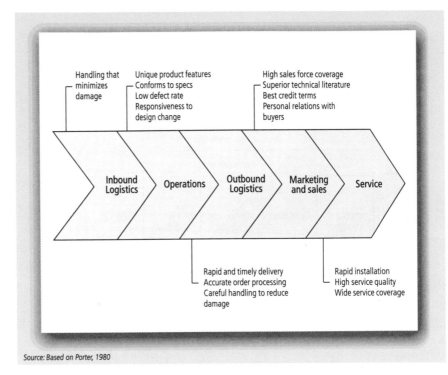

Figure 6.8
Sources of differentiation in the value chain

Source: Based on Porter, 1980

Tangible benefits	Product solution	Analysis and comment
Increased revenue		
Increased sales volume		
Enhanced product line		
Cost displacement		
Reduced labour costs		
Reduced equipment costs		
Reduced maintenance costs		
Lowered stock costs		
Reduced energy costs		
Cost avoidance		
Reduced new personnel requirement		
Eliminate planned new equipment		
Intangible benefits		
Customer goodwill		
Improved decision making		

Figure 6.9
Value chain analysis summary

1 *Reduce the life cycle/Alter the cost mix*. Customers are often willing to pay a considerably higher initial price for a product with significantly lower post-purchase costs.
2 *Expand value through functional redesign*. For example, a product which increases the user's production capacity or throughput, a product which enables the user to improve the quality or reliability of his or her end-product, a product which enhances end-use flexibility or a product which adds functions or permits added applications.
3 Expand incremental value by developing associated intangibles. For example, service, financing and 'prestige'.

Mini-case 1:

Value chain analysis for a packaging company

An international chemical company undertook this investigation process using a novel method. They organized a two-day event for eight very senior people from different functions in a large packaging company. These executives included marketing people, a health and safety executive, an environmental specialist, a logistics manager, a manufacturing manager and a couple of directors! These executives were matched by equivalent managers and directors from the supplying company. An independent consultant was asked to chair the two-day event.

The purpose of the event, which was held in a neutral location, was to investigate ways in which the several goods and services of the supplying company were received, used and perceived by the customer. This inquiry was obviously only possible because of the good relationships already enjoyed by the supplier.

While it took a few hours for the independent moderator to break down the natural barriers to honest and open communication, the event had a major impact on the processes and attitudes of the supplier. For example, at one stage the customers were asked to go into a syndicate room and write down all the things they did not like or found inadequate in the supplying company. The sheer size of the list and the contents so shocked the supplier that it immediately agreed to set up a number of functional and cross-functional working groups comprising executives from both sides in order to study how cost-effective improvements could be made.

All issues were investigated openly and honestly, ranging from the strategic issues faced by the customer in its industry, to very tactical issues concerned with processes. The end-result was a dramatically improved relationship which led to substantial benefits to both sides.

It is not suggested that this is the only way to discover the kind of detailed information outlined in Figure 6.9. In many cases, much patience is required over considerable periods of time and the effectiveness and efficiency with which this investigative task can be carried out will be a function of how good and deep the existing relationships are.

Nonetheless, it is difficult to see how improvements can be made without a thorough understanding of the customer's systems and processes. The list of possibilities for improvement for the supplier is now growing quite considerably. However, there are still more aspects of the business which need to be analysed.

Step 7: the customer's buying process

Figure 6.10 outlines the buying process for goods and services. In the remainder of this section, it will be assumed that you are selling a service, although the same process applies equally well to products.

Customer Analysis Form
Salesperson ______ Customer ______
Products ______ Address ______
Telephone number ______
Buy class: new buy / straight re-buy / modified re-buy
Date of analysis ______
Date of reviews ______

Member of Decision Making Unit (DMU) — Buy Phase	Name	Production	Sales & Marketing	Research & Development	Finance & Accounts	Purchasing	Data Processing	Other
1 Recognizes need or problem and works out general solution								
2 Works out characteristics and quantity of what is needed								
3 Prepares detailed specification								
4 Searches for and locates potential sources of supply								
5 Analyses and evaluates tenders, plans, products								
6 Selects supplier								
7 Places order								
8 Checks and tests products								

Factors for consideration: 1 price; 2 performance; 3 availability; 4 back-up service; 5 reliability of supplier; 6 other users' experience; 7 guarantees and warranties; 8 payment terms, credit or discount; 9 other, eg. past purchases, prestige, image, etc.

Source: Adapted from Robinson, Farris and Wind, 1967

Figure 6.10 Buying process for goods and services

Selling to an organization can be a complex process because it is possible for a number of different people to become involved at the customer end. Although theoretically only one of these is the buyer, in practice he or she might not be allowed to make a decision to purchase until others with technical expertise or hierarchical responsibility have given their approval.

The personal authority of the buyer will to a large extent be governed by the following factors:

1 *The cost of the service* – the higher the cost, the higher up in the organization will the purchasing decision be made (see Table 6.1). Please note that, although the level of expenditure figures will have increased substantially during the past sixteen years, the table is included because it is indicative of a hierarchy of purchasing authority.
2 *The 'newness' of the service* – the relative novelty of the service will pose an element of commercial risk for an organization. A new and untried proposition will require support at a senior management level, whereas a routine, non-risky service can be handled at a lower level.

Table 6.1 Responsibility for financial expenditure

Level of expenditure	Level at which decision is taken			
	Board (collective)	Individual director	Departmental manager	Lower management or clerical
Over £50,000	88%	11%	2%	–
Up to £50,000	70%	25%	4%	less than 0.5%
Up to £5,000	29%	55%	14%	2%
Up to £2,500	18%	54%	24%	4%
Up to £500	4%	31%	52%	14%

Source: 'How British Industry Buys', a survey conducted by Cranfield School of Management for *The Financial Times*, January 1984

3 *The complexity of the service* – the more complex the service offered, the more technical the implications which have to be understood within the client company. Several specialist managers might be required to give their approval before the transaction can be completed.

All those involved in the **buying decision** are known as the decision-making unit (DMU) and it is important for the salesperson to identify the DMU in all current and prospective customer companies. Table 6.2 provides some research findings which demonstrate how rarely sales-people reach all component members of the DMU.

A useful way of anticipating who would be involved in the decision-making processes in a company is to consider the sales transaction from the buyer's point of view. It has been recognized that the process can be split into a number of distinct steps known as 'buy phases'. These buy phases will be followed in most cases, particularly for major purchases. It will be obvious that at stages beyond the *cooperative* key account management (KAM) stage, the incumbent supplier will have an inside

● Definition: All those involved in the buying decision are known as the decision-making unit (DMU).

Table 6.2 Buying influences by company size

Number of employees	Average number of buying influences (the DMU)	Average number of contacts made by salesperson
0–200	3.42	1.72
201–400	4.85	1.75
401–1000	5.81	1.90
1000 plus	6.50	1.65

Source: McGraw-Hill

track and, hence, an advantage, throughout the process. In many cases, customers do not even bother to put their proposed purchase requirements out to tender, preferring to deal with their current trusted partner.

Buy phases

(This section of the text owes much to the original research conducted by the Marketing Science Institute in the USA under the guidance of Patrick J. Robinson.)

1 *Problem identification* – a problem is identified or anticipated and a general solution worked out. For example, the marketing planning department finds that it has inadequate information about sales records and costs. It needs better information made available on the computer.

2 *Problem definition* – the problem is examined in more detail in order to grasp the dimensions and, hence, the nature of the ultimate choice of solution. Taking our earlier example of the international chemical company further, investigation shows that the supplier's original software system was not devised with the customer's current marketing planning requirements in mind. A new system is required which can also provide the option for the inclusion of other new data.

3 *Solution specification* – the various technical requirements are listed and a sum of money is allocated to cover the cost of investing in new software.

4 *Search* – a search is made for potential suppliers, in this case those with the capability of devising a 'tailor-made' system to meet the above requirements.

5 *Assessment* – proposals from interested suppliers are assessed and evaluated.

6 *Selection* – a supplier is selected and final details are probably negotiated prior to the next step.

7 *Agreement* – a contract/agreement is signed.

8 *Monitoring* – the service is monitored in terms of meeting installation deadlines and performance claims.

> If we happened to be running a computer programming service to industry, we could deduce from the buying process that the DMU at this company might well contain the following people: a marketing planner, a sales director, a sales office manager, the company computer specialist, the company accountant, the company secretary and perhaps even the managing director depending on the nature of the contract and the buyer. Sometimes the buyer might be one of those already listed and not exist as a separate role.

We could also speculate with some certainty that each of these people would need to be satisfied about different aspects of the efficiency of our service and we would need to plan accordingly.

For now, it is enough to recognize that, when selling to an organization, the person with the title of buyer is often unable to make important decisions on their own. Although he or she can be a useful cog in the company's purchasing machine, he or she is often not a free agent.

The person with the title of buyer is often unable to make important decisions on their own.

Pressures on the buyer

When we purchase something for the home we know from our own experience how difficult it can sometimes be. Even if we are only buying a carpet, we have to agree whether or not it should be plain or patterned, what colour, what price, what quality and so on. Even seemingly straightforward considerations like these are clouded by issues such as whether the neighbours or relatives will think we are copying them or whether we are being too chic or too outrageous. The buying decision makers in a typical company are faced with a greater multitude of pressures which come from two directions: from outside the company and from inside the company.

External pressures

External pressures can be many and various and may involve important issues such as the following:

1 *The economic situation* – what will be the cost of borrowing? Are interest rates likely to rise or fall? Is it a good time to invest in a new service now? Is the market decline really over or should we wait for more signals of recovery?
2 *Political considerations* – how will government fiscal policy affect our business or that of our customers? Will proposed legislation have an impact on either us or our markets?
3 *Technology* – how are we as a company keeping up with technological developments? How does this new proposal rate on a technological scale? Is it too near the frontiers of existing knowledge? How long will it be before a whole new phase of technology supersedes this investment?
4 *Environmental considerations* – will this new service be advantageous to us in terms of energy conservation or pollution control? Does it present any increase in hazards to our workforce? Will we need more room to expand? Is such room available?
5 *The business climate* – how do our profit levels compare with those of companies in general and those in our type of business in particular? Are there material cost increases in the pipeline which could reduce our profits? Is the cost of labour increasing?

Any one of these external issues could put pressure on the buying decision maker – and this is only half the picture.

Internal pressures

Another set of pressures evolve from within the company itself such as the following:

1 *Confused information* – it is often difficult to obtain the correct information to support a buying decision. Either the information does not exist or it has not been communicated accurately from the specialist department. Sometimes it is not presented in a convenient form and this leads to confusion and misunderstanding.
2 *Internal politics* – the relative status of individuals or departments can sometimes hinder the buying process. Personal rivalries or vested interests can create difficulties about priorities or standards. The 'politics' might entail non-essential people being involved in the decision-making process, thereby elongating the communication chain and slowing down decision making.
3 *Organizational* – how the company is organized can affect the efficiency of its buying process. It is essential for everyone within the company to be aware of their role and level of authority if they are to perform effectively.

Personal pressures

Buyers can be pressurized by a number of personal matters, some real, others imagined. They might be unsure about their role or how their colleagues accept their judgement. They might lack experience in the buying role and be unsure of how to conduct themselves. They might prefer a quiet life and therefore be against change, preferring to continue transactions with tried and tested suppliers – even if it can be clearly demonstrated that there are advantages in changing them. They might be naturally shy and not enjoy first meetings. They might find it difficult to learn new information about technical developments or the special features of your particular service.

> All of these pressures, both external and internal, have a profound bearing on the behaviour of the buyer and, if the account manager is to relate to the buyer, he or she must try to understand them.

By way of summarizing this section on business-to-business selling, it can be demonstrated that the successful account manager needs to be aware of all these things when approaching a buyer acting on behalf of an organization. All of the following elements need to be known and understood:

- The relative influence of the buyer in the context of the particular product or service being offered.
- What constitutes the DMU in the buying company.
- How the buying process works.
- The pressures on the buying decision maker.

With this information, the account manager is in a better position to plan his or her work and to adopt appropriate conduct when face-to-face with the buying decision maker(s). Exactly how this information should be used will be covered later in the chapter.

Buy classes

Whether or not the account manager is selling to an individual or to an organization, the decision-making processes of the prospects can be divided into what are termed 'buy classes'. There are three types of buy class

1 *New buy* – in effect, all the foregoing discussion has focused on the new buy category. It is here that those people who make up the DMU are fully exercised as the buy phases unfold. In the new buy class, the needs of all decision makers must be met and influenced by the salesperson. Not surprisingly, this takes time and so it is not unusual for a lengthy period to elapse between the initial discussion and contract closure.

2 *Straight rebuy* – once the salesperson has had the opportunity of demonstrating how the service can help the customer, further purchases of the service do not generally require such a rigorous examination of all of the buy phases. In fact, should the customer merely want a repeat purchase of the same service, then their only concerns are likely to be about issues such as has the price been held to the same level as before, will the standard of the service be unchanged and can it be provided at a specific time? Such issues can generally be resolved by negotiation with the buyer.

3 *Modified rebuy* – sometimes a modification of the product or service might be necessary. It might be that the supplier wants to update the product or service and provide better performance by using different methods or equipment. Alternatively, it could be the customer who calls for some form of modification from the original purchase. Whatever the origin, all or some of the buy phases will have to be re-examined and again the salesperson will have to meet with and persuade and satisfy the relevant members of the DMU.

There are often advantages for an account manager in trying to change a straight rebuy into a modified rebuy. They are twofold:

1 A modified rebuy reactivates and strengthens the relationship with the various members of the customer's DMU.

2 The more closely a supplier can match its service to the customer's needs (and remember this matching only comes about as a result of a mutual learning, as communication and trust develop between the supplier and the customer), the more committed the customer becomes to the product or service.

The higher the commitment the customer has to the particular product or service and the supplier, the more difficult it becomes for competitors to break in.

The higher the commitment the customer has to the particular product or service and the supplier, the more difficult it becomes for competitors to break in.

Identifying the decision maker

Recognizing that there is a DMU is an important first step for the account manager but, having done this, it is essential to identify who actually has the power to authorize the purchase. No matter how persuasive the arguments for buying your service, if you are not reaching the key decision maker then all your efforts could well be in vain. Identifying this person is too important to be left to chance and yet many account managers fail to meet with them. Sometimes they just have not done enough research about the company to obtain an accurate picture of its character and key concerns. It is important that the account manager research the company sufficiently in order to obtain a thorough understanding of its operations, personnel and priorities.

If you are not reaching the key decision maker then all your efforts could well be in vain.

> Alternatively, many account managers prefer to continue liaising with their original contacts in the client company, the ones with whom they feel comfortable and have come to regard as friends, rather than to extend their network to include more influential client representatives. Because many purchase decision makers will hold senior positions, the thought of meeting them somehow seems a daunting prospect, particularly to complacent or ill-prepared account managers.

Yet many of these fears are groundless. There is no evidence that senior executives set out to be deliberately obstructive or use meetings to expose the account manager's possible inadequacies. In fact, quite the opposite appears to be true.

Certainly, the decision makers will be busy people and so will want discussion to be to the point and relevant. At the same time, they will be trying to get the best deal for the company and it is only natural that they should.

Step 8: your sales history with the client

Figure 6.11 is a very simple analysis of your sales over a designated period of time working with the customer. The purpose is merely to summarize your business history, share and prospects with this customer.

Your sales history with the client					
Products		T-2	T-1	T-0	Trend
Customer volume (Total)					
YOUR volume					
YOUR share volume					
YOUR share value					
Sales analysis					
Products		T-2	T-1	T-0	Trend
	Val				
	Vol				
	%				
	Val				
	Vol				
	%				
	Val				
	Vol				
	%				
	Val				
	Vol				
	%				
	Val				
	Vol				
	%				
Comments					

Figure 6.11
Sales analysis and history

Competitive comparison	Importance Rating	You	Competitor 1 2 3	Implications
Product quality				
Product range				
Availability				
Delivery				
Price/discounts				
Terms				
Sales support				
Promotion support				
Other				

Importance rating
(by customer)
A – very important (essential)
B – important (desirable)
C – low importance

Rating
(customer view)
1 – consistently/fully meets needs
2 – meets needs inconsistently
3 – fails to meet needs

Competitors' strategy	
Competitor	Strategy
1.	
2.	
3.	

Figure 6.12 Competitive comparison and competitor strategy

Step 9: competitive comparison and competitor strategy

Figure 6.12 shows one of a number of possible ways of establishing how well you are meeting the customer's needs in comparison with your competitors. It is obviously better if this is done using evidence obtained from independent market research, but providing the analysis suggested in this chapter is carried out thoroughly and with diligence, it should be possible to complete this part of the analysis internally with sufficient accuracy.

Definition: ●
A SWOT is an analysis of your strengths and weaknesses compared to competitors and of the opportunities and threats by a key account.

Some people prefer to carry out this analysis using a more traditional SWOT (strengths, weaknesses, opportunities and threats) format as given in Figure 6.13.

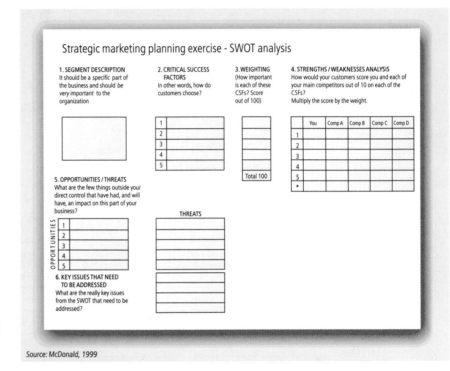

Figure 6.13
Strategic marketing planning exercise – SWOT analysis

Source: McDonald, 1999

The main point of course is that any organization hoping to get and keep business with a major account needs to provide superior customer value and this can only be achieved by comparisons with the best that competitors have to offer.

Next steps

Definition: ●
Customer critical success factors are those factors which are critical to the customer's future success.

The painstaking key account analysis is now complete and a number of customer critical success factors will have been accumulated, together with specific ways in which your products or services and processes can help.

Figure 6.14 describes a useful way of categorizing your business solutions and approaches to your client prior to producing a strategic marketing plan for your customer, which will be explained in the next chapter.

The applications portfolio comprises four quadrants. The quadrants at the bottom left and right are labelled avoiding disadvantage. While the meaning of this label might be self-evident, it is nonetheless worth providing an example of this category.

> Take, for instance, a bank considering buying automatic teller machines (ATMs) for use by customers outside bank opening hours. Not having ATMs would clearly place the bank at a disadvantage. However, having them does not give the bank any advantage either. The majority of commercial transactions fall into this category.

The bottom left quadrant represents key operational activities, such as basic accounting, manufacturing and distribution systems. The bottom right quadrant might include activities such as producing overhead slides for internal presentations.

In contrast, the top two quadrants represent a real opportunity for differentiating your organization's offering by creating advantage for the customer. The top right quadrant might be beta testing a product, service or process prior to making a major investment in launching it for the customer.

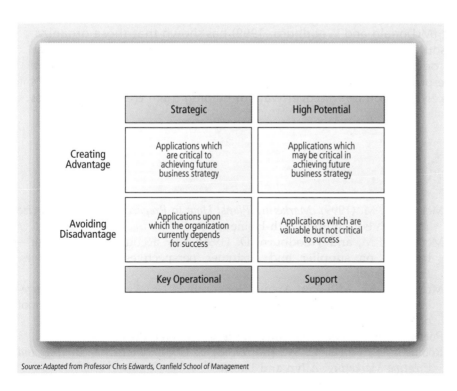

Source: Adapted from Professor Chris Edwards, Cranfield School of Management

Figure 6.14
The applications portfolio

Mini-case 2:

Gaining advantage

A classic example of a high potential application was Thompson's computer systems in the leisure/holiday market where the company was able to place its own holidays at the head of all travel agents' lists.

> The reality of commercial life is that most of what any organization does falls into the 'avoiding disadvantage' category.

The reality of commercial life is that most of what any organization does falls into the avoiding disadvantage category. However, leading companies adopt a proactive business approach. They work hard at developing products, services and processes designed to deliver advantage for their major accounts, for it is clear that creative, customer-focused suppliers will always be preferred over those who merely offer 'me too' products and trade only on price.

The KAM Best Practice Research Club at Cranfield has strong evidence to suggest that, once such an audit on a key account has been completed, if it is presented formally to senior managers in the account, the response is extremely favourable and, further, that additional confidential information is likely to be provided by the customer to enable the supplier to prepare a strategic marketing plan. This is the main topic addressed in Chapter 7.

Summary

Research at Cranfield (McDonald and Woodburn, 1999) has shown that those organizations which invest resources in detailed analysis of the needs and processes of their key accounts fare much better in building long-term profitable relationships. We have termed this stage pre-planning. Armed with a detailed knowledge of your customer's business, it is more likely that you can discover ways of helping them create advantages in their marketplace.

References

McDonald, M. (1999). *Marketing Plans: How to Prepare Them, How to Use Them*, 4th edn. Butterworth-Heinemann.

McDonald, M. and Woodburn, D. (1999) Key account management – building on supplier and customer perspectives. *Financial Times*, Prentice Hall.

McDonald, M., Millman, A. and Rogers, B. (1996) *Key Account Management – Learning from Supplier and Customer Perspectives*. Cranfield School of Management.

Porter, M. E. (1980). *Competitive Strategy*. The Free Press.

Robinson, J., Farris, C. W. and Wind, Y. (1967). *Industrial Buying and Creative Marketing*. Allyn and Bacon.

Chapter 7

Planning for key accounts and measuring profitability

Introduction

The purpose of this chapter is threefold: to explain the key elements of marketing planning, to position key account planning within this context and to show how to measure key account profitability. These themes are set out in three sections. The first section describes the nature of marketing planning and outlines the main steps involved in the marketing planning process. The second section locates key account planning within this process and explains its fundamental characteristics. The third section examines the significance of key account profitability and the importance of measuring it accurately.

No matter where a key account is positioned in the relationship development model (RDM) (see Figure 3.1), if a supplier has aspirations for building a relationship with a customer over time, then some kind of plan setting out a strategy for how this is to be achieved will be necessary. The problem with this is that most organizations are not very good at or even very knowledgeable about planning. Thus, this chapter will also explain how to prepare a strategic plan for a key account. However, key account planning must be placed firmly in the context of strategic marketing planning, otherwise it will not be effective.

> The problem with this is that most organizations are not very good at planning.

> However, key account planning must be placed firmly in the context of strategic marketing planning, otherwise it will not be effective.

Strategic marketing planning

Marketing planning contributes to business success by both providing a detailed analysis of opportunities for meeting customer needs and by promoting a professional approach to making available those products or services which deliver the benefits customers are seeking to well-defined market segments.

> Marketing planning should not be confused with budgets and forecasts. Marketing planning is specifically concerned with identifying what and to whom sales need be made in the longer term to give revenue budgets any chance of succeeding.

There is no such thing as a 'market' – only people with needs and money.

There is no such thing as a 'market' – only people with needs and money. An organization must offer something to those prospective customers which will make them want to buy from it rather than from any other supplier. Nowadays, markets are generally over-supplied and customers have a wide choice. So, if an organization is to persuade people to part with their money, it has to understand their needs in depth and to develop specific 'offers' with a differential advantage over competitors' offers. These offers are not just physical products or services; they are to do with the totality of the relationship between supplier and customer and include the organization's reputation, brand name, accessibility, service levels and so on.

In the less complex environments of the 1960s and 1970s, which were characterized by growth and the easy marketability of products and services, a 'production' orientation was possible, largely because demand seemed limitless. During the late 1980s, when demand was less buoyant, financial husbandry began its ascendancy. Indeed, it seemed to work for a while: profits continued to rise as costs and productivity increased.

Alas, the ratio-driven, cost-cutting, margin management mentality persisted. Every product had to make a prescribed margin over what it cost to produce it, otherwise prices were raised or it was taken off the market. Too little attention was paid to the number of times products were turned over, so low margin products were sacrificed. However, overheads either remained or were rationalized as organizations drove themselves towards fewer, more profitable products. Eventually 'anorexia industrialosa' (an excessive desire to be leaner and fitter, leading to emaciation and death) set in.

Companies went bankrupt at an unprecedented rate and even the latest innovative approaches (total quality management (TQM), balanced scorecards, business process re-engineering (BPR), relationship management, knowledge management, customer relationship management and so on) were unable to halt the rot that had set in.

> Indeed, over a fifteen-year period, most of Britain's highest return on investment public limited companies either disappeared, downsized or got into severe financial difficulties. Nor was the contagion confined to Britain. According to Pascale (1990), author of *Managing on the Edge: How Successful Companies use Conflict to Stay Ahead*, only six of Peters and Waterman's (1982) 43 excellent companies in *In Search of Excellence: Lessons from American Best-run Companies* would have been considered excellent a mere eight years later.

It became increasingly clear that, sooner or later, corporations were going to have to turn their attentions to addressing their markets and their customers instead of tinkering with their own internal processes – and this is where strategic marketing planning comes into its own.

There is now a substantial body of evidence to show that requisite marketing planning not only results in greater profitability and stability over time, but it also helps to reduce the friction and operational difficulties which arise within organizations.

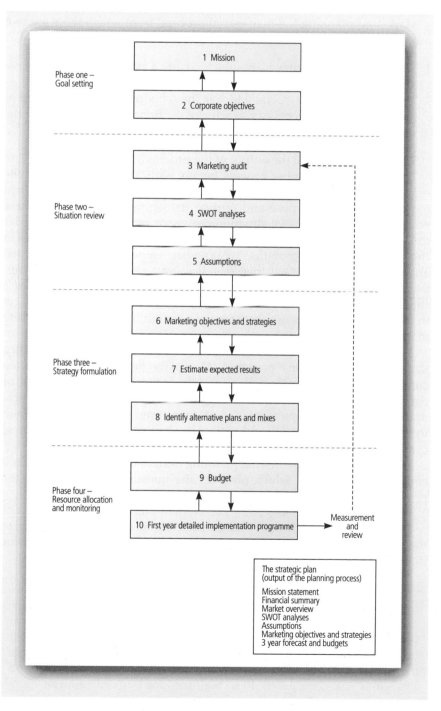

Figure 7.1
The ten steps in the strategic marketing planning process

Definition:
Marketing planning is a logical sequence of activities leading to the setting of marketing objectives and the formulating of plans to achieve them.

Marketing planning is a logical sequence of activities leading to the setting of marketing objectives and the formulating of plans for achieving them. It is a management process which is conceptually very simple. As a planning system, it is a way of identifying options, of making them explicit, of formulating marketing objectives which are consistent with the organization's overall objectives and of scheduling and costing out the activities most likely to achieve the objectives.

Marketing planning is a managerial process, from which there are two outputs:

1 The strategic marketing plan, which covers a period of between three and five years
2 The tactical marketing plan, which is the scheduling and costing out of the specific actions necessary to achieve the first year's objectives in the strategic marketing plan.

The process itself and the output of the process are shown in Figure 7.1

The marketing planning process begins with an identification of the organization's mission and financial objectives, which serves to confirm the organization's purpose and outline its aspirations. The next phase embodies a comprehensive situation review or marketing audit in order to establish inherent problems and potential. This involves summaries in the form of SWOT (strengths, weaknesses, opportunities and threats) analyses for main products/markets, leading to the making of assumptions and the setting of draft marketing objectives and strategies for a

Definition:
A marketing objective is a quantitative statement about sales volume, value, market share or profit.

three to five year period. At this stage, other functional managers get involved in order to ensure that the organization is capable of resourcing marketing's requirements.

Alternative plans and budgets are then finalized and, eventually, tactical marketing plans prepared. Company headquarters will often consolidate both the strategic plans and the tactical plans into business or corporate plans. At the start of the organization's fiscal year, the tactical marketing plan is implemented and monitored via the management information system, until the whole process begins again in the next fiscal cycle.

This strategic and operational planning system can be represented as a circle (see Figure 7.2), which obviates the question about whether the process is top down or bottom up for, clearly, it is continuous.

The contents of a strategic marketing plan are listed in Table 7.1.

Definition:
A marketing strategy is a statement of how the marketing objectives are to be achieved using the 4Ps (product, price, place and promotion).

The plan can be made as formal or informal as necessary according to the particular circumstances. The main point is that it should combine thoroughness with creativity.

Over twenty scholarly research studies have identified hostile corporate cultures and financially driven systems and procedures as the main barriers to implementing effective marketing planning. It is clear that, until organizations learn to grasp the nettle of customer orientation, financial husbandry will dominate corporate life, despite the fact that it has caused so many casualties during the 1980s and 1990s and will continue to do so well into the new millennium.

Table 7.1 Contents of a strategic marketing plan

1. A mission or purpose statement

2. A financial summary

3. A market overview
   What the market is
   How it works
   What the key segments are

4. A SWOT on each segment
   What value does each require?
   What value can we create to persuade customers to buy from us?

5. A portfolio summary of the SWOT
   This classifies segments according to our relative strengths and the
   potential of each for growth in profits over the next three years

6. Assumptions

7. Marketing objectives and strategies
   Prioritized in accordance with the portfolio summary

8. A budget
   For three years

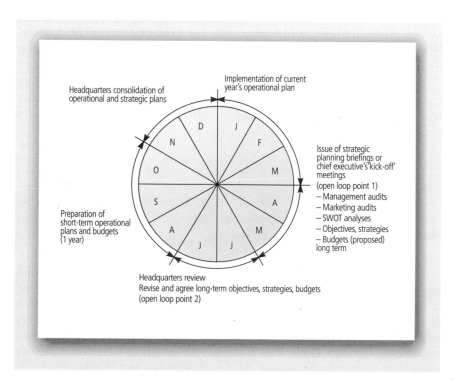

Figure 7.2
Strategic and
operational
planning

Definition:
Attributable costs are the major items of operating and overhead expenses which can be directly attributed to dealing with a particular customer.

However, financial orientation aside, it is a sad state of affairs that, in 2000, companies still fail to allocate attributable interface costs properly and, hence, have little idea which are their profitable and unprofitable customers.

Another endemic problem in business is the depth of ignorance about what marketing actually is. This is graphically illustrated by the comment of one managing director, who announced aggressively at a public seminar that 'There is no time for marketing in my company until sales improve!'

The simple truth is that, while it is the marketing people who work out the value required by customers, it is the whole company which delivers this value.

> Companies which persist in organizing themselves around tribes of personnel, such as accountants, engineers, information technology (IT) specialists, salespeople and so on, cannot by their very nature achieve this integrated delivery of customer value.

How can any organization achieve customer focus while it continues to organize itself around what it makes rather than around its customers or its markets?

Such groups will never subjugate their own tribal goals to the broader aims of customer satisfaction and retention. In addition, how can any organization achieve customer focus while it continues to organize itself around what it makes rather than around its customers or its markets?

Many corporate cultures are, in the main, hostile to the marketing ethic. Directors who got their job as a result of professional behaviour considered appropriate in the 1960s, 1970s, 1980s and 1990s do not know how to respond to increased competition and static or declining markets. Their natural reaction is to resort to traditional measures, one of which is to cut costs without addressing the fundamental issue of growth. However, crucially, growth requires customers who want to buy things from us rather than from our competitors.

It also takes intellect, confidence and courage to take a strategic rather than a purely tactical approach. Unsuccessful organizations do not bother with strategic marketing planning at all; instead, they rely on sales forecasts and associated budgets.

> The problem with this route is that many salespeople sell the products they find easiest to sell (usually at a maximum discount) to those customers who treat them the nicest. Thus, by developing short-term budgets first and then extrapolating them, companies only succeed in extrapolating their own inadequacies.

Preoccupation with short-term forecasts is typical of those companies which confuse this approach with strategic marketing planning. Such companies are being left behind by companies led by directors with a pioneering spirit anchored in practical expertise. These business frontiers men and women lead the effort in understanding their markets and customers, for they know that it is only by creating superior customer value that their companies will be able to survive and thrive.

Transforming 'vision' into reality is where strategic marketing planning comes in, enabling a number of plans or models to be developed which spell out quantitatively and qualitatively the value that each employee must create in order to achieve collective prosperity.

Key account planning

Referring to Figure 7.2, it will be clear from the planning cycle that key account planning must take place at the same time as or even before draft plans are prepared for a strategic business unit.

Mini-case 1:

Key account planning in a medical supplies company

If this is not clear, the following example of a medical supplies company servicing the needs of a national health service should help.

It will be seen from Figure 7.3 that there are four 'markets' within hospitals to be served:

1 Medical.
2 Administration.
3 Catering.
4 Energy.

The supplies company will service a number of hospital groups or key accounts, referred to here as A, B, C, D, etc. Each of these hospital groups may well have its own key account manager who has to plan for the group. Thus, for example, the key account manager for hospital A has to prepare a draft plan across all four markets and this would clearly be a key input to the planning process shown in Figure 7.1.

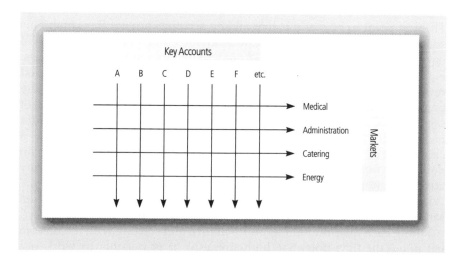

Figure 7.3
Hospital groups and key account managers

The position of key account planning in strategic marketing planning

All planning should start with the market where the customers are. Indeed, in anything other than small organizations it is clearly absurd to think that any kind of meaningful planning can take place without the committed inputs of those who operate most directly with customers.

Figure 7.4 shows a hierarchy of planning with key account planning at the base. Every principle outlined in this chapter applies right down to the individual key account. Thus, the planning process shown in Figure 7.1 would be first applied to key accounts. From this point onwards in the chapter the discussion of strategic and tactical planning will focus on key accounts.

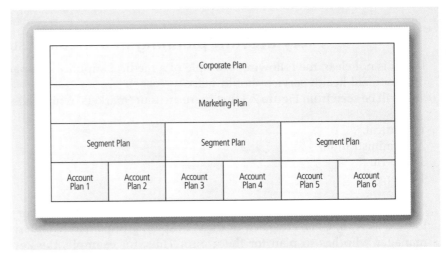

Figure 7.4
The planning hierarchy

Guidelines for setting key account objectives and strategies

The first point to be made is that all key accounts are not the same. This adage applies at two levels. First, it is obvious that all organizations will have preferred markets and preferred segments within these markets. Figure 7.5 (given earlier as Figure 5.6) shows the current and projected revenues from different segments within a single market. Clearly, any organization without a distinct policy towards each of these market segments is unlikely to be able to make a success of key account management (KAM). On the understanding that our organization has a clear and well-communicated policy for each of its target markets, we can now turn our attention to setting objectives and strategies for key accounts within each segment.

Let us take another look at the key account portfolio matrix given earlier as Figure 5.9 and repeated here as Figure 7.6.

Taking each quadrant in Figure 7.6 in turn and starting with the bottom left quadrant (low-potential/high-strength), it is possible to work out

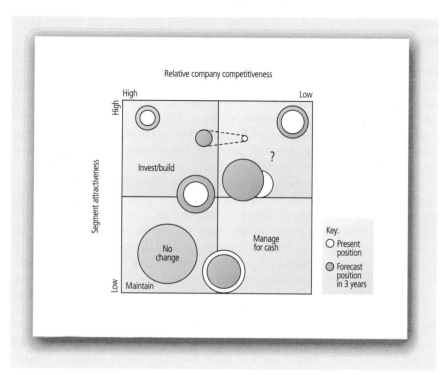

Figure 7.5
Prioritizing and selecting segments

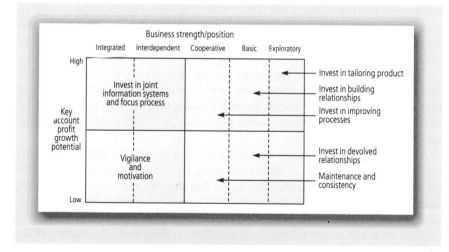

Figure 7.6
Portfolio analysis matrix

sensible objectives and strategies for each key account. Accounts meeting the profile of the first quadrant are likely to continue to deliver excellent revenues for some considerable time, even though they may be in static or declining markets. Good relationships are already enjoyed and should be preserved. Retention strategies are therefore advisable, incorporating prudence, vigilance and motivation. More importantly, as the supplying company will be seeking a good return on previous investment, any further financial input here should be of the maintenance kind. In this

Definition: ●
The cost of capital is usually taken to be the weighted average return on investment of all competitors in a specific sector. Any organization generating returns in excess of the cost of capital are enhancing shareholder value.

Definition: ●
NPV calculations work on the principle that cash received in future periods will be worth less than cash received today. Future revenues are therefore discounted at a rate usually equalling the cost of capital.

To do so would be a bit like pulling up a new plant every few weeks to see whether it had grown!

Definition: ●
Net free cash flow is cash generated in excess of cash used.

way, it should be possible to free up cash and resources for investing in key accounts with greater growth potential.

The quadrant to the top left (high-potential/high-strength) represents accounts with the highest potential growth in sales and profits. These warrant a quite aggressive investment approach, providing it is justified by returns. Net present value (NPV) calculations may be used as a basis for evaluating these returns, using a discount rate higher than the cost of capital to reflect the additional risks involved. Any investment here will probably be directed towards developing joint information systems and collaborative relationships.

Accounts situated in the quadrant to the top right (high-potential/low-strength) pose a problem, for few organizations have sufficient resources for investing in building better relationships with all of them. To determine which ones justify investment, net revenue streams should be forecast for each account for, say, three years and discounted at the cost of capital (plus a considerable percentage to reflect the high risk involved). Having made these calculations and selected the promising accounts, under no circumstances should financial accounting measures such as Net present value (NPV) be used to control them within the budget year. To do so would be a bit like pulling up a new plant every few weeks to see whether it had grown! The achievement of objectives should instead be monitored using terms such as sales volume, value, 'share of wallet' and the quality of the relationship, enabling selected accounts to be moved gradually towards partnerships and, in some cases, towards integrated relationships. Only then will it become more appropriate to measure profitability as a control procedure. Accounts which the company cannot afford to invest in should be managed in a similar way to those residing in the final quadrant to the bottom right.

Accounts found in the quadrant to the bottom right (low-potential/low-strength) should not occupy too much of a company's time. Some of these accounts can be handed over to distributors while others can be handled by an organization's sales personnel, providing all transactions are profitable and deliver net free cash flow.

All other company functions and activities should be consistent with the goals set for key accounts according to the general categorization given in Figure 7.6. This rule includes the appointment of key account managers to key accounts. For example, some key account managers will be extremely good at managing accounts in the *exploratory*, *basic* and *cooperative* KAM stages where their excellent selling and negotiating skills are essential, whereas others will be better suited to the more complex business and managerial issues surrounding interdependent and integrated relationships. The implications for key account managers are examined Chapter 8.

Developing a strategic marketing plan for key accounts

Earlier in the chapter, we outlined the contents of a strategic marketing plan in Table 7.1. Let us now consider each of them more fully in chronological order.

Mission/purpose statement

While it is not essential to produce a formal mission statement in all cases, it is useful if the person preparing the marketing plan makes at least a brief statement about the position of the particular key account in the organization's key account portfolio. For example, if the account is in the top right quadrant of Figure 7.6, an investment plan is called for, whereas an account located in the bottom right quadrant would dictate a transaction-by-transaction approach justified on the basis of net free cash flow. An account in the top left quadrant would also warrant an investment approach, but one requiring an acceptable profit. Finally, an account positioned in the bottom left quadrant should be managed for sustained profits, using prudence and management judgement.

It is important that these expectations should be verbalized up front in the marketing plan in order to make clear the strategic context of the key account plan that follows.

● Definition:
A mission statement should state what the role of the key account is in the portfolio of key accounts and what the future indications are for the supplying company.

Financial summary

The financial summary is merely a graphical representation of the revenue and costs for the three years of the plan. It is effectively a summary of the more detailed budget which appears later in the marketing plan.

Key account overview

The key account overview is somewhat like a market overview and should contain a summary of the more important facts about the customer's markets, competitors and prospects.

Client's critical success factor analyses summary

The critical success factor (CSF) analyses summary brings together the client's CSFs which emerged from the earlier analysis outlined in Chapter 6.

Applications portfolio summary

The applications portfolio summary, as explained previously, categorizes the supplier's product/service solutions according to their importance to the client's business.

Assumptions

As in a strategic marketing plan, there are certain key determinants of success in all companies about which assumptions have to be made before the planning process can proceed. Thus, the assumptions specify the conditions necessary for the plan to happen. Assumptions should be relevant and few in number.

Objectives and strategies

Figures 7.7–7.9 set out the objectives and strategies for the key account. It is important to remember that key account objectives are principally about sales, profits and account penetration. Strategies outline the principal elements of the supplier's offer during the planning period.

Products		Last year	T+1	T+2	T+3
	Val				
	Vol				
	%				
	Val				
	Vol				
	%				
	Val				
	Vol				
	%				
	Val				
	Vol				
	%				
	Val				
	Vol				
	%				
	Val				
	Vol				
	%				

Figure 7.7
Sales objectives

Other objectives
(consider customer attitude, account penetration, new product/application development and customer's business performance improvements)

Figure 7.8
Other objectives

Objectives	Strategy
1	
2	
3	
4	
5	
6	
7	
8	

In developing strategy consider:

Product	include new products/quality/product mix/technical service/literature
Price	include pricing against competition/volume vs. price/terms and conditions
Place	include packaging/lot sizes/distribution/customer service
Promotion	include entertainment/advertising/displays, etc.

Figure 7.9
Strategy
considerations

Budget

The budget will be drawn in accordance with the particular requirements of the supplying organization and should set out the details of revenues and costs during the three-year planning period.

Action programme and account review

Figures 7.10 and 7.11 complete the planning circuit and translate the key account strategic marketing plan into a more detailed scheduling and costing out of the specific actions for achieving the first year of the plan, together with their regular review.

Research at Cranfield has shown that very few companies know the profitability of their key accounts. This is evident in Figure 7.12, which

Month	Objectives and main activities	Responsibility	Budget
January			
February			
March			
April			
May			
June			
July			
August			
September			
October			
November			
December			
Support required (technical, management, etc.)			

Figure 7.10
Action programme

Month	Activity to review	With whom
January		
February		
March		
April		
May		
June		
July		
August		
September		
October		
November		
December		

Figure 7.11
Account review

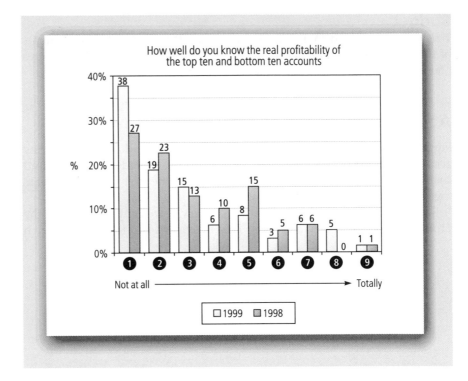

Figure 7.12
Knowing the real
profitability of key
accounts

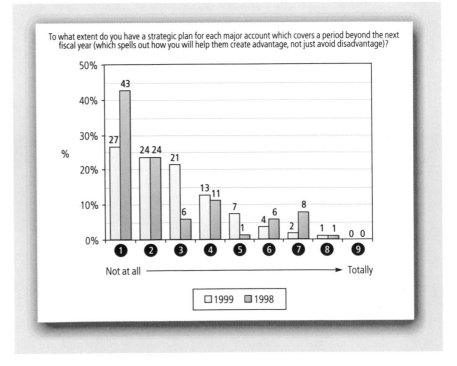

Figure 7.13
Preparing strategic
plans

reveals the extent to which companies are ignorant of the profitability of their top and bottom accounts. Disconcertingly, the contrast between the figures for 1998 and 1999 would suggest that the position is getting worse rather than better!

Cranfield research (McDonald and Woodburn, 1999) has also shown that few companies prepare strategic plans for their key accounts, as can be seen from Figure 7.13.

It is hoped that this section of the chapter has succeeded in demonstrating that the key account planning process is complex and time-consuming – but vital. Without all this dedicated and detailed effort, it is unlikely that any supplier will be able to provide superior value to its key accounts and, hence, achieve sustainable competitive advantage.

> Sustainable competitive advantage is the making of profits on an ongoing basis in excess of the weighted average return on investment of all competing organizations in a sector.

Measuring key account profitability

Before exploring key account profitability, it is necessary to ensure that readers fully understand the concept of 'sustainable competitive advantage' and how it must be measured. Therefore, let us enter into an explanation of some of the basic principles inherent in this concept.

Customer retention and profitability

It has been suggested that it costs up to five times as much to win a new customer as it does to retain an existing customer. Despite this finding, many organizations have traditionally focused their marketing activity on acquiring new customers rather than retaining existing customers. The costs of capturing market share are not always easy to gauge, but there are many companies who now regret earlier strategies based upon the blind pursuit of sales volume. While strong evidence exists to suggest a link between market share and profitability, there is equally strong evidence to show that it is the quality of the market share which counts. In other words, does our customer base comprise, in the main, long-established, loyal customers or is there a high degree of customer turnover or 'churn'? If the latter is the case, then the chances are that we are not as profitable as we might be.

> It has been suggested that it costs up to five times as much to win a new customer as it does to retain an existing customer.

The international consultants Bain & Company have suggested that even a relatively small improvement in the customer retention rate (measured as the percentage of retained business from one defined period to another) can have a marked impact upon profitability. They have found that, on average, an improvement of five percentage points in customer retention can lead to profit improvements of between 25 and 85 per cent in the NPV of the future flow of earnings.

So why should a retained customer be more profitable than a new one? According to Reichheld and Sasser (1990), there are several reasons. First, the costs of acquiring new business may be significant and, thus, it may take time, even years, to turn a new customer into a profitable customer. Second, the more satisfied customers are with the relationship, the more likely they are to place a larger proportion of their total purchase with us, even to the extent of single sourcing. Third, as the relationship develops, there is greater mutual understanding and collaboration which serves to reduce costs. Retained customers become easier to sell to and economies of scale produce lower operating costs. These customers are also more willing to integrate their IT systems (for example, their planning, scheduling and ordering systems) with ours, leading to further cost reductions. Fourth, satisfied customers are more likely to refer others to us, which promotes profit generation as the cost of acquiring these new customers is dramatically reduced. Finally, loyal customers are often less price sensitive and less inclined to switch suppliers because of price rises.

These factors collectively suggest that retained customers generate considerably more profit than new ones. Figure 7.14 summarizes this connection between customer retention and profitability.

> A study of the North American car industry found that a satisfied customer is likely to stay with the same supplier for a further twelve years after the first satisfactory purchase and during that period will buy four more cars of the same make. It is estimated that, to a car manufacturer, this level of customer retention is worth $400 million in new car sales annually.

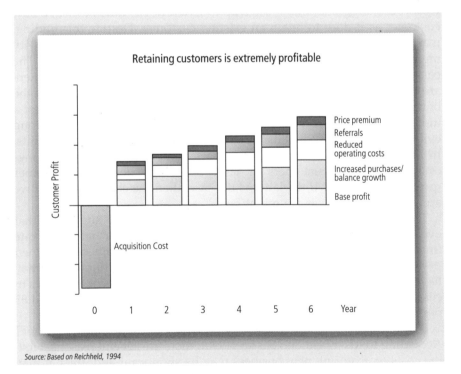

Figure 7.14
Customer profit
contribution over
time

Source: Based on Reichheld, 1994

There is a direct linkage between the customer retention rate and the average customer lifetime, meaning the lifetime of a customer relationship. For example, if the customer retention rate is 90 per cent per annum (meaning that we lose 10 per cent of our existing customer base each year), then the average customer lifetime will be ten years. If, on the other hand, we manage to improve the retention rate to 95 per cent per annum (meaning that we lose 5 per cent of our customers each year), then the average customer lifetime will be twenty years. In other words, a doubling of the average customer lifetime is achieved for a relatively small improvement in the retention rate. Figure 7.15 illustrates the relationship between the retention rate and customer lifetime.

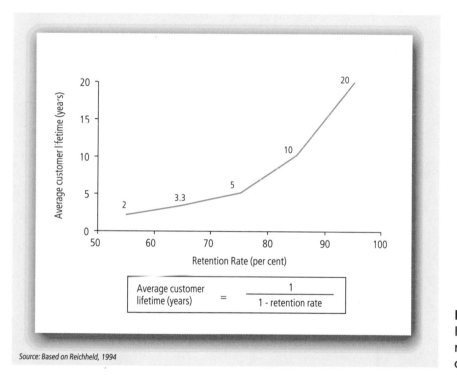

Source: Based on Reichheld, 1994

Figure 7.15
Impact of customer
retention rate on
customer lifetime

An important statistic that is not always measured is the *lifetime value* of a customer. Put very simply, this is a measure of the financial worth to the organization of a retained customer. If customers are loyal and continue to spend money with us into the future, then clearly their lifetime value is greater than that of a customer who buys only once or twice from us and then switches to another brand or supplier.

Measuring the lifetime value of a customer requires an estimation of the likely cash flow to be provided by that customer if he or she achieves an average loyalty level. In other words, if a typical account lasts for ten years, then we need to calculate the NPV of the profits which would flow

If customers are loyal and continue to spend money with us into the future, then clearly their lifetime value is greater than that of a customer who buys only once or twice from us and then switches to another brand or supplier.

from that customer over ten years. We are now in a position to calculate the impact that increasing the retention rate of customers will have upon profitability and also what the effect of extending the customer lifetime by a given amount will be. This information provides a sound basis for marketing investment decision making, indicating how much it is worth spending for either improving the retention rate or extending the life of a customer relationship.

The key question is who to retain and who to invest in.

Let us revisit the hierarchy of key relationships model presented earlier as a pyramid in Figure 3.2 and redrawn here (Figure 7.16) in a similar format to the original Millman and Wilson model (1994).

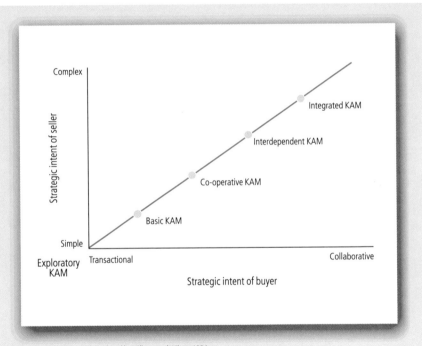

Figure 7.16
Relationship
development model

Source: Adapted from a model developed by Millman and Wilson, 1994

The development of profitable key accounts begins with the development of the key account relationship. Having qualified 'prospective' key accounts and selected certain accounts for investment strategies, the next step is to implement the marketing planning process.

Once a sale has been made, then we have a *basic* customer. For many companies, the closing of a sale is regarded as the culmination of the marketing process. However, smart marketers realize that this only the beginning of a process of building customer loyalty leading to potentially lucrative, long-lasting customer relationships.

> For many companies, the closing of a sale is regarded as the culmination of the marketing process.

To convert the customer into a *cooperative* client requires that we establish a pattern of repeat buying by making it easy for the customer to do business with us. However, being a *cooperative* client does not

necessarily signal commitment. For example, banks have regular customers who might be termed *cooperative* clients. However, many of those
customers may express high levels of dissatisfaction with the service they
receive and, if it were possible to move accounts easily, would defect to
another bank. What is required is for us to develop such an effective
customer-oriented approach that these *cooperative* customers become
interdependent customers, meaning they are pleased with the service they
receive. In fact, if they are really impressed with the quality of the
relationship, they may become *integrated* customers who are moved to tell
others about their satisfaction with our offer. Given the power of word of
mouth, this type of advocacy can be worth more than any amount of
advertising.

The *integrated* customer relationship reaches the ultimate rung on the
ladder of customer loyalty. It marks the achievement of a mutually
rewarding relationship where neither party intends to leave the other.
Increasingly, the idea of 'partnership' is being accepted as a desirable goal
of business relationships. This is particularly the case in industrial
marketing and business-to-business marketing.

The RDM, while a simple idea, can provide a practical framework
around which to build specific customer retention strategies. The first of
these strategies concerns financial risk and business risk, as represented
in Figure 7.17.

Box 1 in the matrix denotes high financial risk combined with high
business risk, an often lethal combination.

> The *integrated*
> customer relationship
> reaches the ultimate
> rung on the ladder of
> customer loyalty.

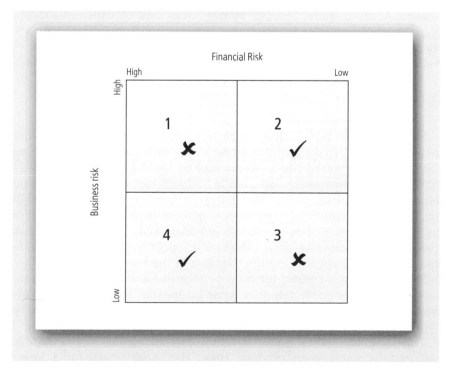

Figure 7.17
Financial risk versus
business risk

Mini-case 2:

High financial and business risk

Consider Sir Freddie Laker's Sky Train venture in the 1980s. With a very high financial gearing, given the high cost of entering the airline business, he entered the most competitive market in the world – the London–North Atlantic route. Furthermore, his strategy against the mighty global airlines was one of low price, which, given Laker's high break-even point, became unsustainable in the long run against special price promotions mounted by the top airlines to counteract the impact of SkyTrain.

A similar impact was experienced in the UK housing market of the late 1980s and early 1990s. As home owners borrowed more and more money against the hope that property values would continue to rise, millions of people were left with negative equity when house prices plunged dramatically.

Mini-case 3:

High business risk, low financial risk

Turning now to box 2 (low financial risk/high business risk), compare this situation with Richard Branson's market debut with Virgin Airlines. He entered the market with very few planes and low financial gearing, initially leasing his aircraft. Like Sir Freddie Laker, he also entered the lucrative North Atlantic route, but his strategy was one of differentiation, something he has very successfully sustained ever since. There is no doubt that Virgin's service is fundamentally different from that of other airlines, particularly Virgin Upper Class, which the younger travellers find particularly appealing. Virgin Airlines continues to go from strength to strength.

Now consider box 3 (low financial risk/low business risk). Any organization in this delightful position would be ill-advised to hoard the cash! For many years, Marks & Spencer adopted this type of strategy until the company cleverly invested in higher business risk ventures and repositioned itself in box 2. On the other hand, in situations of high financial risk, it would seem prudent to make at least some investment in low-risk businesses (box 4). A low business risk, high financial risk position would describe organizations such as Olympia and York before the property market fell through the floor in the late 1980s.

Having briefly examined the concept of business and financial risk, we can now begin to appreciate why some businesses do better than others over extended periods of time. The world's stock exchanges can be represented by the line of best fit shown in Figure 7.18.

This diagram shows financial return plotted against financial risk. Successful organizations produce either the same return for a lower

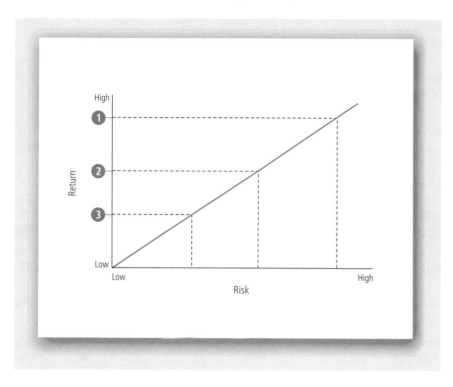

Figure 7.18
Return versus risk

perceived risk or a higher return for the same risk or both. Being north west of the line of best fit year after year is the mark of organizations whose shares continuously outperform the sectors to which they belong. Taking the cost of capital and using this as a discount rate against future earnings to produce a positive NPV is indicative of super profits or sustainable competitive advantage.

> This is not to be mistaken for producing super profits in one single year, which can be achieved relatively easily by cutting costs, limiting capital expenditure or even by selling off some of the company assets. The trouble with this short-term strategy is that financial markets today are much too sophisticated to be taken in by this, so it is a common phenomenon to see the capital value of the shares fall after an increase in a single year's profits and an increased dividend.

The following two examples illustrate the tenuous nature of the future profitability of many organizations. Table 7.2 shows the performance of a fictitious company in which it appears to be excelling on virtually every business dimension. Table 7.3, however, shows the same company's performance compared with the market as a whole. Here the performance figures reveal severe under-performance, indicating that the company is heading for disaster.

Table 7.4 is taken from Hugh Davidson's book, *Even More Offensive Marketing*, and is reproduced here with his kind permission. The table shows two companies making the same return on sales on the same

Table 7.2 Example of market growth performance: InterTech's five-year performance

Performance (£ million)	Base year	1	2	3	4	5
Sales revenue	£254	£293	£318	£387	£431	£454
Cost of goods sold	£135	£152	£167	£201	£224	£236
Gross contribution	£119	£141	£151	£186	£207	£218
Manufacturing overhead	£48	£58	£63	£82	£90	£95
Marketing and sales	£18	£23	£24	£26	£27	£28
Research and development	£22	£23	£23	£25	£24	£24
Net profit	£16	£22	£26	£37	£50	£55
Return on sales (%)	6.3%	7.5%	8.2%	9.6%	11.6%	12.2%
Assets	£141	£162	£167	£194	£205	£206
Assets (% of sales)	56%	55%	53%	50%	48%	45%
Return on assets (%)	11.3%	13.5%	15.6%	19.1%	24.4%	26.7%

Table 7.3 Example of market-based performance: InterTech's five-year market-based performance

Performance (£ million)	Base year %	1 %	2 %	3 %	4 %	5 %
Market growth	18.3	23.4	17.6	34.4	24.0	17.9
InterTech sales growth	12.8	17.4	11.2	27.1	16.5	10.9
Market share	20.3	19.1	18.4	17.1	16.3	14.9
Customer retention	88.2	87.1	85.0	82.2	80.9	80.0
New customers	11.7	12.9	14.9	24.1	22.5	29.2
Dissatisfied customers	13.6	14.3	16.1	17.3	18.9	19.6
Relative product quality	+10.0	+8.0	+5.0	+3.0	+1.0	+0.0
Relative service quality	+0.0	+0.0	−20.0	−3.0	−5.0	−8.0
Relative new product sales	+8.0	+8.0	+7.0	+5.0	+1.0	−4.0

Table 7.4 Quality of profits

%	Virtuous plc (%)	Dissembler plc (%)
Sales revenue	100	100
Cost of goods sold	43	61
Profit margin	57	39
Advertising	11	3
R&D	5	–
Capital investment	7	2
Investment ratio	23	5
Operating expenses	20	20
Operating profit	14	14
Key trends ⟶	Past five year revenue growth 10% pa Heavy advertising investment in new/ improved products Premium priced products, new plant, so low cost of goods sold	Flat revenue, declining volume No recent product innovation, little advertising Discounted pricing, so high cost of goods sold

Note: This table is similar to a P&L with one important exception – **depreciation**, a standard item in any P&L has been replaced by **capital expenditure**, which does not appear in P&Ls. In the long-term, Capex levels determine depreciation costs. Capex as a percentage of sales is an investment ratio often ignored by marketers, and it has been included in this table to emphasize its importance. (Reichhold and Sasser (1990)).

	The make-up of 14% operating profits	
Factor	Virtuous plc (%)	Dissembler plc (%)
Profit on existing products over three years old	21	15
Losses on products recently launched or in development	(7)	(1)
Total operating profits	14	14

From Hugh Davidson's 'Even More Offensive Marketing' 1998

turnover, but even a cursory glance at the two sets of figures clearly shows that Dissembler plc is heading for disaster. Financial institutions around the world are rarely fooled by so-called 'successful' annual results.

> The latest Cranfield/*Financial Times* research report into KAM (McDonald and Woodburn, 1999) concluded that there is much supplier delusion about the stage of development customer relationships have reached and that much of the profitability of key accounts is leaked away through the provision of levels of service which are not justified by the revenue (Pascale, 1991).

This is perfectly in order if it is done deliberately as an investment strategy in key accounts selected as having the best potential over, say, a three-year planning horizon. However, where there is no such proactive strategy, money is being lost without justification.

Let us examine Figure 7.19. The line of best fit indicates a perfect match between the strategic intent of both the supplying and buying companies. In Figures 7.20 and 7.21, however, we see an obvious mismatch and it is likely that both companies are losing money unnecessarily.

This judgement of the situation of course presupposes that supplying organizations have systems which can measure *attributable* costs, that is to say those costs which are directly related to a particular account. Alas, our database at Cranfield shows that a very substantial majority of Western European companies do not measure attributable costs (see Figure 7.22).

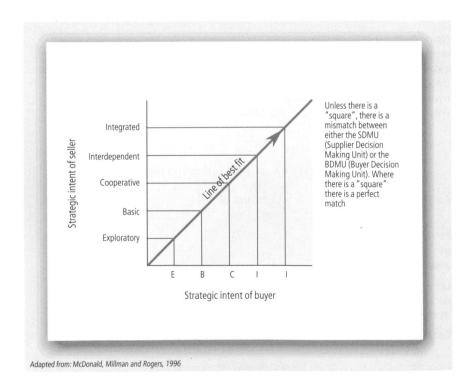

Figure 7.19
A match between buyers and sellers

Adapted from: McDonald, Millman and Rogers, 1996

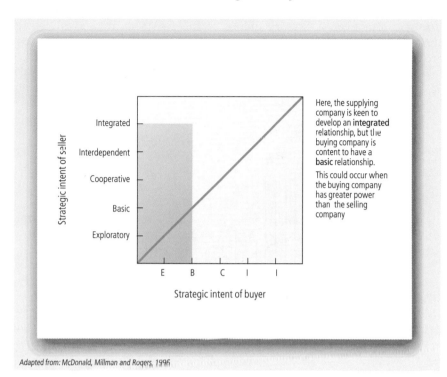

Here, the supplying company is keen to develop an **integrated** relationship, but the buying company is content to have a **basic** relationship.

This could occur when the buying company has greater power than the selling company

Adapted from: McDonald, Millman and Rogers, 1996

Figure 7.20
A mismatch between buyer and seller

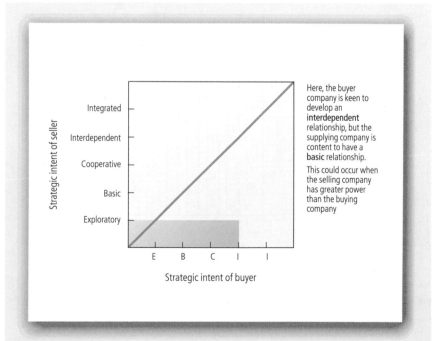

Here, the buyer company is keen to develop an **interdependent** relationship, but the supplying company is content to have a **basic** relationship.

This could occur when the selling company has greater power than the buying company

Adapted from: McDonald, Millman and Rogers, 1996

Figure 7.21
A mismatch between buyer and seller

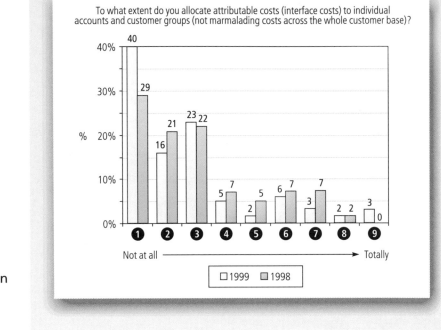

Figure 7.22
Cranfield survey on
key account
profitability
(1988–99)

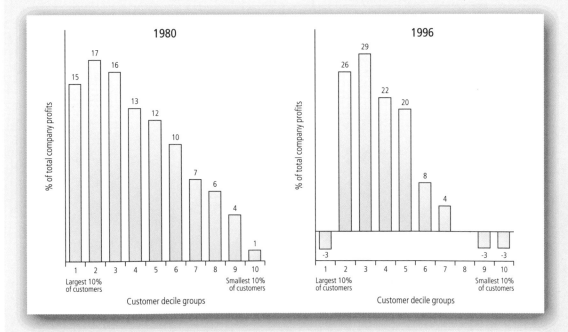

Figure 7.23   The widening rift between profitable and unprofitable customers

Mini-case 4:

Attributing costs to serve

Take the case of a soft drinks company supplying two major supermarket groups with two million dozen tonic waters each. Group A insists on daily, just-in-time, store-by-store deliveries, whereas group B takes delivery at its own distribution centre. Group A insists on calls by representatives to all stores, whereas group B decidedly does not want this. Group A takes 140 days to pay its accounts, whereas group B pays its accounts within fifty days. It does not take a genius to work out which of these two supermarket groups is the most profitable.

Yet suppliers still persist in operating systems which spread the overheads across the customer base according to turnover, in effect penalizing customers who are easy to serve and rewarding customers who are difficult and costly to serve.

Figure 7.23 shows the current profitability of the top 10 per cent of customers of a major European print company as compared with fifteen years ago.

This comparative example is taken from Wilson's (1998) excellent book and confirms the Cranfield research finding highlighted in Figure 7.12 that most companies today fail to keep a prudent check on key account profitability. This disturbing trend must be of particular concern to chief executives and also to finance directors. To understand and measure key account profitability is to direct/define the destiny of your customer relationships and, thus, your business future!

Summary

Few organizations in Western Europe either measure key account profitability or prepare strategic plans for selected key accounts. Those organizations which do fare considerably better financially and also succeed in profitably retaining those customers with whom they have elected to have close ongoing relationships.

References

Davidson, H. (1998). *Even More Offensive Marketing*. Penguin.

McDonald, M. and Woodburn, D. (1999). Key account management – building on supplier and customer perspectives. *Financial Times*, Prentice-Hall.

McDonald, M., Millman, A. and Rogers, B. (1996). *Key Account Management – Learning from Supplier and Customer Perspectives*. Cranfield School of Management.

Millman, A. F. and Wilson, K. J. (1994). From key account selling to key account management. In *Tenth Annual Conference on Industrial Marketing and Purchasing*.

Pascale, R. T. (1990). *Managing on the Edge: How Successful Companies use Conflict to Stay Ahead*. Viking.

Peters, T. J. and Waterman Jr, R. H. (1982). *In Search of Excellence: Lessons from American Best-run Companies*. Harper & Row.

Reichheld, F. R. (1994). Loyalty and the renaissance of © marketing. *Marketing Management*, **12**(4), 17.

Reichheld, F. R. and Sasser Jr, W. E. (1990). Zero defections: quality comes to services. *Harvard Business Rev.*, September–October, 105–11.

Wilson, C. (1998). *Profitable Customers: How to Identify, Develop and Keep Them*, 2nd edn. Kogan Page.

Chapter 8
Organizing for key account management

Introduction

The purpose of this chapter is to examine the positioning of key account activity in organizations and to explore opportunities for enhancing key account management (KAM) through organizational change. The chapter looks first of all at how companies have traditionally organized themselves and contrasts these structures with modern interpretations of customer-focused organizations. The challenge of operating globally is then considered, followed by a description of current practice in the setting up of global account teams. Finally and briefly, the scenario of value management occurring throughout the supply chain is presented to highlight the potential for the evolution of KAM into a transorganizational role.

KAM can prove difficult for relatively small companies where the sales, service, delivery, manufacturing and accounting departments may all hold a different view of a single customer. As the scope of the company's operations broadens, particularly geographically, the scale of the KAM task becomes even greater. It is therefore crucial that companies, large and small, organize themselves in such a way that the treatment of customers, particularly key customers, is made clear and consistent throughout the organization.

Understandably, company directors ask 'How should we manage ourselves to achieve the full benefits of KAM?' However, this focus on internal issues as being the route to KAM success does not enlighten the heart of the matter. Customers are not interested in suppliers' management structures and procedures. In fact, they are heartily sick of being given 'that is not my department' as the reason why a supplying company representative cannot help them. As marketing practitioners we know that this frequent response is neither suitable nor helpful and that some sort of customer-focused organization is needed. The difficulty is that, with so many types of organization to choose from, how do we determine what approach is best. In most cases, adopting any one type of organizational focus is too limiting. Different customers want different kinds of service and support, and suppliers therefore need to be flexible and accommodating.

For a company to perform successfully, its infrastructure must address a number of important considerations. First, all key accounts base their selection processes on the supplier's ability to deliver on time and to the agreed specification. To meet these criteria, the supplier must practice relationship management, possess technical expertise and demonstrate process excellence. Second, the customer will be looking for a relevant degree of interfunctional coordination within the supplying company. For global accounts, this requirement will extend to cross-divisional, multinational coordination. Lack of internal coordination is not only inefficient and wasteful of resources, but it can result in suboptimal performance enabling competitors to gain the advantage. A comparison of traditional and relatively new organizational structures serves to highlight the importance of having an appropriate and well-functioning infrastructure.

> Lack of internal coordination is not only inefficient and wasteful of resources, but it can result in suboptimal performance, enabling competitors to gain the advantage.

Historical precedents – national organizations

In the beginning, the structural nature of organizations was fairly simple and straightforward (see Figure 8.1). Sales representatives had geographical territories, which generally comprised a few customers who ordered in large volumes and a number of customers who ordered in small volumes. These salespeople reported to regional managers who 'ruled' their respective regions. The regional sales managers reported to a sales director who in turn reported to a managing director.

In some countries sales representatives continue to serve the small/ medium enterprise (SME) sector in this way, although they are increasingly being replaced by call centres. For the most part, business growth in the 1970s highlighted the limitations of this model and pushed strategic

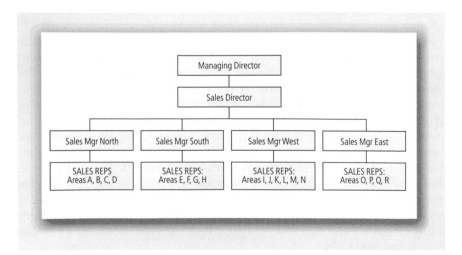

Figure 8.1
Sales organization by geography

decision-making processes to national level. Companies selling to national corporations assigned senior sales representatives to look after the largest accounts. Organizationally, few selling companies changed: hierarchical boundaries and functional silos remained. However, some farsighted brand leaders replaced their geographically based structures with more customer-oriented structures, but even these displayed remnants of the traditional geographical branch system (see Figure 8.2).

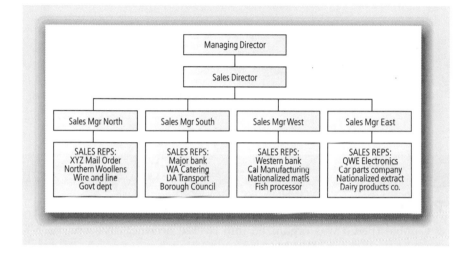

Figure 8.2
Hybrid of account focus and regional sales organization

The 1980s saw greater diversity in the way businesses were organized. While many companies maintained their geographical orientation, big companies were getting bigger through mergers and acquisitions and were outgrowing their traditional organizational structures. Both suppliers and customers now had their own different product divisions. While a shift from regional to national product divisions was evident in some markets, it rarely represented a match between customers' divisional structures and those of suppliers. A customer could be faced with a collection of product sales representatives, some of whose offers might be in direct competition with those of a sister company. Purchasing decision makers still complain about the arcane structure of many supplying organizations. Outdated policies and outmoded practices have given rise to confusion and contempt. Naturally, a supplier who is perceived to be 'difficult to do business with' is less likely to win the customer's favour (see Figure 8.3).

Where specialist buyers are concerned, the attraction of a product specialism may prove strong enough to counteract any organizational weakness on the part of the supplier. For example, large retailers generally sell to buyers from specific consumer goods categories, such as fresh baked goods, dairy products, household cleaning materials and so on. Yet even in the retail industry, some suppliers are more strategically driven than others, adopting a collaborative business approach in order to maximize benefit for both parties.

> A customer could be faced with a collection of product sales representatives, some of whose offers might be in direct competition with those of a 'sister' company.

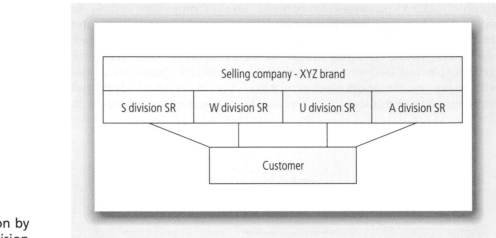

Figure 8.3
Organization by
product division

Procter & Gamble organized to focus on Wal-Mart

Prior to 1988, Proctor & Gamble (P&G) was organized into twelve product divisions, each with account managers who called on Wal-Mart. The relationship was adversarial, transactional and short-term and was managed only at the sales–purchasing interface. P&G had no way of measuring the total sales of each of its customers, let alone attributing customer costs. It was a classically *basic* relationship. Sam Walton, Wal-Mart's chief executive, was never able to get hold of P&G's chief executive.

A new vice-president of sales at P&G visited Sam Walton and suggested that their two great companies could do better business together. In 1988, P&G set up a team specifically dedicated to the Wal-Mart account. The companies later reported a jump in joint business growth from US$375 million to US$4 billion. Significant cost reductions were also achieved through the sharing of technologies which underpinned the collaborative effort. Technology has since played a key role in joint performance measurement, helping to reduce costs further through the automation of processes and sharing of data, including data about consumer needs and behaviour (Graen, 1999).

Current models of key account management

KAM offers an alternative to organizing business activities around a geographical or product base. By adopting a focus on the management and performance of its key accounts, the supplying company can better identify and pursue a strategic direction commensurate with market trends. The supplier can also achieve closer relationships with its most valuable customers, which can serve to raise its profile as well as its profit levels.

A number of KAM models have been identified in recent years, most notably with respect to internal reporting channels. These include sales line reporting, marketing management reporting and executive management reporting.

Sales line reporting

The traditional view of the key account reporting line would assume that key account managers report to sales and marketing, perhaps via a regional hierarchy (see Figure 8.4).

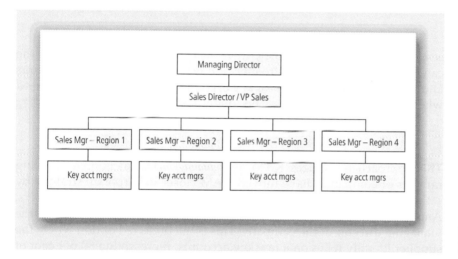

Figure 8.4
Sales reporting line

Few companies these days can afford so many layers of management. The persistence of KAM in the sales hierarchy within sales recognizes only a small part of its full role and potential, although the arrangement seems to work well for some companies. For instance, if the supplying company is operating in a market where the majority of its key accounts behave transactionally and opportunistically, then a selling and negotiating focus would be considered appropriate. While sales line reporting has clearly survived, other types of reporting structure have thrived.

> If the supplying company is operating in a market where the majority of its key accounts behave transactionally and opportunistically, then a selling and negotiating focus would be considered appropriate.

Marketing management reporting

In some organizations KAM is treated as an extension of marketing, perhaps to emphasize that it is strategically and indelibly linked to the company's long-term marketing plan (see Figure 8.5). Many large companies have a mixed portfolio of key accounts and customers with low buying frequencies. Ensuring that the different customer types are managed via different reporting lines can be a useful way of ensuring appropriate handling of the accounts and, thus, optimizing their

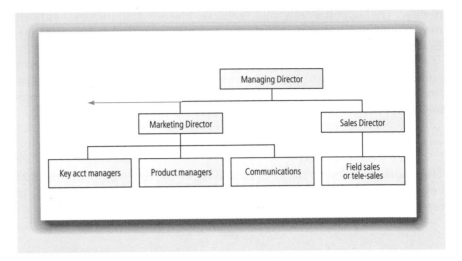

Figure 8.5
KAM as an element
of strategic
marketing

respective potential. Obviously, there has to be some flexibility in the categorization to allow low-frequency buyers to grow into key accounts and to enable underperforming key accounts to be relegated or released when mutual strategic interest no longer justifies key account status.

Executive management reporting

This approach recognizes KAM as a *management* function. A growing number of companies have moved KAM closer to corporate strategy by setting up key account divisions which report to general managers. Another variation has key account managers reporting directly to the managing director of the company. This is the preferred option where the supplier literally relies on a few key accounts, representing 80 per cent of revenue, volume or profit (see Figure 8.6).

Smart senior managers recognize the importance of being in direct contact with their key account managers, for it not only expedites the

Smart senior managers recognize the importance of being in direct contact with their key account managers.

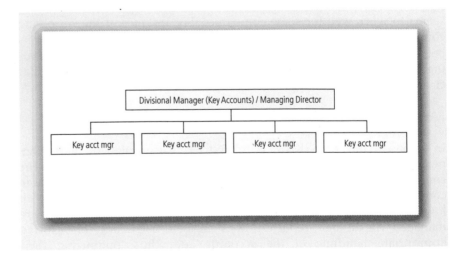

Figure 8.6
KAM as a
management
function

management of crucial accounts, it also demonstrates to the customer that the account manager has the respect and support of his or her company. Purchasing decision makers naturally tend to assume that account managers who are too far removed from the real power base do not carry sufficient authority and status for getting things done. That perception in turn may affect the key account manager's ability to access senior people in the customers' organization.

Ideally, the key account manager should have a main contact at director level and regular contact with other senior management. The key account manager will also be expected to liaise with the company's executive directors and to have the requisite calibre of skills and professionalism.

In all of these structures, questions are raised about the relationship between KAM and traditional marketing roles, such as brand management and product management.

The relationship between key account management and marketing

Most companies which focus on key accounts assign equal or greater status to key account managers as compared to product or brand managers. Even in consumer goods manufacturing, the increasing power of retailers in the supply chain has ensured that the professionals who manage key accounts have a critical role in their company's success, regardless of the 'demand pull' which brand managers may be able to generate (see Mini-case 1: Procter & Gamble organized to focus on Wal-Mart).

In so-called 'industrial' markets or those markets located further up the supply chain near to and including raw materials extraction, account management often dominates marketing activity and can even eclipse or exclude it. While some buying companies appreciate strong branding and merchandising in business-to-business marketing, they tend to give greater weight to the key account manager's relationship with their decision-making unit (DMU). Further, the tough economic conditions of the early 1990s encouraged companies to cut back on marketing expenditure where effectiveness could not be measured easily. Spending on general advertising and exhibitions was reduced in favour of relationship-building activity targeted at particular customers or prospects.

The marketing department can still make a crucial contribution by briefing and updating the account manager on market activity, trends and opportunities. In addition, the value of a selling company's general marketing activity to a key account is the knowledge, information and expertise it can offer, which might enable supplier and buyer to work together on promotions to the next set of customers in the supply chain.

The marketing department still needs to fulfil its traditional functions, even where KAM has a high profile. The value of branding is working its way up supply chains, for example in the generation of 'demand pull' from end consumers, to encourage customers to prefer the company and its brands. The 'Intel inside' campaign is an illustration of the power of component branding.

From hierarchies to networks

The growing trend towards a transition from hierarchical structures to networks is a consequence of changes in market conditions and the nature of customers. Market maturity and customer sophistication are just two of the many reasons why companies need to achieve success on more than one organizational axis (see Chapter 1). Figure 8.7 helps to illustrate the supplier's complex task of managing a range of customer accounts while meeting consistently high standards of quality and value.

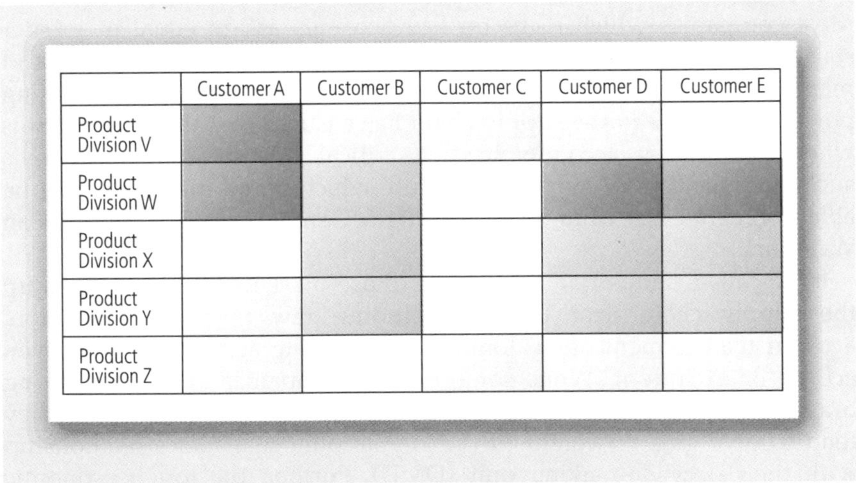

	Customer A	Customer B	Customer C	Customer D	Customer E
Product Division V					
Product Division W					
Product Division X					
Product Division Y					
Product Division Z					

Figure 8.7
Matrix of divisional and customer lines of management

The various shaded areas represent the amount of business that each division has with each customer, with black signifying that the customer uses the company for 100 per cent of purchases of a product type and white indicating that the customer does not use the company at all for that product type. While it is the role of the key account manager to turn the matrix ever darker in all applicable boxes, it is the responsibility of product managers to ensure that the company's products are ahead of the competition in terms of functionality and quality.

Matrix management requires the highest standards of communication and objectivity from everyone within the supplying organization. In the case of a sufficiently large supplier, there might be one manager for each product-for-account box reporting to a divisional manager and the key account manager. In fact, if we were to add a third dimension of geography/culture there might be one manager per product/customer/region cube.

Companies who are developing matrix management tend to set objectives for the unit managers as members of the key account team. Their product-oriented or region-oriented role may be the subject of some required activity. Conflicts between product interests, regional interests and the interests of the key account are usually resolved in favour of the key account.

Successful KAM is identified by the following criteria:

1 A plan per key account for all its business and capabilities, which can be delivered consistently at a macro and micro level and which ideally would be shared with the key account for forward management of the supply chain.
2 Company-wide recognition of each key account as 'key' and widespread understanding of each key account's decision-making criteria.
3 Prices and terms for each key account are harmonized across all divisions/localities where relevant.
4 Key account involvement in product and process development.
5 Account-specific financial reporting so that local/divisional and overall profit and loss per account is known.

Organizing key account teams

The existence of cross-functional key account teams is one of the surest and earliest indicators to a customer that the supplier takes their business seriously. The more formalized the teamwork structure, the more likely it is that processes can be aligned with those of customers.

'Papering over the cracks'

In most selling companies, key account managers do not have formal or informal teams and yet they are expected to have influence in the company to get things done for their customer. In practice this means that key account managers are constantly bidding for resources. The managers of the key account managers may assert that 'they can pull in who they need', but buying companies will perceive that, if the key account manager has to beg for required materials and expertise on an ad hoc basis, then the supplier has a tactical and begrudging attitude to fulfilling their needs.

Equally, buying companies do not consider the traditional company organization, in which account managers have no leverage over colleagues other than escalation from manager to manager, to be

In most selling companies, key account managers are constantly bidding for resources.

Buying companies do not consider the traditional company organization to be appropriate for meeting their often complex needs.

appropriate for meeting their often complex needs. As we have already discussed, buyers expect key account managers to have sufficient status and authority in order to be able to 'deliver'. Further, cross-functional bidding for resource or silo-style escalation restricts the supplier's ability to develop the potential of key accounts. The benefits of interdependence and integration cannot be realized if the supplying company architecture insists on dragging the relationship back to basic level.

Semi-formal key account teams

In terms of current best practice, 'semi-formal' key account teams are delivering significant benefits. In this arrangement, operational staff report to functional managers but have dotted line responsibility to a key account manager for a particular key account (see Figure 8.8).

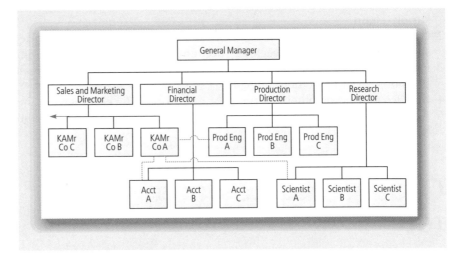

Figure 8.8
Reporting structure for semi-formal key account teams

Members of semi-formal key account teams meet regularly with the key account manager and the key account. They pursue objectives relating to general customer requirements but devote a percentage of their time to servicing their key account. Such teams normally exhibit some degree of shared motivation and reward, where account perform-ance is linked to the career development and job security of team members. In most cases of 'dotted line' responsibility, operational staff are required to report to the key account manager as well as their line manager about contacts with buying companies. It is imperative that key account managers are able to plan and monitor all communications relating to their key accounts.

Buying companies often expect semi-formal key account teams to include a company director as mentor. Their presence adds status to the team, ensures widespread understanding of the importance of the key account focus and improves customer perceptions of the company.

Team members may spend a lot of time with their customer contacts, depending on the customer's required level of technical support, logistics

Such teams normally exhibit some degree of shared motivation and reward, where account performance is linked to the career development and job security of team members.

planning, systems integration or involvement in research and development (R&D). It is the key account manager's responsibility to coordinate or 'orchestrate' what happens at each interface of the buyer–seller relationship.

The key account manager must ensure that the key account team is informed and up to date about the customer's strategic and tactical objectives. Members of the team will be encouraged to meet with their counterparts even when there is no immediate need to work closely with them, as frequent contact is seen to promote trust and reinforce the relationship. It is important that team members feel committed enough to the account to explain to their line managers on occasion that a key account activity must take priority over their normal functional duties.

Besides supervising communications and interactions, the key account manager has to make sure that the team and individual team members persistently do things that demonstrate value to the customer. For example, one key account manager we interviewed (McDonald, Millman and Rogers 1996) asked for one small gesture from each member at every team meeting which would help get the company closer to the customer, for example redesigning a report. Strong leadership skills are obviously an essential attribute of successful key account managers.

Semi-formal key account teams need to be reassured in their efforts by company feedback, recognition and reward. The giving of awards such as 'dinner-for-two' coupons or shopping vouchers can be enormously motivating. If companies want staff to be customer focused, then rewards for customer-focused effort have to be available.

Formal key account teams

Some companies have gone further in developing their KAM set-ups and have completely converted key account managers into line managers (see Figure 8.9). Functional professionals, such as engineers and accountants, are dedicated to a particular customer and report to the key account

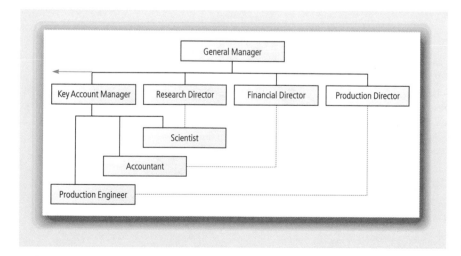

Figure 8.9
Reporting structure for formal key account teams

manager while maintaining dotted line responsibility to functional managers. Thus, the formal structure of the organization is focused on customers.

Formal key account teams are effective in project-oriented businesses such as consultancy and have been used successfully in make-to-order manufacturing and finance companies. It is also feasible to adopt this organizational model in dedicated key account divisions. Clearly, it would be very difficult if not impossible to operate it in sectors such as process manufacturing.

The use of formal key account teams is not universally popular. Some professionals may feel threatened or fear that their functional excellence is being diluted. However, key customers tend to welcome the attention and perceived benefits of having fully dedicated resource teams looking after them.

Cross-boundary teams

Integrated relationships between suppliers and customers are characterized by the existence of regular teams working together at different levels in the two organizations. These 'cross-boundary' key account teams set their own agendas and solve their own problems with little direction from but in communication with the key account manager.

Considerable numbers of personnel from both the selling company and the buying company can be involved in cross-boundary teams, as illustrated in Figure 8.10. The borders between the selling company and the buying company have become blurred. Delineations between internal functions and organizational levels have also disappeared. There is even anecdotal evidence of the members of such cross-boundary teams actually swapping jobs, from selling company to buying company and vice versa, for short periods of time.

In this type of cross-boundary integration it is the focus teams that matter most because they are making things happen for the end customer. As discussed in Chapter 3, focus teams are drawn from supplier and

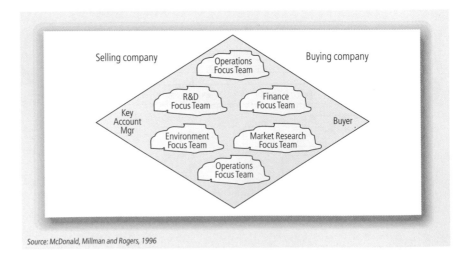

Figure 8.10
Cross-boundary
teams

Source: McDonald, Millman and Rogers, 1996

account personnel in order to tackle specific issues or projects or to introduce motivational forces. While some of these personnel may be dedicated to the supplier–customer relationship, others may be placed with focus teams for their specialist skills or expertise. Team members work to improve or develop particular interfaces between the two organizations, such as accounting transactions, stock transfer and so on. In this way, internal tribalism and role ambiguity is avoided, the two companies are drawn closer together and everyone along the supply chain benefits.

By working together, the selling company and the buying company are able to tackle higher risk activities more successfully than they could individually. Collaboration also makes it easier to improve processes, trial new products and boost financial performance. In order that the key account manager and his or her main contact in the buying company can recommend process changes and gain authorization for their implementation, existing and proposed processes between the two companies need to be examined. A technique known as 'mapping' can be used to indicate where costs could be reduced or quality improvements could be achieved. Mapping involves identifying all the activities at the supplier–customer interface and all their dependencies. Both companies will benefit if these activities can be simplified, eliminated or improved. In an integrated buyer–seller relationship, the partnership performance index might comprise forty to 200 measures, which leaves plenty of scope for focus team activity.

> By working together, the selling company and the buying company are able to tackle higher risk activities more successfully than they could individually.

Both companies will also note improvements in the ability of team members to solve problems and contribute to developments. The establishment of cross-boundary teams formalizes the sharing concerns and ideas so that team members have a better understanding of each other's roles and organizations and a greater willingness to take responsibility for getting things done. Such integrated dyads foster mutual loyalty and trust. Measures to monitor performance provide the necessary feedback to ensure a level of quality that both parties can be proud of.

The challenge of managing cross-boundary teams is to maintain their momentum. Putting teams in place can cause expectations to rise, which can make it harder for team members to feel that they are achieving significant goals. Additional pressures may be added when one or both parties face resource constraints. For instance, one company may find it difficult to release certain individuals to take part in the teams or to allocate appropriate funds and materials to see through some of the team's suggestions.

> Putting teams in place can cause expectations to rise, which can make it harder for team members to feel that they are achieving significant goals.

Piloting organizational change

We are all human and naturally seek to minimize the impact of change. Change can be uncomfortable. Companies who try to achieve organizational change, even if it is universally recognized as change for the better, will no doubt face some degree of resistance. Attempts to elevate the role and status of account managers and account teams need to be made very carefully to avoid any potentially adverse consequences. Changes must be introduced with a high degree of reasoning, commitment and exhortation. There must be a clear understanding of what will be rewarded and what will be rebuked in the new order.

To test the potential and acceptability of proposed internal developments, companies often undertake pilot projects using a small and select group of key accounts. These will likely include those few accounts that warrant a partnership approach or are most strategically well-matched and perhaps one or two disaster recovery situations which require an element of task force activity. The pilot team will comprise diverse representation in order to ensure a balanced range of views and competencies. Advocates of change will have to work alongside sceptics and the 'converted' can then join the campaign to convince others of the worthiness of change. A cooperative aptitude and attitude will be vital in all key account teams.

As well as involving the right people in a pilot, new processes and information technology support will need to be incorporated. Redesigning an organization's flow chart to achieve greater potential for supplier–customer integration is one thing; organizing supplier and customer information systems and capabilities so that they are capable of serving innumerable and complex requirements across internal and inter-company boundaries is quite another. However, as successfully integrated companies well know, the exercise is worth the effort.

Increasing a customer's access to information across the whole supplying company and vice versa may significantly improve communications and mutual business. Integrating technology also ensures that sufficient performance indicators can be used to monitor the success of the relationship, thus aiding the accuracy of analyses and the effectiveness of planning activity. The sharing of technology and information can also influence the terms and conditions of trading, making them more conducive to the companies' capabilities and the market environment. Openness about pricing will require suppliers to do even more to demonstrate their superiority in providing added value for the customer. In the P&G/Wal-Mart case referred to earlier, technology is seen to have played a major role in enhancing joint performance measurement and reducing costs through the automation of processes and the sharing of data, including data about consumer behaviour and needs.

Monitoring the performance of a pilot and applying rewards to reinforce success are the acid test of learning from such projects. Where it is evident that difficult problems can be solved through alterations to organizational structure, culture or operations, the challenge of implementing wider organzational change is made much easier.

Global account management models

Yip (1999) described global account management as an organizational form and process by which the worldwide activities serving a given multinational customer are co-ordinated by one person or team within the supplying company'. Achieving global scope in the organization of key account activity is the ultimate challenge; the 'Olympics' for key account strategists.

During the 1970s and 1980s, companies which had migrated from exporting to establishing subsidiaries in overseas markets in the 1950s and 1960s were becoming complex 'multinationals'. Towards the end of the 1980s, these companies recognized that they had replicated the old geographical fiefdoms, only on a larger scale. In many cases they had also created a product- or service-specific focus which meant that a variety of sales representatives were serving a single customer within a designated geographical territory.

Purchasing professionals faced the same dilemma of multiple servicing/service overlap in buying local products and services through national subsidiaries. Worldwide companies often found themselves buying from a plethora of disparate suppliers offering different service levels at different prices.

● Definition:
Global account management is an organizational form and process by which the worldwide activities serving a given multinational customer are coordinated by one person or team within the supplying company.

Changes in the way purchasing is organized

In a recent research project global account managers were asked why their companies felt the need to develop global account management (Yip, 1999). A clear majority indicated that accelerating customer demand for it was an over-riding factor. Therefore, understanding how the purchasing profession is approaching global supplier management is an important prerequisite to considering desirable organizational structures for global account management. Some companies with a presence in many countries, such as the pharmaceutical giant Wyeth-Ayerst, are trying to organize their buying globally.

Mini-case 2:

Global purchasing

Wyeth-Ayerst has 58 manufacturing sites worldwide and purchases $4 billion of goods, services and capital products per annum. Historically, most purchasing had been done at plant level, where local buyers were responsible for the negotiation of prices and purchasing terms. In 1993, a team of strategic purchasing staff was created at the company's headquarters in Philadelphia in order to handle core purchases. These purchases, which were initially trans-USA, soon became worldwide. The expansion of the purchasing remit was preceded by a rigorous assessment of buyer performance and was followed by an intensive training regime for those chosen to comprise the strategic team. Between 1994 and 1998, the team achieved $89 million worth of cost savings.

However, the innovative programme was not just about cost reduction. Supply chain analyses, strategic source planning and the extension of value-based metrics to include 'intangibles' were also achieved. A hierarchy of purchasing activity had been established. As a result, the company's long-term strategy and supporting management and monitoring processes are now designed at a global level. Global suppliers are managed from the company's headquarters in Philadelphia. Regional and local buyers are responsible for tailoring the global framework for local implementation (Nolan, 1999).

Globalization can also affect service industries. For example, in 1994 IBM fired its forty advertising agencies located around the world and appointed Ogilvy and Mather as its global agency.

However, not all global companies see centralization as the right corporate purchasing strategy.

Mini-case 3:

Diageo decentralizes purchasing

Drinks giant, Diageo has rejected centralization. The conglomerate has local and regional buying operations and six global centres of excellence. However, it is not assumed that global is best and even where an item is purchased globally, this occurs in collaboration with local buyers. In addition, lead buyers for particular product categories may be drawn from any part of the global organization. Eric Evans, director of operations procurement says 'You cannot have some cowboy sitting in the centre of London telling the guy in the Philippines who his supplier is going to be and what the spec should look like. You must have this "think global, act local" dimension.'

Having an empowered structure is one aspect of Diageo's overall purchasing strategy. Diageo also works on the basis of 'being the customer of first resort' to ensure best price, security of supply and access to innovation. Supplier audits, disaster recovery plans, performance monitoring and risk management are also part of the corporate recipe (Nolan, 1999).

An alternative model for organizing cross-boundary purchasing has been described as network purchasing.

Mini-case 4:

Compass adopts network purchasing

Compass, the multinational contract catering group, adopts a different structure, which group purchasing director Didier Coutte calls a 'global network'. The central purchasing staff are responsible for facilitating a network of purchasing expertise located in different local markets. For example, a reduction in the number of coffee blends stocked Europewide (from 154 to eight) was initiated following a study in The Netherlands which the central team rolled out with the help of a coffee specialist and a project manager (Nolan, 1999).

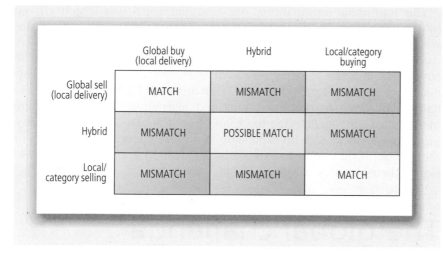

Figure 8.11
Marketing structures across the dyad

The way in which customers organize their buying clearly has an impact on how suppliers organize their account management structures. Figure 8.11 helps to illustrate the complex challenge facing suppliers when they have to satisfy a portfolio of customers with radically different views on how they want to be supplied.

To avoid the pitfalls of choosing one approach to adopt as standard and, thus, becoming inaccessible to the remainder of customers, global companies may have to create different divisions in order to align themselves most usefully to key customers.

One thing is certain; the country-centric organization model which seemed to work so well in the past (see Figure 8.12) is being radically modified in most international companies. Whether it is a case of total realigning reporting lines or creating special divisions and networks, companies are visibly responding to current marketing challenges by becoming more customer led in the way that they organize and operate.

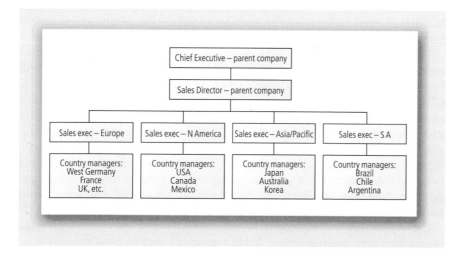

Figure 8.12
The traditional multinational organization model

This traditional multinational organization model was largely driven by the expansion of US companies into Europe. The earliest examples were established in the 1930s, but the model survived into the 1970s. US companies were used to serving a massive single market which could be covered from a few regional offices or even centrally. In Europe, it was necessary to set up local offices in a large number of countries in order to address differing market conditions and legislation. This added huge overheads. Companies trying to expand from the base of a small country faced costs associated with expansion as well as the potential dilution of their brand if they tried to expand by acquisition and were not able to export their business culture.

The global challenge

The challenge for businesses today is to seek global synergy. It is no longer necessarily effective to have country general managers operating culturally unique variations of the company. Global branding, which is attractive to companies in some industry sectors, requires global values.

The current business community regards the nation state as less relevant. Even the largest national markets are too small when the global economy is driven by the technology of nano-second transfer rates for data, image and voice communications. The concept of nations as markets, which emerged only relatively recently in the nineteenth century, is no longer relevant in many industry sectors. Markets of globally dispersed customers are calling for the same or similar products and services, forcing suppliers to rethink, regroup and react appropriately. Global brands, such as Coca-Cola, Sony and Guinness, have established themselves firmly and formidably. Transport and communications costs have been drastically reduced and many tariffs and other barriers to international trade have been removed. Nowadays, most types of manufacturing can be done anywhere in the world. 'Globalization' is on the agenda of every major company and, through the auspices of the Internet, it even features on the agendas of small companies and business start ups.

> The concept of nations as markets, which emerged only relatively recently in the nineteenth century, is no longer relevant in many industry sectors.

Up to 100 people in a selling company could be directly involved in managing business with a particular global buying company. They will be talking different languages and working in different business cultures. Global account managers report that conflicts between national and global interests are the main problem in implementing key account programmes. Managing multinational teams is also regarded as problematic. Mirror-image problems on the customer side of the dyad also have repercussions for the global account manager. Where the customer's national interests conflict with the company's global interests, the global account manager will have to deal with a 'knock-on' challenge from national account managers in his or her team.

Cross-cultural management is undoubtedly the most difficult task facing business people today. Multinationals used to be a collection of national companies which were either commonly owned by one of the companies or dominated by the culture of the country in which the parent company was based. Now, consumers expect a global brand to have consistent values which all its customers can 'buy into'.

It has been argued that global account management and global supplier management are 'Western' concepts which are being imposed worldwide. However, Americans and Europeans often regard the interdependence or integration of companies which tends to be associated with global synergy between suppliers and customers as 'Eastern' in origin. It could also be argued that global account management is where Western drive for efficacy and Eastern values of loyal business relationships come together.

'Recruit people from all the countries you operate in, connect them to each other, move them around regularly and in thirty years' time you will have built a truly international management group' (Schlumberger, US–French oil company, quoted in Hall and Poots (1996)).

Insight

What is a global account?

Since relatively few companies are involved in global dyads, it is worth considering what constitutes a global account and what circumstances demand a global response to KAM.

A global account is most commonly identified as being 'big' (large and prominent) in lots of countries simultaneously. However, not every company of that description is thinking or acting 'globally'. Companies which are interested in leveraging their worldwide power are most likely to adopt global purchasing strategies.

● Definition:
A global account is most commonly identified as being 'big' (large and prominent) in lots of countries simultaneously.

Companies which expect global scope from their suppliers must first ensure that their own company capabilities are in good order and strong enough to withstand global competition. To be attractive as a global account, a buying organization must exhibit competencies which represent a good fit with those of the global supplier. Integrated manufacturing or commercial operations across two or more geographical regions provide a good indication that a customer is successfully pursuing global aims.

Although it is not impossible for a global account to be *basic* in terms of relationship development, it is more usually the case that it has reached a level of maturity where interdependence or integration is evident. Unless potential exists for a close relationship, account penetration and joint investment, there is little incentive for a supplier to want to service a customer globally.

What is a world-class supplier?

Purchasing professionals in companies who are 'going global' often talk about receiving consistent levels of service worldwide. This might mean that any or all of the following attributes are qualifiers for globally aspirant suppliers:

- The same product/services and features are available in all countries.
- The same product/service quality exists, regardless of where it was made.
- The same terms and conditions prevail per customer, regardless of delivery location.
- The same back-up is provided, regardless of where the service is delivered.
- A fair and stable level of 'cost of ownership' of the product is maintained worldwide.
- Consistent lead time and due date performance exist.
- Consistent and stable process excellence exists.
- Consistent and stable levels of technical expertise exist.
- Consistent levels of corporate ethics and evidence of community responsibility exist.

It may not be a popular view, but in order to achieve and maintain such consistent performance standards requires a high level of central direction because the customer who believes in global economies of scale is going to be standardizing their requirements as much as possible.

Most companies on the globalization trail take one step at a time. One account management organizational model is frequently encountered in the initial stages of globalization and this is given in Figure 8.13. Here the supplier's global capabilities are defined at head office, but the global framework for each key account is negotiated in the customer's 'home' country. In this way, agreements within each key account's global framework can be tailored for local conditions and managed according to the geographic market concerned.

With this approach, responsibility for a global account rests with the supplier's national subsidiary in the country where the customer's headquarters are located. In the example given in Figure 8.13, a Spanish company requires its Australian subsidiary to manage the global partnership framework for an Australian-owned multinational company. Local delivery is managed by negotiation between the key account

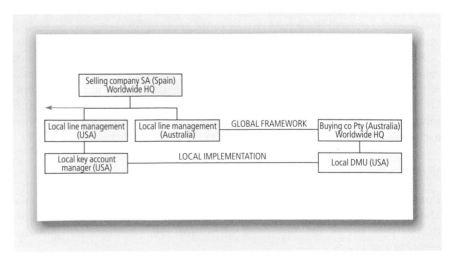

Figure 8.13
Global KAM –
initiation model

manager in the Spanish company's US subsidiary and the purchasing professional in the US unit of the Australian company. This style of global account management is perceived to have advantages because the selling company is always addressing buying companies within their own business culture.

Mini-case 5:

Citibank – semi-formal global account management

Citibank has a global account management system for nearly 500 customers. The 'parent' account manager is located in the customer's home country and a 'field' account manager handles the local relationship. Some individuals find themselves with account portfolios involving both roles (Yip, 1999).

This 'initiation' model clearly represents a convenient first step in an organization's transition from multinational to global status in an effort to meet the needs of key accounts which operate globally. An ambitious further step, of which there are a few examples, is much more purist in its emphasis on global organization (see Figure 8.14).

In this model, local account managers are directly responsible to the company's global account manager and have only dotted line responsibility to local management. Leading global companies in the services sector have successfully implemented this model or variations of it (see Mini-cases 6 and 7). It may still be the case that the global account manager is a national of the customer's 'home' country and is located close to the customer's headquarters. Nevertheless, he or she will report to the supplier's head office or global account division and not his or her own local country manager.

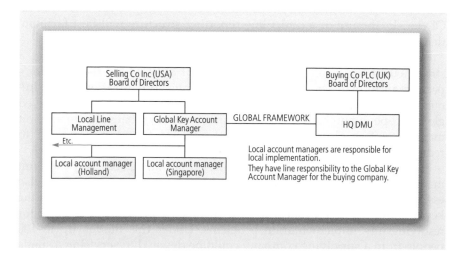

Figure 8.14
Global KAM – line responsibility oriented to key accounts

Mini-case 6:

DHL – a dedicated global accounts division

At DHL, regional-level functional support, such as operations, billing, logistics and information technology, together with country account managers, report to regional account managers who report to the global account manager. Today, DHL have only twenty-eight global accounts, served by a dedicated global accounts division (Cranfield KAM Conference, 1999).

Mini-case 7:

BOC – functional managers reporting to global account managers

At BOC Gases, global key account managers supervise zonal key account managers and beneath them are supply site managers who are responsible for day-to-day account maintenance issues such as contract management and continuous improvement (Cranfield KAM BP Club, 2000).

The global account manager may have to have a budget from which local organizations can be paid on in-company transfer prices for the local service provided to his or her account. This ensures that the local subsidiaries receive a reward for efforts made on behalf of global accounts. The ability to distribute reward also establishes the global account manager's authority.

The Global Forum, a benchmarking group of companies including IBM, ABB, Young and Rubicam, Reuters, Dun and Bradstreet, Cable and Wireless and Xerox have established that the global account manager must be given the authority to manage the company's worldwide team. Obviously, the use of a direct line reporting structure will best facilitate that authority.

While the management model shown in Figure 8.14 demonstrates a strong customer focus, it will be successful only where the supplier's performance matches the buying company's organizational requirements. At the time of writing, few companies have genuinely achieved global scope in purchasing. Thus, the incidence of global scope in account management is also limited. Hewlett Packard found it necessary to reduce its portfolio of global accounts from 250 to ninety-five in 1997.

This 'global control' model requires that all global key account managers possess excellent cross-cultural management skills. It is also essential that a steering committee at board level works together with the key account team and that functional teams are given responsibility for resolving any implementation problems. Under this model, up to 100 people from a supplying company could be devoted to servicing a single global key account. Above all, global KAM requires close attention to the coordination of activities and acute sensitivity to the trade-off between global integration and local flexibility (Millman, 1999b).

Company leagues

The organization of global businesses is important and glamorous, but its significance can be over-played. By the early 1990s there were 37 000 transnational companies which controlled one-third of the world's private sector assets. That meant that two-thirds of the world's private sector assets were held nationally or locally. Of these local assets, the public sector accounted for up to 40 per cent of gross national product in most developed economies. Therefore, the majority of the world's citizens, while they might well be touched by the Coca-Cola or Sony global brand, will be buying it from a local or at most national retail outlet. Apart from the omnipresent McDonalds and Pizza Huts, the majority of the services they consume will be bought from local companies or provided by local or national government.

It seems likely that, in the short term, buyer–seller dyads will form into a league table scenario of supply chain activity (see Table 2.4). The differences in demand and capability for supplying will polarize global and local/niche players, with regional and national companies taking up the intermediate ground. For example, XYZ UK might have a good and longstanding relationship with a UK national supplier. However, if XYZ Inc. wants to move towards purchasing goods or services on a global basis, it will drop the UK supplier in favour of a global supplier. While supplier rationalization normally means that larger buying companies will opt for global suppliers, occasionally buying companies will operate a programme of supplier development and help small suppliers to grow with them.

Alternatively, if a UK company, ABC Ltd, is a key customer of XYZ UK and XYZ Inc. (the worldwide organization) decides to concentrate its resources on global accounts, ABC Ltd may lose the services of or its status with XYZ UK. The obvious response would be to switch to a smaller supplier to whom it will be more important.

Future organizational structures

Future organizational structures for managing key accounts are likely to be based on joint value management where purchasing professionals work together with other key account professionals throughout the value chain. In the words of John Needell, the supply manager for BOC Gases, 'Specifically, we wanted our complete supply chain – original equipment manufacturer through to distributor – to face us as one single entity with a common set of goals and objectives and not as individual businesses with their own agendas' (Arkin, 1999).

The assertion that it is supply chains which compete, not the companies within them, has been made for some time. The focus of cross-boundary teams and the incidence of job swapping will no doubt be transferred from dyadic relationships to multiple relationships and extend from the raw materials processor to the end consumer (see Figure 8.15).

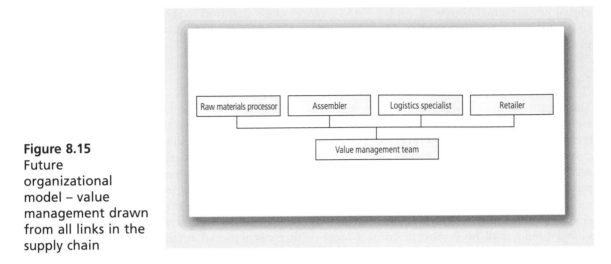

Figure 8.15
Future organizational model – value management drawn from all links in the supply chain

Mini-case 8:

Value management throughout the supply chain

In the early 1990s, the UK Government researched the advantages of supply chain integration and pilot activity to trial its implementation delivered impressive results. In 1995, 110 companies in the aerospace industry and the Ministry of Defence (MOD) signed up to the Supply Chain Relationships in Aerospace (SCRIA) project, which is partially funded by the Department of Trade and Industry. SCRIA's aim is to set standards of best practice within supply chain operations in order to improve the competitiveness of products and enhance customer value. The project involved an analysis of how closely and cooperatively different functions worked together, including design, engineering, production, procurement and marketing.

As a result of the SCRIA's findings and subsequent guidelines, changes were made and dramatic improvements were achieved. The MOD adopted 'integrated product teams' as part of its drive for smart procurement. The UK share of the world market for aerospace increased from 9.3 per cent to 12.5 per cent during the period from 1993 to 1998. SCRIA members have reported 20–30 per cent cost savings, a 54 per cent improvement in delivery, a 50 per cent increase in the accuracy of demand forecasting and substantial growth in evident levels of trust in their business relationships (Varley, 1999).

Summary

There is no set formula for the positioning of key account activity within overall business management. However, successful KAM is governed by a few basic tenets which may be summarized as follows.

- Intercompany collaboration – successful key account strategists counsel the avoidance of feudal and tribal sentiment in customer-facing teams and, therefore, the emphasis of organization at macro and micro levels is on encouraging diversity and cooperation through the use of cross-cultural management, matrix management, multidisciplinary teams, cross-boundary teams, job swapping and so on.
- Operational flexibility – key account practitioners and decision makers also recognize that a balance must be achieved between the need to be competitive and the need to be secure. Greater flexibility and adaptability can work to deliver product superiority and business stability.
- Organizational appropriateness – mismatches with the customer's organizational pattern and their expectations of the supplier's organizational make-up must also be avoided. It must always be understood that the supplier's organizational problems are irrelevant to decision makers in key accounts.
- Demonstrable authority (vested in the key account manager) – the key account manager, despite who he or she reports to or has reporting to him or her, must be perceived by the customer and colleagues as possessing authority as well as accountability. Buying companies often complain that key account managers appear to be accountable for problems which they do not have the authority to solve.
- Long-term perspective – key account activity must be organized with a view to the future. Cooperative value management throughout the supply chain is an emerging trend and this involves the removal of traditional barriers. The process usually starts with multidisciplinary key account teams in the selling company and progresses to cross-boundary teams comprising representatives of both selling and buying companies.

Companies often rush to meet business challenges through structural reorganization. Dramatic changes in the character and volume of customer requirements means that suppliers must adjust and adapt in order to achieve and maintain customer focus. The nature of the business will dictate how total the organizational transformation can and should be.

Suppliers also need to note that the delegation of authority and determination of rewards have to change to reflect changes in organizational policies and practices. New KAM structures must be handled with strategic care, rather than tactical speed. Any reorganization for KAM today should seek to achieve value management throughout the supply chain tomorrow.

References

Arkin, A. (1999). Fuelled for take-off. *Supply Manage.*, 18 November.

Graen, M. (1999). Technology in manufacturer–retailer integration. *Velocity*, spring.

Hall, K. and Poots, A. (1996). Global warming. *Supply Manage.*, 4 July.

Kobrin, S. (n.d.). *Globalisation and Multinationals. Financial Times.*

McDonald, M. and Rogers, B. (1998) *Key Account Management – Learning from Supplier and Customer Perspectives.* Butterworth-Heinemann.

McDonald, M., Millman, A. and Rogers, B. (1996). *Key Account Management – Learning from Supplier and Customer Perspectives.* Cranfield School of Management.

Mailplan (1999). Working as one. *Mailplan*, autumn.

Matthews, J. and Michels, B. (1999). Dispensing change. *Supply Manage.*, 22 July.

Millman, A. F. (1999a). From national account management to global account management in business-to-business markets. *Fachzeitschrift für Marketing THEXIS*, 16(4).

Millman, A. F. (1999b). How well does the concept of global account management travel across cultures? In *Third International Conference on Selling and Major Account Management*.

Nolan, A. (1999). On top of the world. *Supply Manage.*, 18 February.

Schindler, F. (1999). Lessons from a global account management benchmarking group. In *Third International Conference on Selling and Major Account Management*.

Stevens, K. (1997). World class perceptions. *Supply Manage.*, 30 January.

Supply Management (1999). Team approach gains ground with suppliers. *Supply Manage.*, 4 February.

Varley, P. (1999). Model relationships. *Supply Manage.*, 15 April.

Waller, A. (1998). The globalisation of business – the role of supply chain management. *Manage. Focus*, winter.

Wilson, M. (1999). The building blocks for successful global account management. In *Global Account Management Conference*.

Yip, G. S. (1999). Global account management: strategic issues and evidence. In *Third International Conference on Selling and Major Account Management*.

Yip, G. S. and Madsen, T. L. (1996). Global account management: the new frontier in relationship marketing. *Int. Marketing Rev.*, 13(3), 24–42.

Chapter 9

The key account manager

Introduction

This chapter explains how the key account manager's role evolves with the progressive development of the buyer–seller relationship and presents the wide portfolio of skills expected of key account managers and how they might be best developed. It also considers what support the key account manager needs from the rest of the organization in order to fulfil this demanding role and explores issues of recruitment, development and reward.

Role and responsibilities

The role of the key account manager is critical, not just to selling companies but to buying companies as well. Buying companies have a lot to gain from excellence in account management and those in partnership relationships with suppliers are increasingly relying on it. Of course, selling companies hold the main responsibility in terms of recruiting and developing successful key account managers and their first challenge is to define the job description and person specification.

What does a key account manager do? Most studies agree that, although key account managers must have a high profile in the customer's organization, the majority of their activities involve dragooning the resources of their own companies to meet customer needs. Success with the customer depends on success internally and vice versa.

Standard bearer

As discussed in Chapter 3, customers often seek the benefits of having a single point of contact within the selling organization. However, a first-rate clerical progress chaser will not suffice: the key account manager role demands much more than organizational ability and efficiency. Key account managers *represent* their company to the customer. Their behaviour and demeanour are inextricably associated with the character and reputation of the supplier. In the past, some companies were admired for the uniformity of their representatives' appearance and conduct. These days purchasing decision makers are suspicious of 'clones'. However, some degree of conformity and professionalism must be combined with the individuality of the key account manager in order to uphold quality standards and to promote a sense of confidence and security. While the outward appearance of key account managers is important, credibility from the boardroom to the postroom is not vested in the suit and the firm handshake, but in being seen to deliver on promises.

The promises key account managers make to their customers are in essence the promises of the supplier. Key account managers carry responsibility for generating and maintaining trust between the two organizations. This is by no means a simple task for key account managers are often held accountable for actions beyond their control. Some commentators describe the key account manager's representative role as 'being the customer's punchbag'. Customers tend to exhibit a 'negativity bias': anything that goes wrong in the relationship is taken out of proportion to everything that goes right. This means that suppliers are only as good as their last delivery. The whole of the supplying organization must substantiate the customer's belief in the integrity and authority of the key account manager in order that the key account manager can exert influence in the customer organization to mutual advantage. The back-up resources which the supplying company allocates to its key account in terms of expertise and systems will serve to elevate or diminish the standing of the key account manager. A selling company cannot expect a key account manager to be a successful standard-bearer of the company if he or she is denied the authority and status of one. A whole section is devoted to this important point later in the chapter.

Value creator

In addition to sustaining constructive relations with customers, key account managers are responsible for developing the relationship's business potential. They are charged with identifying and realizing opportunities for applying the company's products and services to the customer's needs. However, key account management (KAM) is not simply about 'shifting kit'; it is about creating mutual value.

Mutual value can be observed when the buying company is achieving its objectives through using the supplier's products/services and the selling company is achieving its objectives by supplying the customer. As emphasized throughout this book, business benefit must be mutual for the relationship to succeed. If the supplier is losing money by supplying a customer, the whole supply chain may suffer in the long run. In order to maximize influence in the account while not exposing the company to 'non-core', high-risk or low-profit activities, many supplying companies configure whole solutions for customers and manage their implementation on the customer's behalf.

Mini-case 1:

Unbiased value creation

Mail is a vital communications component for Boots the Chemist. The company's head office deals with 20 million items of incoming mail per annum. The company developed a partnership with the Royal Mail, who delivered tailored training for mailroom staff, streamlined customer service and seconded an operations manager to enable the company to meet its objectives in terms of postroom efficiency. In some cases, the Royal Mail account manager had to present solutions which did not entail Royal Mail products or services. Clearly, an unbiased view of value creation has helped to integrate this supplier–customer relationship.

Another example of solution delivery is the oil company which was the first to offer a strategic account a consignment stock arrangement, thus taking the stock management hassle away from the customer.

Such a holistic view of the creation of mutual value is possible where both supplier and customer are committed to a long-term view of business development. It is unlikely to thrive in an environment where the key account manager is rewarded on the basis of achieving short-term goals. The direct connection between company incentive schemes, profitability and value enhancement is explored later in the chapter.

Communicator

As the predominant interface between the company and the customer, key account managers are expected to communicate effectively and appropriately within the customer's organization as well as their own. Their communications should be accurate, honest, open and courteous. They must be good listeners and responsive managers. To fulfil their duties successfully, key account managers have to generate a good opinion of themselves and their company.

Many key account managers are trained in the techniques of powerful communication, such as creating images through illustrations and anecdotes and generating an aura of fun. Since key account managers may spend over 75 per cent of their working day engaged in different types of communication, it makes sense for their employers to provide them with development support. There are not enough 'born communicators' who are also naturally adept at undertaking the multiplicity of activities required of key account managers.

Planner

The decisions taken by the key account manager are often directly connected to the company's profitability. As we have argued earlier in this book, customers not products or plants or geographies generate profit. As a manager of people, information and processes, the key account manager has to be able to envisage and prepare the pathway in order to ensure the delivery of the mutual value expected by both supplier and customer. Key account managers must therefore be excellent planners capable of producing and implementing strategic and tactical plans for their accounts. They must demonstrate the ability of managing and analysing information and formulating effective strategies from it.

Each key account plan should provide competitive advantage by differentiating the company from its competitors. A good strategy usually springs from good insight. Insight should be driven by an in-depth understanding of the customer's critical success factors (CSFs) based on sound information, which in turn should generate new perspectives which open up other opportunities for serving customers better.

Manager

More challenging perhaps are the tasks of progress chasing and project management which are required to implement the key account plan. Key account managers also have to monitor and measure plan fulfilment. One key measure will not do – you would not fly with a pilot who only looked at one dial in the cockpit. Shaw (1998) of Cranfield University has argued for a structured approach to the measurement of strategic plans which links cause and effect. Companies need to measure and understand the link between inputs, how they generate changes in customer motivation and behaviour and the output which is consequently produced. Where effort is not measured and its effectiveness is not monitored, it usually fails.

Some commonly identified examples of the components of Shaw's (1998) model follow:

1 Input
- Process improvement.
- Innovative product/service.
- Risk management.
- Employee awareness.
- Service levels.
- Acquisition investment.
- Attributable costs.
2 Customer motivation
- Perceptions of brand values.
- Perceptions of quality.
- Perceptions of relative competitive performance on CSFs.
- Customer satisfaction.
3 Customer behaviour
- Share of purchases for this category.
- Length of customer relationship.
- Reduction in complaints/returns/queries.
4 Output
- Profit/return on investment.
- Sales volume.
- Reduction in waste.
- Brand valuation.

Key account managers need to use the measurement system in order to facilitate learning and improvement, for example by detecting performance killers, testing assumptions and identifying potential performance enhancers. Interpreting the results of account investment in financial terms in order to demonstrate the relationship between account success and profitability also forms part of the key account manager's role. Therefore, the key account manager must have an understanding of the following:

- The drivers which create customer asset value.
- How to calculate the lifetime value of the account.
- Realistic net cash flows at different stages of account development.
- The differing financial measures applicable at different stages of account development.
- The level of financial risk versus business risk in the account and its relationship to returns.
- How risk changes over time.
- The relationship between fixed costs and variable costs in maintaining the account.
- The costs and benefits of investing in the account.

In the course of managing the account and its performance, the key account manager will need to be proactive in handling cross-over relationships with other departments, which brings us to the next essential aspect of the role.

Leader

> I think you can be a terrific manager and come up with all the right financial numbers and make your gross profit and everything else, but still be a crummy leader.
>
> William Pagonis,
> Executive Vice-President of Logistics, Sears Roebuck.

Leaders set goals and work with their followers in order to achieve them, showing the way forward and helping to remove obstacles. Key account managers have to demonstrate leadership to influence line staff, peers, senior managers and other stakeholders in their own company, as well as stakeholders in the customer's organization and possibly other third parties, in order to achieve the goals established for their accounts. Rarely can key account managers lead by exercising seniority, for they generally have little positional power. All their 'buy-in' has to be won through consultation and persuasion. In addition to demonstrating concern for the people involved with the account, the account manager also needs to be driven by a desire to achieve the task and inspire that desire in the account team.

The matrix given in Figure 9.1 is the popular Blake and Mouton (1964) managerial grid, which demonstrates the inter-relationship between concern for people and concern for the task.

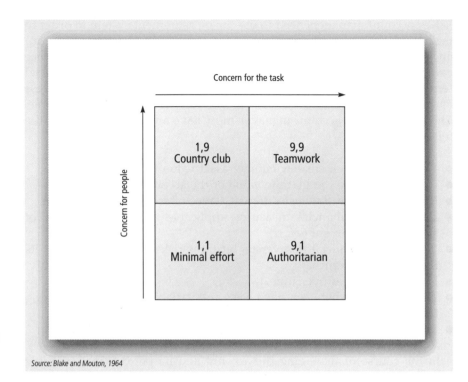

Figure 9.1
Blake and Mouton
(1964) managerial
grid

Source: Blake and Mouton, 1964

The 9,9 teamwork option shown in Figure 9.1 is generally believed to be the most desirable, but there are many challenges in the work of a key account manager which require something else. For example, when there is a panic about a potential over-run on a project, concern for the task becomes the primary focus. The 'concern for people' approach is always associated with greater follower satisfaction, but it is not always associated with higher productivity! It can be time-consuming, it may be lacking in clarity or it may give the customer the impression that the achievement of their objectives has to be wheedled out of supplier personnel.

Leadership is strongest where relationships are good, tasks are structured and the leader has positional power, that it to say control of rewards and punishments (Fiedler, 1967). Key account managers need to be given some influence in the reward and discipline of members of key account teams in order to gain command and respect. They should also have some influence in selecting the key account team. The success of informal leadership usually depends on the maturity of the followers (Hersey and Blanchard, 1982). Those who have job maturity (ability and experience) and attitudinal maturity (motivation) are more likely to respond to informal leadership than those who are inexperienced, unsure of themselves or lacking in initiative.

Insight

When everyone else is blaming each other about missed deliveries, a leader is getting on the van and finding out what is happening.

Knowledge systems manager

Key account managers have responsibility for managing strategic knowledge about their accounts or determining how operational data is collected, collated and used. They are probably also involved in managing how information is shared and processes are integrated between the two organizations.

Although colleagues may research some of the external data, key account managers will certainly be responsible for the accuracy and currency of customer-specific data. They will also be the prime organizers of all strategic, operational and integration information. However, key account managers do not own the information. The company owns it and there should be a company-wide framework establishing who has access to what information. Usually, all senior managers and all members of the relevant key account team will have access to the database for the particular account.

Strategic information

Table 9.1 outlines the sort of strategic information that the key account manager will need to manage. In many companies, there is an intranet site per key account, with site access granted on a 'need-to-know' basis.

Operational information

A vast amount of data is generated about accounts within company systems, but few of the systems are constructed so that it is easy for

Table 9.1 Strategic information

Information relevant to assessing and selecting the account	Account attractiveness factors The account's perceptions of the suppliers' business strengths (critical success factors)
Information and analysis which underpins the account plan	External information such as: industry forces, customers' competitive position, how their customers rate them and relative sources of power in the supply chain. Customer-specific information such as: the decision-making unit and purchasing behaviour, purchasing processes, trends within the customer organization (e.g. centralization or delegation) and the customer's culture.
How success against the plan is measured and controlled	Investments made in the account Changes in customer motivation, judged by improvements in critical success factor scores Changes in customer behaviour, e.g. increased share of spend. Improvements in sales and profitability

account team members to access operational information, such as customer-specific transaction histories. For each key account there should be on-line access to data concerning:

- orders,
- sales,
- service calls,
- credits,
- returns,
- deliveries,
- costs,
- performance indicators,
- recent contacts.

Key account managers cannot be expected to programme these 'intelligence' systems themselves, but they do need to be involved in their design, maintenance and development. As guardians of what other people in the company may need to know about their account, key account managers also need to advise colleagues about how they want the information to be used and what feedback is required from them.

Integration

If an account is strategically very important, it is likely that both companies will want to integrate operational data. Where full integration is desirable, process fulfilment will become a significant factor. In highly collaborative supplier–customer relationships, the integration of processes will typically start with fast-tracking communication links and then move on to the managing of operational dependencies, such as scheduling, logistics and project control. The key account manager acts as facilitator of the integration process.

Role development

The role of the key account manager differs according to the position of the buyer–seller relationship in the relationship development model (see Figure 3.1). This does not mean to say that the post holder has to be changed as the relationship evolves. Many key account managers grow in stature and ability as they build their accounts. In other cases, senior key account managers may be tasked with converting a key prospect into a new customer so that they can revisit the skills required in building new business and, using their wealth of experience and expertise, ensure the rapid development of that business.

The diagram shown in Figure 9.2 serves to illustrate how the key account manager role changes as the supplier–customer relationship evolves.

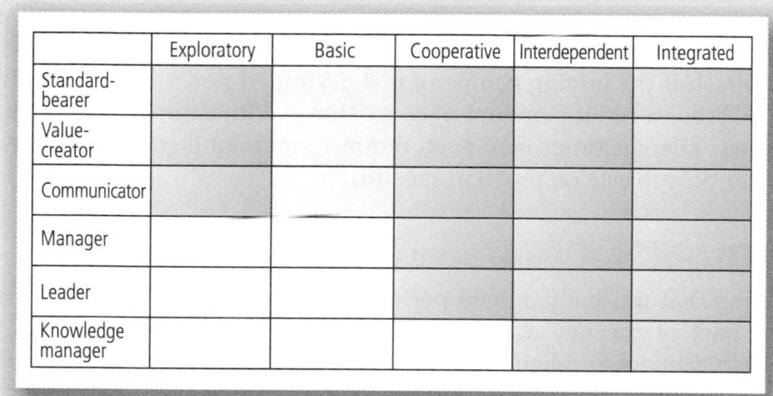

	Exploratory	Basic	Cooperative	Interdependent	Integrated
Standard-bearer					
Value-creator					
Communicator					
Manager					
Leader					
Knowledge manager					

Figure 9.2
How the role evolves with the account relationship

Exploratory

At the *exploratory* stage, the key account manager's role as standard-bearer and value creator is dominant. If prospecting is ever to dislodge an incumbent supplier, the priority must be to influence the customer's decision-making unit (DMU) successfully. Securing the DMU's favour will primarily depend upon the key account manager's ability to persuade the DMU's members that the company's product and/or service is superior to that of competitors in terms of offering more competitive advantage.

Basic

If a key account gets stuck at the *basic* stage as a result of customer preference or supplier indolence, the role of the key account manager is weak. The emphasis on individual transactions which characterizes this stage of relationship development means that the key account manager mainly functions as an order taker and price negotiator. In some extreme cases, regardless of volume, suppliers might be better off conducting the customer's business via a call centre.

Cooperative

Where the key account has reached the *cooperative* stage, it is likely that the purchasing decision makers will have placed a value on the account management role. In choosing a preferred supplier, they might reasonably expect their account manager to have the authority and aptitude to get things done for them. Contacts between supplier and buyer will be established at all levels in order to handle the increasing scale of business between them. The whole key account team will assume importance to the buying company and the role of the key account manager will be critical.

The key account manager's objective in a *cooperative* relationship is most likely to be to increase account penetration (see Chapter 3). His or her strengths as a standard-bearer and value creator will be tested as he or she makes contacts in other divisions or departments within the buying company. However, return on time and effort invested will start to diminish if the buying company is determined never to single source, in which case a certain amount of co-existence with competition has to be accepted. The customer may even request competing suppliers to work together on projects or problem resolution.

Interdependent

Ensuring that mutually agreed performance criteria are met will form a major part of the key account manager's day-to-day activities at the *interdependent* stage. Here the management emphasis shifts from value creation to value delivery. The key account manager will be producing long-term plans jointly with the key decision makers in the buying company. Effort will also be concentrated on streamlining processes between the two companies in order to improve quality standards and reduce costs.

Integrated

At the *integrated* stage, vigilance, monitoring and measuring will be critical, as the 'partnership index' might include up to 200 performance criteria as more and more processes are scrutinized. Achieving these criteria should be business as usual and the key account manager should be primarily concerned with resolving exceptions. The supplier will still need to be able to withstand any market test the customer might choose to impose, so value auditing will continue to be necessary.

Skills and attributes

Insight

One sales and marketing director quipped that it was easy to spot the ideal key account manager. An ideal key account manager walks on water and leaps tall buildings at a single bound.

With such a varied and significant role to play, the successful key account manager will certainly require a broad portfolio of capabilities. Narrowly focused selling skills will clearly be inadequate, particularly at the higher relationship levels. As outlined in Table 9.2, our research indicates much diversity of opinion on the prioritization of the skills, knowledge and qualities considered desirable in key account managers.

According to the study's findings, buying company contacts value integrity and technical product knowledge the most, followed by knowledge of their business. The importance of selling and negotiating skills is the most widely contested area: the managers of key account managers and the key account managers themselves rated them highly (62 and 67 per cent, respectively), whereas only 9 per cent of buying

Table 9.2 Desirable attributes of key account managers

n = number of respondents *Desirable skills/knowledge/qualities*	*Managers of key account managers* *n = 13* %	*Key account managers* *n = 9* %	*Customer contacts* *n = 11* %
Integrity/honesty	15	11	64
Product knowledge — technical	54	33	64
Understanding of buying company's business	46	56	54
Product knowledge — applications	31	0	45
Communication/interpersonal	85	56	45
Knowledge of markets/environment	85	33	45
Creativity	15	22	36
Financial	46	33	27
Strategic thinking/consultancy	69	56	28
Credibility from boardroom to postroom	15	33	18
Listening	8	0	18
Flexibility	0	11	18
Selling/negotiating	62	67	9
Administration/organization	38	11	9
People management/leadership	38	11	9
Legal knowledge	8	11	9
Resilience	46	0	0
Planning	23	11	0
Computer literacy	23	0	0
Persuasion	31	0	0
Languages/cultural skills	15	0	0

Source: McDonald, Millman and Rogers, 1996

decision makers even mentioned them. Administrative, strategic and leadership skills appear to be valued more by managers of account managers than by the buying company contacts, although this is likely to change as customers reveal a greater reliance on supplier expertise due to the rationalization of their own resources.

Managers of key account managers quoted the greatest number of desirable attributes, but the mismatch between their views and those of the customer decision makers should be a matter of concern. It is reasonable to assume that, as strategists for the supplying company, the managers of key account managers should be thinking ahead and pre-empting customers' needs and expectations. However, they appear to be missing some important messages from customers. Some supplier decision makers argue that they would not put integrity on their list of desirable attributes because it is a quality which key account managers would obviously and automatically possess. However, many customers do not share this view and suppliers would be wise to recognize the need to reinforce their reputation continually through demonstrations of honesty, willingness and sound business judgement.

Table 9.3 summarizes the core elements of the contrasting views of customers and suppliers and key account managers which suppliers must try to reconcile.

Table 9.3 Summary of differing views on the key attributes of key account managers

	Buying company view	*Selling company strategic view*	*Key account manager's view*
First	Integrity	Knowledge of business environment	Selling/negotiating
Second	Product knowledge – technical	Communications	Communications
Third	Understanding our business	Strategic thinking	Understanding customer's business
Fourth	Product knowledge – applications	Selling/negotiating	Strategic thinking
Fifth	Communications	Product knowledge – technical	Technical/financial/ markets/credibility

The nearest we can get to a definition of the ideal key account manager, 'the unattainable', would be a collection of all the skills and qualities desired by selling companies and buying companies at higher relationship levels. The portfolio of essential attributes of a key account manager would thus include the following:

1 'People' skills.
   - Communication skills including listening and persuasion.
   - Leadership.
   - Credibility – boardroom to postroom.
2 Thinking skills.
   - Analytical skills.
   - Creativity and flexibility.
   - Strategic thinking.
   - 'Boundary spanning'.
3 Administration/project management skills.
4 Relevant knowledge.
   - Technical knowledge – product and applications in the customer's business.
   - Subject knowledge.
     - Industry/market understanding.
     - Financial understanding.
     - Computer literacy and appreciation of information systems.
     - Cultural skills and languages.
     - Legal understanding.
5 Personal qualities.
   - Integrity.
   - Selling/negotiating skills.
   - Resilience/persistence.
   - 'Likeability'.

'People' skills

Communication skills including listening

The importance of verbal fluency, presentation skills and the ability to exercise influence in meetings are widely appreciated by all those involved in key account relationships. Advanced interpersonal skills, particularly communication skills, are considered a 'must' for key account managers. While these skills can be introduced on courses, key account managers will also need abundant opportunities for practising them with colleagues before practising them on customers.

Buying company decision makers are emphatic that listening skills are distinct from other communication skills. Some key account managers are able to present their products beautifully, but are unable to absorb the buying company's response or to put themselves in the buying company's position in order to appreciate their priorities. It is also vital for key account managers to be able to listen and respond appropriately to members of the account team, influential colleagues and senior management.

Leadership

In order to motivate dotted line teams and get things done for the customer, key account managers must be able to exercise leadership within their own companies in order to promote the account internally. They may also be required to direct or supervise buying company personnel on specific projects or in cross-boundary focus teams.

Historically, people have assumed that leaders are born not made. Thus, leadership traits have been researched – for about seventy years! That research suggests that there is a correlation between leadership ability and certain common personal traits, such as intelligence, dominance, self-confidence, high energy levels and task-relevant knowledge. The great mystery is the relationship between cause and effect. Do people become leaders because they have those traits or do they become leaders and acquire those traits as a result? Whatever the correct answer might be, these common leadership traits might not be appropriate in every business situation. No doubt some eminent military and political leaders would have made awful key account managers!

Credibility from the boardroom to the postroom

In a mature buyer–seller relationship, the key account manager is not only striving to convince purchasing professionals, but he or she is also seeking to gain buying company commitment at the board level. In the Cranfield study (McDonald, Millman and Rogers, 1996) key account managers and buying companies recognized the need for key account managers to command respect from anyone at any level in either the selling or buying company who had a direct interest in their proposed solutions. They must have credibility from the boardroom to the postroom.

Thinking skills

Analytical skills

The assumption is usually made that key account managers today are of sufficient intelligence and educational attainment to have well-honed analytical thinking skills. Indeed, KAM is becoming a popular choice of career for graduates and MBAs. While analytical skills are certainly needed, one of the main attractions of the job is that it is not the only thinking mode that is required.

Creativity and flexibility

In our study, 36 per cent of buying company decision makers indicated that creativity was a desirable attribute in a key account manager. In fact, they were more likely to criticize key account managers who displayed a lack of mental flexibility. Problem-solving techniques such as brainstorming are of limited value when customers demand immediate and innovative solutions to their problems. Key account managers need to be able to question and to reconfigure situations using analogy and scenario planning.

Strategic thinking

The more experienced the key account manager is at developing and implementing key account plans, the more likely it is that he or she will be able to maintain a long-term view, even when engaged in the immediacy of tactical detail. The ability to think strategically and establish practical pathways for achieving long-term objectives is strengthened through regular practice. The planning process, incorporating the establishment of the company's mission, final performance challenges, operating environment and customer and competitor activity, should be revisited at least annually and the plan produced reviewed at least quarterly.

'Boundary spanning'

Insight	You only know a man when you have walked a mile in his moccasins. (Native American saying).

Senior managers in selling companies often worry about key account managers identifying more closely with their customer than they do with their employer. It is understood that this is more likely to occur when the customer ascribes high value to a key account manager who lacks status or authority within his or her own organization. Such a situation leads the key account manager to feel a closer affinity to the customer's point of view than the supplier's.

It is essential that the key account manager should be able to adopt different mindsets, but be able to control from which perspective he or she is working and to decide on its appropriateness. This skill is called 'boundary spanning'. The key account manager will need to be able focus on the interests of a range different people at different times, including those of senior management, individuals within the buying company and end consumers. Sometimes the key account manager may have to approach a situation as an unbiased external observer.

Breaking out of the monoculture of one's own company can offer a wide and powerful spectrum of understanding. The hopes, fears, pride and prejudices of the customer and all aspects of their internal frames of reference can be grasped as well as their policies and processes. A top key account manager will be able to appreciate a diversity of behaviours and business styles springing from different philosophies and historical perspectives. A truly successful manager needs to 'feel' as well as to know. Empathy with other points of view may be gained through role-play or achieved through job swaps.

Administration/project management skills

It has been emphasized throughout this book that the key account manager is indeed a manager. The armoury of management skills required by key account managers may be taught in part, but they must be strengthened and supported in-house through internal organization, mentoring arrangements and regular practice.

The attention to detail required to administer and organize key account activity is the least glamorous aspect of the key account manager's job, but it is very important to their managers and is usually quite helpful to the customer as well. The key account manager's meticulousness, conscientiousness and managerial competence will need to be under-pinned by a resolute determination to succeed.

Relevant knowledge

Facts about products, markets and business in general can be learnt, which suggests that imbuing key account managers with requisite subject knowledge is one of the easiest aspects of professional development and one which can have immediate results in terms of improving customer satisfaction. It is how that knowledge is applied which determines its value to the customer.

Technical knowledge

Product

There is no doubt, particularly in the early stages of relationship development when the key account manager is the single point of contact, that it is very important for him or her to be able to handle technical questions. A majority of the buying company's technical questions ought to be within the key account manager's technical product knowledge, although a minority of buying companies place more emphasis on the key account manager's ability to accomplish tasks and obtain appropriate technical support. Access to technical databases might be an expedient support tool. As relationships between the supplier and customer become more complex, direct contact between the two companies' technicians should reduce the amount of technical information that the key account manager needs to know.

Insight	In the early days of question and answer databases, information systems companies had a great opportunity for demonstrating to key accounts how they practised what they preached. Account managers would receive telephone calls from customers about almost anything and could turn to their screens, enter a few key words and, usually, find an answer for them. They did not need to be technically expert on every aspect of the customer's installation, provided they were expert at searching the databases!

Applications

Besides knowing the features of a product, the key account manager must understand how the product works and what it does for the customer. This is a relatively new requirement. The effects of downsizing and the accelerating pace of change have meant that buying companies are increasingly reliant on the key account manager knowing enough about their business to be able to present solutions with customer-specific benefits. Opportunities of bestowing knowledge of product applications can be used by key account managers in highlighting company and product superiority in terms of delivering mutual competitive advantage.

Insight	A hygiene services firm presented its value add to customers and prospects on the basis of output measurement rather than input measurement. The company proposed its services not on how many times a specific type of room needed to be cleaned, but the standard of cleanliness to which it needed to be kept. Services would be concentrated on key areas, such as the toilets and reception area and less emphasis would be placed on non-critical cleaning jobs, such as vacuuming the offices. The firm was relatively expensive as it offered high wages in order to retain good staff. The firm's approach meant maximizing value to customers while maintaining competitiveness.

Subject knowledge

Industry/market understanding

In addition to having an understanding of the buying company's business, the key account manager must also possess understanding of the industry and markets in which the customer operates (see Chapter 7). Buying companies expect the key account manager to be as familiar with the political, economic, social and technological factors affecting their business as they are themselves.

Insight	'We have to admit, our key account manager knows more about our business environment than we do. . .' (a buying company decision maker acknowledging part of what made a particular supplier strategically important).

Financial understanding

The key account manager's ability to present a sound financial case within a proposal is crucial to both parties in a contract negotiation. It is sorely missed when it is not available. Buying company decision makers say that they would value more financial input from suppliers, although the willingness of the supplier to provide it is dependent on the customer's willingness to reciprocate by offering their financial analyses. Regardless of how much reciprocity can be achieved, the key account manager needs at least to have a financial understanding of the situation, particularly the link between activities and cost. This involves knowing the following:

- How to read and analyse company accounts.
- How to construct a business case, including techniques such as discounted cash flow.
- How to analyse customer profitability.
- How to recognize the elements of cost in customer and supplier processes and devise options for reducing them.

Computer literacy and appreciation of information systems

It is almost inconceivable that anyone in business today could survive without some degree of computer literacy and information technology (IT) proficiency. Key account managers must be able to employ information systems effectively, particularly for communication purposes, as well as exploiting their full potential for improving integration processes.

Cultural skills and languages

The greatest errors in military history have been made because the strategists failed to understand the point of view of their opponents. In modern business strategy, quality can be achieved by acquiring a thorough understanding of the customer's point of view as well as competitors. This quality must encompass a variety of national and corporate cultures.

Facts can be learnt about doing business in different parts of the world. This is the first step in acquiring an understanding of cultural diversity and other people's points of view. Many global companies are now giving business executives extended assignments in different parts of the world so that facts can be backed up by experience. The practice has been common in oil companies for some time. For example, Schlumberger argues that it takes decades of moving staff around the globe to create truly international management.

Although English is widely used as a business language in many companies that are not US or UK owned and global account managers are usually nationals of the country in which their customer's headquarters is based, it is still desirable for global account managers to be fluent in more than one language. Government embassy staff are immersed in the language of their new postings sometimes before they even start any other research about the country. Businesses which are serious about global reach will also train their professionals to be great communicators in languages other than their own.

Legal understanding

Although companies in *interdependent* relationships will often claim that the relationship is in trouble if the contract has to come out of the drawer, in all commercial exchanges a contract is in place or implied. Contracts are ultimately the responsibility of lawyers, but it is helpful for the key account manager to understand the basics of commercial law, including contract law, employment law, competition law and consumer protection law. For a global key account manager, the priority need is to understand the legal framework of the country whose laws governs agreements between the selling company and the buying company in addition to the laws of the country in which he or she is based.

Personal qualities

It is often assumed that personal qualities cannot be developed in an account manager; a company has to recruit for them. Perhaps 'developing personal qualities' sounds too much like the parent–child relationship. Nevertheless, it is not unusual for companies to have a framework of behavioural expectations of employees or to invest in training in self-awareness or relating to others.

Integrity

Buying company decision makers emphasize the importance of being able to trust the key account manager as an individual, as well as expecting suppliers to demonstrate corporate integrity. Delivering on promises has already been described in the role of the key account manager. The difficulty faced by key account managers is the perceived paradox between integrity and selling. Buying company decision makers express their distaste at being sold to. The two are not mutually exclusive. Key account managers can and do sell honestly!

Selling skills

The modern key account manager is more a secular evangelist than an out-and-out salesperson. Selling actually takes up a small proportion of a key account manager's time. It may constitute as little as 10 per cent of the key account manager's activity in an *interdependent* relationship. Selling effort also depends on the pace at which the supplier is introducing new products. Nevertheless, key account managers fear that if they forget about selling they will forget their role in generating profit for their employer. Their job is about making money for the selling company and they need to invest some emotion in that, even though they recognize the importance of a 'soft' sales approach.

Negotiating skills

While salesmen have only to negotiate with purchasing managers, key account managers use their negotiating ability with buying decision makers and many others, including the following:

● Their own management.
● Colleagues in the account team.
● End-users of their product/service in the customer.
● Other influencers and gatekeepers in both organizations and beyond them.

Negotiation is a process of preparation, debate, proposing, bargaining and looping back to debate if necessary before reaching agreement. It ought to be rationally viewed as a normal part of life, but it is often distrusted as a process in which one side loses and the other gains at their expense. Therefore, the distinction between the concept of streetwise negotiation and principled negotiation must be made.

Streetwise negotiation, the game of winning as much as you can, potentially at the expense of the other parties, is totally out of place in the selling company which has embraced account management as a way of doing business. This category of negotiation is characterized by the use of ploys such as 'you need to order soon or we might run out' or 'if you order before Friday we can give you a much bigger discount' and counteracted by purchasing ploys such as 'you had better offer a lower price, we have offers pending from your competitors'.

Streetwise negotiation is often associated with bullying, particularly where one party has much more power than the other does. For example, in the case of negotiating with colleagues, a desperate key account manager might take the approach of threatening a junior colleague with trouble from his immediate boss. Such behaviour ensures that the task is done with bad grace, which is not in the best interests of the supplier or the customer.

Harvard lawyers Roger Fisher and Bill Ury originally defined principled negotiation based upon theories of rational decision making. It is based on objective criteria and the search for options for mutual gain. Where the following four principles are observed, a 'win–win' situation is more likely to be achieved:

- Separate personalities from the issue and concentrate on the issue and do not react to provocation.
- Focus on the interests of parties, not on their position.
- Search for options for mutual gain.
- Insist on objective criteria.

Resilience and persistence

The need for key account managers to possess resilience and persistence is noticed mostly by their managers who seem to be more conscious of the strains of the job than the account managers themselves or buying company decision makers. There ought to be no doubt that the role requires mental strength and stamina. Customer acceptance is not always achieved quickly and obtaining buy-in from colleagues and senior managers can also take longer than anticipated.

'Likeability'

Buying company decision makers talk a lot about the 'likeability' of key account managers, but find it difficult to describe. It is a quality characterized by optimism, enthusiasm, tolerance, thoughtfulness, courtesy and being interesting. Likeable key account managers are inclusive in the way they conduct meetings. They are calm under pressure and do not abuse their power. Selling companies need to exercise care in recruiting confidence but not arrogance, customer care but not obsequiousness and communication skills which include listening and sociability.

Issues of personal chemistry or fit clearly do play some part in the successful achievement of account objectives. Indeed, a buying company decision maker might make sure that conditions were not right for doing business if he or she did not like the key account manager. However, care must be taken in order to ensure that personality profiling has no adverse impact on equal opportunities. The desire for buying decision makers to have key account managers who fit in culturally or socially may exclude some candidates unfairly. Take, for example, the case of a woman account manager who was asked to leave the venue of a business lunch because the club was men only. In this instance, the people responsible were embarrassed by their gaffe, but arguably they should have been more aware. There are risks for all parties.

Suppliers do not have to provide buying decision makers with a mirror image of themselves as key account managers. Each contact is like a central jigsaw piece which has four or five points of 'fit' around it.

In summary, key account managers require a wide portfolio of skills and qualities. Table 9.4 links these attributes to the different elements of the key account manager's role.

Table 9.4 How the requisite attributes serve the key account manager role

Standard-bearing	Personal qualities
Value-creating	Subject knowledge — technical Thinking skills
Communicating	People skills Cultural and linguistic knowledge*
Managing	Administrative/project management skills Subject knowledge — general
Leading	People skills Thinking skills
Knowledge management	Management skills Thinking skills Subject knowledge

* Mainly relevant in global account management

The attributes required of key account managers change according to the nature of the buyer–seller relationship, as described in Figure 9.3. The darker the shading, the more critical the attribute. Technical subject knowledge and personal qualities are dominant success factors in the *exploratory* and *basic* stages of relationship development. Accounts at the *cooperative* stage require a broader spread of skills, notably the skills

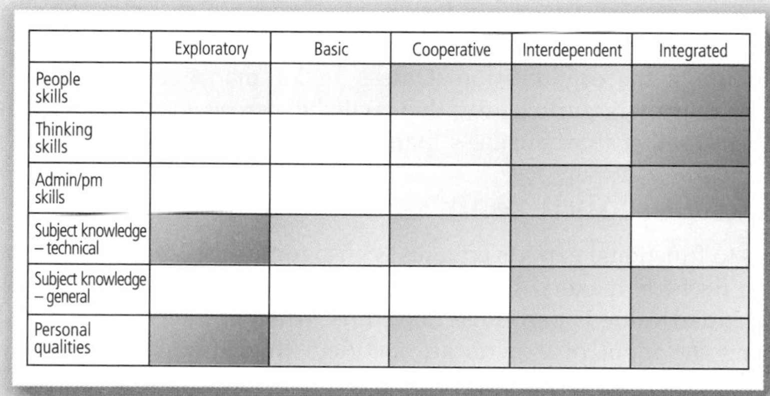

	Exploratory	Basic	Cooperative	Interdependent	Integrated
People skills					
Thinking skills					
Admin/pm skills					
Subject knowledge – technical					
Subject knowledge – general					
Personal qualities					

Figure 9.3
How the skills requirement changes as the relationship evolves

required to manage the key account team. *Interdependent* relationships demand skills right across the board. The achievement of integration places an emphasis on managerial skills and technical subject knowledge is noticeably less relevant.

In-company support
Authority

'We do not want to deal with a postman who has to trot back to his boss every time we ask a question' (purchasing manager).

Insight

Despite growing recognition of the importance of adopting a customer focus, key account managers seldom have the level of professional authority and status that they need and deserve and customers expect. A senior marketing manager in an international high-tech company told us recently that if a certain member of his key account managers with first-rate influencing skills fell under a bus, this would create a huge issue with the customer. That was not just because of his influence with the customer, but because it was unlikely that his successor would be able to pull the same strings with relevant colleagues to get things done for the customer.

Successful KAM requires top-level backing. Organizational structures and operations must work to assist key account managers in the fulfilment of their responsibilities. It is a challenge indeed to lead teams of people from other disciplines and departments where only informal or 'dotted line' authority exists. Key account managers are rarely line managers, although they are increasingly so in project-based service companies. There are a few instances of global suppliers serving global customers who have made their key account managers line managers, usually to counterbalance to the power of country managers (see Chapter 8).

Key account managers generally find it difficult to agree unique arrangements with buying companies because of the limitations placed on their power which leave them little room for manoeuvre except on price. Consequently, their position as the main liaison is easily undermined if buying company decision makers seek to deal with someone higher up in the organization. Unless senior managers empower key account managers sufficiently, they will be perceived as the despised 'postman', rather than business managers.

The key account team

Access to functional experts equates with significant added value to most buying decision makers. The question for key account managers is how much added value is perceived and, thus, whether the costs involved in securing the input of experts are justified. In addition to contributing valuable expertise and status, key account teams working at multiple organizational levels boost supplier visibility and intercompany bonding. They afford greater opportunities for the exchange of information and ideas and promote a sense of continuity even where there are occasional changes of personnel.

The use of key account teams in supporting customer relationships and developing tomorrow's key account managers is becoming widespread. The organization of selected individuals into informal or semi-formal teams serves to create synergy on the customer's behalf (see Chapter 8). It also provides a mechanism for training future key account managers and developing customer service skills throughout the company. Buying companies certainly appreciate linkage between old and new key account managers.

The key account team must be multidisciplinary in order to ensure that all corners of the selling company appreciate the value of the key account and strive to improve the account's performance. Ideally, team members should represent all of the relevant skill areas necessary to meet the customer's requirements and expectations. Participating functions might include engineering, research and development, technical support, customer service, finance, logistics, operations and IT. Depending on the nature of the selling company, merchandising, human resources and purchasing might also be represented.

Within the team itself, members can practise team roles as well as helping others understand their own specialisms. Rotas can be established for the roles of facilitator, progress chaser, researcher and recorder. The key account manager should take the role of coach and foster a spirit of mutual encouragement. Teams will also need to develop their own frameworks for undertaking activities such as problem resolution, idea generation, account planning, time management and cost management.

Senior management must create a 'big game' atmosphere in which key account teams can see that their efforts really matter. This should be reinforced by frequent feedback on team performance and the distribution of rewards associated with team achievement. Critical success factors for key account teams might include the following:

● Contact with customers for all members of the team – customer visits, social events and so on.

- Monthly targets, however small.
- Monitoring/measurement/feedback and reward.
- A balance of skills appropriate to the customer's requirements.
- A spirit of mutual encouragement.
- Open consideration of strategic as well as tactical issues.
- Leadership by key account manager.

Company infrastructure

Higher relationship stages are unlikely to be achieved in a company where professionals operate with a departmental 'silo' mentality. Only a company which creates an ethos of customer focus and provides enough systemic flexibility to implement customer focus can truly convince customers that it is 'easy to do business with'. As discussed in Chapter 8, there are various organizational options available for companies developing a KAM approach. The processes for implementing KAM are covered in the Chapter 10.

Information technology

The importance of knowledge management to the role of the key account manager cannot be underestimated. Most companies today require sophisticated IT support in order to facilitate the rapid accumulation and analysis of data from a variety of sources. The Internet has considerably enhanced access to information and has enabled the instantaneous exchange of communications.

Mini-case 2:

Hewlett Packard – communicating by intranet

Hewlett Packard have an intranet page per account, so that the account team worldwide have access to a database of information about the customer. Customers have access to Hewlett Packard's technical support information databases, automatic software fixes, download of print drivers, personalized product information, order and delivery status, configurations and pricing, news, company information, contact lists and so on. The company even has an on-line relationship assessment process which provides feedback on Hewlett Packard's performance against the customer's critical success factors.

Mini-case 3:

Pioneer – value creation via IT

Pioneer Hi-Bred International is a global leader in agricultural seeds. Their field information system provides account managers with access to product comparisons, articles and news, performance data, communication with agronomists, latest market prices and links to the newest satellite technology for information on weather patterns. The account manager can create an impressive crop plan for the buying decision maker and the company has successfully differentiated itself by using this expertise (SAMA Awards, 1999).

Recruitment

Large and complex customers today require unprecedented levels of leadership and administration support from their suppliers. Indeed, managers of strategic accounts are now recognized by suppliers and customers alike as critical members of staff. Historically, the top-performing field sales representative was rewarded with a strategic account. This was a common mistake. The promotion of an excellent salesperson to the more demanding role of account manager without first providing them with significant training and development often resulted in failure and regret.

The first step in recruiting good key account managers is to define the character of the role and the ideal candidate. While we have made some generalizations here about the nature of the job in different types of relationship, it is imperative that employers identify the specific account for which an account manager or account manager designate is required and match the post holder accordingly. What does the customer want and need? What skills and qualities will be essential and desirable? Only 44 per cent of the firms surveyed by Wotruba and Castleberry (1993) took customer requirements into account when recruiting key account managers. Senior managers responsible for recruitment should also consider industry best practice and the views of other stakeholders, such as the sponsoring director, the account team members and the human resources manager. Disturbingly, only 42 per cent of the companies in the Wotruba and Castleberry (1993) survey based the job qualifications on the job analysis.

The recruitment and selection process should proceed only after the job and individual requirements have been established. According to Wotruba and Castleberry (1993), the majority of key account managers (84 per cent) are recruited internally, mostly from sales roles, but also from non-sales roles. We have come across a significant minority of ex-engineers and even ex-accountants. Ironically, only 50 per cent of companies have a programme for developing their employees as key account managers, so half of these people switching professions have to learn by trial and error.

As well as recruiting internally, applicants may be found through recommendations, referrals and other word-of-mouth sources. However, an increasing number of key account manager posts are being advertised or filled via recruitment consultants and headhunters.

Having shortlisted the most suitable candidates, the recruiter's attention should turn to selecting the most appropriate assessment techniques. In the Wotruba and Castleberry (1993) study, interviewing was rated as the best method. Generally, human resources professionals advocate the application of a wider range of techniques, including informal contact with the account team, simulations, references and aptitude and psychographic tests.

Training and development

The prospect that only half of the world's key account managers receive any kind of training or development is a sobering one. However, since the Wotruba and Castleberry (1993) survey, significant advances have been made in the study of KAM which have led to wider understanding of how account managers need to be developed and how this can be achieved.

It is clear that a variety of methods need to be employed in order to equip key account managers with the tools and techniques of effective KAM. A pragmatic approach which we have found to be successful combines self-study with workshop-style training, reinforced by team dynamics mentoring and experience.

Status, appraisal and reward
Status

Assuming that near perfect key account managers can be moulded from ready and willing candidates, it seems only natural that they will expect to be treated in a manner befitting their strategic importance to the company. The status attributed to the key account manager largely depends on the behaviour of colleagues above them and below them in the organizational hierarchy. Key account managers are status conscious and for good reason.

A key account manager justifiably expects recognition as confirmation of his or value to the company and to the customer. In most business-to-business selling companies, KAM is regarded as much more important than general marketing. This is in line with the views of buying companies which consider their relationship with their key account manager to be more crucial to business success than general marketing activity.

Sometimes the status of key account managers within their own company is derived from the relative size and power of their key account. For example, in fast-moving consumer goods suppliers, key account managers for the top few supermarkets have the highest status among their peers.

Status symbols are often used to determine and display relative importance. Key account managers expect to be given powerful company cars, equipped with all the paraphernalia of an executive who spends a lot of time on the road. The quality of their office equipment, at base and for teleworking, demonstrates their status as well as contributing to their productivity. Key account managers also need to be very visible in internal communications, such as the company magazine. Photo opportunities such as the presentation of awards are part of the status mix.

Appraisal and reward

On the subject of rewards for key account managers, many commentators would say that little has changed since the 1950s. Considerable dissatisfaction among account managers and particularly customers stems from the fact that performance rewards are based on current year sales performance rather than longer-term relationship goals.

Most sales professionals with the job title of key account manager are still paid on the simple basis of salary plus commission. At a conference on global account management held at Cranfield in January 1999, 49 per cent of attendees said that key account managers in their companies were assessed primarily on their ability to generate sales volume (see Figure 9.4).

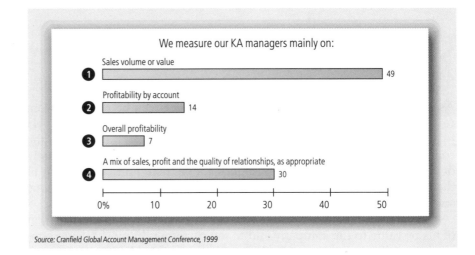

Figure 9.4
Main key account manager performance measures

Source: Cranfield Global Account Management Conference, 1999

Sales managers set sales targets and up to 50 per cent of the key account manager's earnings may depend upon the target being achieved.

Selling companies who practise KAM strategically are more likely to appraise and reward key account managers on a variety of performance criteria such as the following:

- Customer satisfaction ratings.
- Share of spend in the account.
- Account profitability.
- Accuracy of forecasts.
- Resolution of problems.
- Number of new contacts in the account.
- New opportunities identified.

Key account managers whose products are project based may be rewarded on the achievement of milestones and deadlines. In industries marked by cyclical sales, such as capital equipment, key account managers may be remunerated according to the financial value of the key account's portfolio of the selling company's products.

Whatever reward mechanism is used, selling companies with a KAM philosophy want to move key account managers away from counting their commission towards concentrating on mutual long-term interests. In addition, some sales managers believe that it is unfair to judge key account managers' performance on the basis of revenue if they are looking after only one or two key accounts. The customer's market position may slip or the main contact's budget may be cut for reasons beyond the key account manager's control. However, no performance measurement system can make allowances for external impacts. For this reason, a significant minority of key account managers are rewarded with 100 per cent salary, although performance measures are still employed and considered important. High achievement is seen to accelerate promotion.

Table 9.5 Reward mechanisms for key account managers

Reward mechanism	Pros	Cons
100% salary	No constraints to long-term, strategic view No penalties for single account key account managers	Has to be set at a very high threshold in order to be competitive May be demotivating to entrepreneurial personalities
51–80% salary, small percentage bonuses (increasingly believed to be the most suitable and effective)	Key account manager receives some reward associated with particular performance criteria, but can also take a long-term view	A plethora of small bonuses may be complicated to calculate and introduce a hassle factor They may not be sufficient to drive particular activities
30–50% salary, majority PRP (performance-related pay)	Key account manager receives high rewards associated with particular performance criteria which can drive the business	Selection of the appropriate PRP criteria may not be apparent in advance The PRPs may not have a long enough term perspective
Mix of salary and company performance based bonuses	Promotes interest in teamwork Promotes interest in overall company performance	The company bonus may be too remote from day to day activity to be motivating A good performer may be poorly paid when the company overall has a bad patch
50% salary 50% commission on transactions	Direct relationship between sales achievement and reward Drives activity	May not be in customers' best interests The customer may try to exploit this arrangement in sales negotiations

A substantial salary containing a minority proportion of performance-related pay is emerging as the preferred formula in many companies with partnership relationships. Mounting evidence suggests that it is the most effective reward mechanism for key account managers, as it provides incentive to succeed with customers in both the short and long term.

So what sort of earnings might a key account manager expect overall? According to 27 per cent of Cranfield conference attendees, key account managers should be paid more than £80 000, though £30 000–£60 000 was understood to be the norm!

The Strategic Account Management Association in the USA conducts regular surveys on account management compensation. In 1997, the association sampled 248 US companies in 37 industries. Salaries for national account managers were seen to have risen by 4.1 per cent and total reward by 5.7 per cent compared to salary levels in 1996. The median salary recorded was $78 000 and the median total reward was $100 000. One-third of US national account managers are eligible for stock options which boost the value of their remuneration even more. The relative value of key account managers' salary levels is also rising. In the USA national account managers earn more than field sales managers do.

Table 9.5 summarizes Cranfield's findings on the issue of rewards for key account managers.

Summary

The 1990s have seen a marked increase in the knowledge and sophistication of buying decision makers. At the same time relationships between suppliers and customers have become highly collaborative and complex. These changes have served to elevate and expand the role of the key account manager, shifting the job emphasis from mutual value creation to managing and leading relationship development. Consequently, the list of skills and attributes required of key account managers has broadened and this has had implications for the way in which the company is organized. To be effective, today's key account manager needs a range of competencies and unprecedented support and backing from the company.

References

Blake, R. R. and Mouton, J. S. (1964) *The Managerial Grid*. Gulf Publishing.

Fiedler, F. E. (1967). *A Theory of Leadership Effectiveness*. McGraw-Hill.

Hersey, P. and Blanchard, K. H. (1982). *Management of Organizational Behavior*. Prentice-Hall.

McDonald, M., Millman, A. and Rogers, B. (1996). *Key Account Management – Learning from Supplier and Customer Perspectives*. Cranfield School of Management.

Shaw, R. (1998). *Improving Marketing Effectiveness*. The Economist Books.

Wotruba, T. R. and Castleberry, S. B. (1993). Job analysis and hiring practices for national account management positions. *J. Personal Selling Sales Manage.*, 13(3), 49–65.

Further reading

House, R. J. (1971). A path-goal theory of leadership effectiveness. *Admin. Sci. Quart.*, September.

Kennedy, G. and Webb, R. (1996). N is for negotiation. *Supply Manage.*, 19 September.

McDonald, M. and Rogers, B. (1998). *Key Account Management – Learning from Supplier and Customer Perspectives*. Butterworth-Heinemann.

Mailplan (1999). Working as one. *Mailplan*, Autumn.

Millman, A. F. and Wilson, K. J. (1994). From key account selling to key account management. In *Tenth Annual Conference on Industrial Marketing and Purchasing*.

Millman, A. F. and Wilson, K. J. (1995). Developing key account managers. In *Eleventh Annual Conference on Industrial Marketing and Purchasing*.

Millman, A. F. and Wilson, K. J. (1996). Developing key account competencies. *J. Marketing Pract. Appl. Marketing Sci.*, 2(2), 7–22.

National Account Management Association (1998). *1997 Survey of National Account Management Compensation Practices*. National Account Management Association.

Robbins, S. P. (1991). *Organizational Behavior*. Prentice-Hall.

Rogers, B. (1999). The key account manager as leader. *J. Selling Major Account Manage.*, 1(3), 60–66.

Trompenaars, F. and Woolliams, P. (1999). Trans-cultural competence. *People Manage.*, 22 April.

Chapter 10

Processes for implementing key account management

Introduction

Key account management (KAM) processes naturally divide themselves into two types: the processes involved in reaching decisions about which strategies to use for key accounts (what to do and why) as discussed in Chapters 5–7, and the processes required to deliver the strategies (how to make it all happen), which form the subject of this chapter.

Disturbingly, the critical task of putting strategy into practice is often overlooked. This may be because implementing strategy is far more difficult than defining strategy: it requires endless tact, focus, persistence and patience. The implementation of a KAM strategy may involve working with an account team which is dispersed across the globe and with people in other parts of the company who have different agendas and ideas. Alternatively, it may be left to a key account manager working alone without the support of a team or even concerted company backing.

This chapter expands on the considerable range of processes which actually deliver the promises to customers which sales and marketing make. Most of these implementation processes already occur in some way, but their application to key accounts needs to be brought to a higher level of consciousness and dedication in order to be fully beneficial. The chapter also provides some examples of useful tools which KAM practitioners may use and adapt to meet the demands of their particular situation.

Implementation: the graveyard of strategy

'Implementation, rather than structure and strategy, is most often at the root of organizations' problems' (Bonoma, 1985).

Today, the delivery of superior customer value is as much about a company's business processes as it is about the core product or service. Because many markets and products are mature and opportunities for differentiation are few, suppliers have to look further for means of differentiating themselves. Good implementation is a minimum requirement at the key account level: great implementation offers real competitive advantage. Research has shown that key customers overwhelmingly prefer suppliers which are 'easy to do business with' (McDonald, Millman and Rogers, 1996).

Some of the processes involved in the management of implementation for key accounts are fairly generic and they might be used by a number of different functions. Such processes include the following:

- Development of tactical action plans.
- Management of resources.
- Management of information.

Development of tactical action plans

Once a strategic plan for the key account has been prepared and agreed, as outlined in Chapter 7, tactical action plans need to be developed ready for implementation. The extension of strategic planning into action planning should be a familiar process for any company. Standard questions of what, how, who, when, where and how much will all need to be answered. Figure 10.1 is a simple format for the development of a strategy into tactical programmes.

Objective							
Strategy							
Programmes	Action	Principal owner	Resources	Measure of success	Achieved by date	Cost	Review date

Figure 10.1
Tactical planning
for key accounts

Traditionally, salespeople have backed away from planning for individual customers, often using the excuse that customer unpredictability renders the exercise pointless. However, in a high-involvement relationship this fig leaf disappears. Here the customer should be actively involved in the formulation of tactical plans and the action required to fulfil them, thus removing those elements of apparent unpredictability which often stem from the supplier's ignorance of the customer.

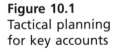

Elements of apparent unpredictability often stem from the supplier's ignorance of the customer.

Management of resources

Finding and managing the human resources necessary to carry out tactical plans is an important part of the key account manager's role. For an ordinary customer, identifying which of the supplier's staff are concerned with the account and how they relate to each other is relatively simple. In fact, the salesperson and functional departments would undertake most of the action. However, in a KAM relationship determining who is involved at any given time is more complicated. The key account manager will be expecting action from an account team whose members may have other responsibilities as well, for example from field sales forces which report on a geographical rather than an account basis. Resource management can be very complex in global accounts as the number of people involved escalates and cross-boundary and cross-cultural issues are added to the cauldron.

Resource management can be very complex in global accounts as the number of people involved escalates and cross-boundary and cross-cultural issues are added to the cauldron.

In order to optimize the use of expertise, the key account manager needs visibility of which people are available, where they are located and what they cost. A systematic record such as that shown in Figure 10.2 is helpful in identifying the people allocated to the account and how much of their time can be dedicated to each customer.

Key account managers need to know how much resource is being applied to which account to avoid the emphasis shifting to the most demanding customer, who may not necessarily be the most rewarding. The framework defined in Figure 10.2 provides a valuable map of who is involved with the account and in what way, as well as what information they should have and what decisions they are authorized to make. In

Title/ position	Role in account/ other responsibility	Authority	Location	Share of time available	Total cost of time	Share of time by customer		
						A	B	C
Key Account Manager	Overall strategy & co-ordination	All decisions relating to Account with implications <£100k	Munich	100%	£200k pa	50	30	20
Sales								
Salesperson 1								
Salesperson 2								
Product specialists								
Product manager 1								
Product manager 2								
Function specialists								
Logistics manager								
Operations manager								

Figure 10.2
Identification of resource available to key accounts

addition, it is a useful management tool for identifying some of those customer costs, rarely attributed to accounts, which may explain the poor levels of real profitability commonly yielded by key accounts (see Chapter 7). The same kind of framework can be used to identify resources of capacity or funds, which are also applied to specific key accounts.

Management of information

As well as managing people and other resources, the key account manager must also manage a wealth of information. If we think about it, we realize that companies probably experience a greater flow of information to and from a single key account than they do about the market in general. Data about markets is often collected at a cost and, therefore, intermittently, while data about key accounts accumulates naturally through daily interactions with the customer. With new technology and low costs, it is now possible to offer Internet access to a whole library of documents about the account via a dedicated website, making information much easier to find and much easier to share.

> Companies probably experience a greater flow of information to and from a single key account than they do about the market in general.

Insight

Hewlett Packard introduced a World Wide Web-based electronic sales partner (see Figure 10.3) which was designed mainly for use by its 5000-strong sales force. Access to some areas in the site is restricted, depending on the individual's role in the account. The account plan is attached and the arrival of new documents is flagged automatically. Everyone is much better informed and productivity savings/increases were estimated to be worth $125 million in the first year alone.

Figure 10.3
Hewlett Packard's website for key customers

Source: Reproduced by kind permission of Mike Cohn, Hewlett Packard

The flexible and accessible nature of electronic formats makes them well suited to management systems for key accounts, particularly for global accounts, making the key account manager's job much easier. Electronic media also excel in accommodating change: alterations are easily made and readily broadcast to everyone who needs to know. All tactical plans should be living documents, of course none more so than those for key accounts. Holding tactical plans in electronic format means that they are more likely to be adapted and used than shelved and ignored.

In addition to these general processes (development of tactical plans, management of resources and management of information), there are other processes which are more specific to KAM or which are implemented in different ways from the norm.

Key account management implementation processes

The processes which underpin KAM implementation can be grouped in various ways. Categorizing them according to the special requirements of KAM helps to highlight the different ways in which they need to be executed to meet the expectations of key accounts. Using this approach, we have identified five groups of implementation processes which are crucial to KAM. These five processes, shown in the flow chart in Figure 10.4,

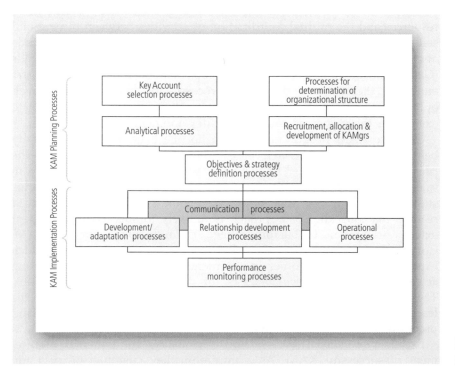

Figure 10.4
KAM processes

together with the analysis and planning processes discussed earlier, consist of the following:

- Communication processes.
- Relationship development processes.
- Development/adaptation processes.
- Operational processes.
- Performance monitoring processes.

Communication is a separate and significant process, one which underpins and supports all other KAM processes.

KAM depends on extended or virtual teams inside both buying and selling companies for its implementation, so *communication processes* are vital. Communication could be regarded as an intrinsic part of each KAM process which should happen automatically. In contrast, Figure 10.4 depicts communication as a separate and significant process, one which underpins and supports all other KAM processes.

Research and observation have shown that, unless specific processes have been developed and used, communication is likely to fall short of requirements. Indeed, satisfactory communication may represent the biggest challenge of the future in any aspect of business. While the quantity of communication has grown to excessive levels, the clarity and quality of communication has often suffered. Messages are sent, but unless they are assimilated by the recipient, and many are not, the communication fails. A long-standing maxim of the army is 'communication is the responsibility of the communicator': it applies equally well to the business world.

Key account relationships are less about attitude and more about material, activity-based, business-developing bonds.

Central to KAM implementation processes are *relationship development processes*. Key account relationships do not evolve independently: they develop through the interactions which implement the dedication of resources and the mutual coordination of activities between buying and selling organizations. Key account relationships are less about attitude and more about material, activity-based, business-developing bonds (Gadde and Snehota, 1999). Relationships with so much substance are entities in themselves and warrant processes for managing and developing them as relationships. Chapter 11 is therefore devoted to examining these specific relationship development processes.

Of those KAM programmes which no one ever hears about, many belong to companies which based their business approach on the premise that being 'nicer' to customers would secure huge increases in sales of the same, standardized products delivered in the same, standardized way. By this stage, this book should have convinced readers that this kind of approach is unlikely to succeed to any great extent. Adaptation to customer need is an intrinsic part of KAM. Companies renowned for their KAM programmes are those which expect to adapt to customer requirements and set up smooth-running *development and adaptation processes* for delivering such modifications.

The most successful companies use their key account programme as the leading edge in the execution of their strategy.

The most successful companies use their key account programme as the leading edge in the execution of their strategy, innovating products and processes through working with customers.

Excellent *operational processes* are obviously a fundamental requirement of successful KAM. As a minimum, key customers expect top quality in all aspects of their transactions with suppliers, even in a *basic* relationship. The hierarchy of relationships shown in Figure 3.2 suggests that collaborative relationships have the supplier's ability to satisfy or even exceed this expectation as their foundation. Indeed, the implication is that a relationship is unlikely to develop beyond the *basic* level if this expectation is not fulfilled (McDonald and Woodburn, 1999). Where a supplier's past performance has proved to be excellent, a strong customer relationship may compensate for poor performance by the supplier in the short term, though not indefinitely. Key account managers who overlook the importance of excellence in everyday operations for their key accounts do so at their peril.

Lastly, there must be efficient and effective *performance monitoring processes* in order to ensure that the whole plan is kept on track. In reality, most companies struggle to collect the data they need, particularly global suppliers. Data from different countries is rarely compatible, nor are the formats in which it is held. Most companies have to resort to frustratingly slow, manual methods of compilation. Many companies cannot even answer the question 'Worldwide, who is your biggest customer?'. In all probability, companies will have to compromise on their requirements for monitoring data in the short term. However, for the longer term, any company with global customers should decide, as a matter of urgency, what it really needs to know and how that information can be captured.

> Many companies cannot even answer the question 'Worldwide, who is your biggest customer?'.

To appreciate better how these KAM implementation processes work, each of the processes in Figure 10.4 is discussed in turn (with the exception of relationship development processes which are covered in the next chapter).

Communication processes

Communication processes with key customers

When the pivotal nature of communication is recognized, it becomes a process in its own right rather than a reactive, belated, rushed and reluctant add-on to another process. Undoubtedly, communication takes time. Equally, good communication prevents the wastage of time and other resources more than any other management process.

> Communication with key customers needs to be treated as a conscious process as much as it is in consumer campaigns. The fact that the target audience is a small group of companies or even just one does not diminish its importance. In fact, each company may contain large numbers of people with whom a supplier wants to communicate and they are just as likely to require different messages conveyed in different ways and in different styles as any consumer programme. Indeed, the task can be a good deal more complicated than in the average consumer campaign, particularly if the relationship does not allow free, direct access to the customer's internal media and staff.

Chapter 3 showed that communication with the customer is a critical determinant of relationships (Krapfel, Salmond and Spekman, 1991; McDonald and Woodburn, 1999) and as such it can be used proactively as a strategy in developing relationships. The first step is the identification of the key people to whom communication should be directed. These primary targets should be the decision makers and/or people who have a major influence on decisions. The section on contacts in Chapter 11 shows a way of mapping contacts within the customer organization, which can be used as a framework for determining where communications should be directed. A similar approach can be taken in identifying customer employees who are likely to have information of interest to the supplier and targeting them as sources. Real communication is a two-way process and suppliers should remember the value of listening as well as transmitting.

Excellent face-to-face communication with buyers is one of the traditional skills of salespeople and it is needed just as much by key account managers. In addition, key account managers must be able to communicate with people in a far wider range of functions than just purchasing and for purposes other than persuading a buyer to place an order. For example:

- The customer's research and development (R&D) staff will need to understand the product's attributes well enough to make the best use of them in designing their own product.
- The customer's sales force will need to appreciate fully the selling points of the product where it forms part of their offer to the next buyer in the supply chain.
- Repair and maintenance people, help-line operators and customer service representatives will all need to be properly trained and kept up to date with developments. With integrated supply chain management the key account manager will direct communication links at every point in the supply chain. Whether the key account manager is communicating directly or managing the communication process, he or she must conduct the symphony of communications from the boardroom to the shop floor (McDonald, Millman and Rogers, 1996).

Many selling companies are still grappling with the problem of addressing all the members of the buying company's decision-making unit.

Many selling companies are still grappling with the problem of addressing all the members of the buying company's decision-making unit. Meanwhile, the really good ones have solved that problem and have moved on to influencing the business downstream, directing positive communications through to a wider audience such as internal users and others handling or administering the product.

Figure 10.5 portrays the essential elements to be considered in the design of smooth-running and cost-effective communications. The development of an explicit communication programme works to address these elements, ensuring that the selection of message, medium, weight and timing is appropriate to the audience and the purpose of the communication. To illustrate how these elements work, Figure 10.6 gives an example of how a new desktop telecommunications service is introduced, post-decision to purchase.

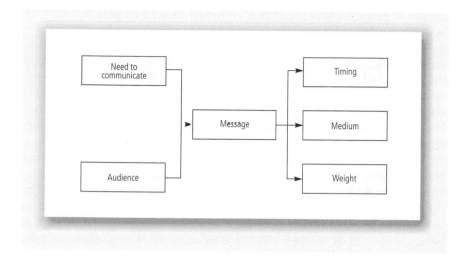

Figure 10.5
Decisions in key customer communications

The role of new electronic media should receive special attention from key account managers. Electronic media will not completely replace person-to-person dialogue and proactive approaches by any means, but they can handle a wide range and large volume of communication, and are fast becoming indispensable to KAM. The profile of attributes of these media can be compared with the elements identified in Figure 10.5 in order to see what they can deliver to the audience defined, which may

Audience	Purchasing	Users: office workers	Trainers	On-site maintenance engineers	IT department	Accounts
Commun-ication need	Keep Purchasing focused on benefits during install hassle	Win over users	Give users support to ensure comfort level reached quickly	Minimize downtime to keep users happy	Drive up new uses for lock-in and extra sales	Pre-empt negative messages to Purchasing
Message	Better connected, fewer calls, save money	Makes your life easier	Initial user training needs follow-up	We will support you: help-line available	New utility: link desk-top computers to phones	Invoices to match your management information needs
Medium	Face-to-face	Buying co trainers Desk-top leaflets Company magazine	Selling co trainer Mail-shot after first training	Binder: everything within Face-to-face with supplier engineers Coffee room noticeboard	Technical seminar Manual Case studies	Face-to-face
Timing	Before, during and after installation	Installation After 3 wks After 6 wks	Pre-installation Immediately post-installation		Asap after purchase decision, pre-installation, on-going	Before first payment due
Weight	Heavy	Heavy	Medium	Medium	Heavy	Light
Budget	-	£5,000	£1,000	£2,500	£5,000	-
Respons-ibility	KAMgr	Jill Baker	Mary Webster	John Smith	Mike Mills	KAMgr

Figure 10.6
Key customer communication programme definition (new desktop telecommunications service)

Electronic media are fast becoming indispensable to KAM.

consist of people inside the selling company as well as people inside the buying company.

For example, electronic media offer interaction to a greater extent than printed material, but to a lesser extent than person-to-person dialogue. On the other hand, a telephone conversation does not currently convey visual material and while printed material can provide very high-quality visuals, they cannot be animated and manipulated as in electronic media. The ease of updating of material held electronically is also a very attractive attribute for account teams who cannot meet very often. So is the fact that electronic media are 'open' at any time regardless of office hours, particularly important for global companies communicating across different time zones.

Figure 10.7 shows Hewlett Packard's website for key customers. It offers them access to more individually relevant information as well as general product developments and specifications. Key customers have secure and exclusive access to the status of their orders, accounts and any special services they receive. This kind of on-line customer support is not a poor substitute for personal service: it offers extra utility for customers who can find the information they want quickly and easily on demand, regardless of office hours or time zones. Obviously, the website must be managed with rigorous discipline in order to ensure that it is consistently kept up to date and complete.

When communication with key customers is highlighted as a process itself, it demands proper planning and coordination as well. Spasmodic, ad hoc activity is unlikely to be efficient or to achieve much retention of

On-line customer support is not a poor substitute for personal service: it offers extra utility for customers.

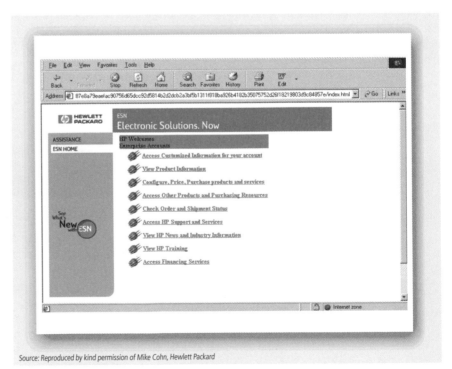

Figure 10.7
Hewlett Packard's electronic sales partner

Source: Reproduced by kind permission of Mike Cohn, Hewlett Packard

messages, whereas the development of an explicit programme will draw out important issues and ultimately build up a far more effective approach. Good planning ensures that all the elements shown in Figure 10.6 are addressed and it also allows the balance across all programmes to be managed. Coordination of the timing and total weight of communication delivered to each audience is important: too much communication received in too short a period or at the wrong time will simply reduce retention and breed confusion.

'Our customer publishes two main catalogues per year, spring and autumn, so all our planning, design and production is based on this six-monthly cycle. They are understandably quite ruthless about deadlines for design samples and delivered product. Approaching these deadlines, it is difficult for either side to talk about longer-term issues' (fashion supplier).

Insight

Through adopting a specific focus on communication to key customers, companies achieve clearer messages, better balance and coordination from the receiver's point of view and usage of a wider range of delivery media, all leading to a far more effective transmission of information.

Internal communication processes

Key account managers need highly developed communication skills in order to work effectively with a huge range and number of people inside their own organization in the fulfilment of their account objectives. Some have dedicated teams, but many act without any direct line authority or share team members who have other demands on their time, so they need substantial powers of persuasion and influence. Timeliness is essential, though often lacking.

At one end of the scale are communications with smaller numbers of senior internal people. The basic principles of communication apply:

- Clarify what you want to convey.
- Gain the attention of your audience.
- Express your message in terms which match the style, language and interests of the recipient.
- Identify what action you require of them.

Communication tends to be unsuccessful when it is based more on what the transmitter wants to say than what the receiver wants to hear. A good deal of wasted time and effort can be saved by employing a very simple device: imagine you are the audience, with all their known pressures and prejudices, and ask what you would want to see and hear before you would commit yourself to the response requested. Focusing on those elements will make communications far easier to produce, more concise and considerably more effective.

Key account managers need to be multilingual in the sense that they are able to speak in the different 'languages' of all these (internal) functions.

As discussed in Chapter 9, key account managers need a broad range of skills for managing all the aspects of their complex role. Of paramount importance is their ability to communicate appropriately with colleagues from various departments: sales, marketing, finance, technical, information technology, logistics, customer service and so on. In effect, key account managers need to be multilingual in the sense that they are able to speak in the different 'languages' of all these functions. Regional and global account managers will need to be multilingual in the literal sense as well.

Timing is likewise a crucial issue in internal communications. The commercial year has a seasonality which is imposed partly by social influences (Christmas, Chinese New Year, Ramadan and summer holidays), partly by the industry sector (agriculture, fashion and pharmaceuticals) and partly by the selling company itself (financial year, sales conference and factory shut down). In addition to pre-set calendars of activity, issues of timing can be subject to irregular and often unexpected internal events, such as product launches, reorganizations and staff reductions. Personal and attitudinal factors can also influence the timing of communications and the key account manager must exercise sensitivity and judgement in choosing 'the right moment'. While business disruptions and attention-occupying events create problems for all key account managers, they exacerbate the already momentous tasks of global account managers who must manage team members in different locations working on different time cycles.

At the other end of the scale are communications with large numbers of people who interface directly with the customer or who take implementation-level decisions and actions which affect the customer. Excellent operating instructions are not enough on their own. An action can be correctly specified and carried out to the letter and yet leave a poor impression on the customer, while, if carried out in the right spirit as well, that same action can really add value for the customer. To make sure that key customers receive the right type of response from anyone, anywhere, in the selling organization, key account managers need to ensure that all relevant staff are well-informed and, more importantly, they need to win their hearts and minds as well.

Insight

'It does not matter any more whether there is solid line, dotted line or no line responsibility at all. You cannot *make* people do anything: those days are gone. You have to get them to *want* to do it' (key account director).

Communications need to reach the furthest outposts of the customer interface in order to deliver the expectations that the key account manager has established with the customer.

Key customers are often piqued to discover that very few staff within their supplier's organization even know that they represent an important account. They are more than irritated when they then receive standard treatment and inappropriate action. Communications need to reach the furthest outposts of the customer interface in order to deliver the expectations that the key account manager has established with the customer.

Successful internal communication requires carefully planned, properly executed processes and programmes whose effectiveness is actually monitored. The same degree of focus and formality that is applied to customer communications should be applied to internal communications (see Figures 10.5 and 10.6). Reliance on the unsupported 'cascade effect' is usually an opt-out. This approach is often ineffective and can even be dangerously misleading.

There is an inclination to think that the job is done when all the decisions have been made and action has been agreed. Internal communication often seems like a burden of questionable value compared with the time it takes to achieve, but it is probably the single most important element of implementation. Not only does the task of communicating need to be done, it needs to be done well, with clarity, repetition and persistence.

KAM employs communication processes specifically for managing the customer's expectations and perceptions. There are no absolutes in performance: delivering to or above expectation is the only way customers can evaluate performance. Selling companies may do an excellent job and yet discover that some misconception has had an adverse effect on the customer's perception of it and, hence, of the relationship. Managing expectations is important internally as well, and it therefore demands a careful and systematic approach.

Where there is a large number of people involved, management of perceptions should be particularly elevated to a conscious process, involving the following:

> Management of customer perceptions should be elevated to a conscious process.

- Intelligence gathering from customer and internal sources to discover what the customer needs, wants and expects.
- Matching this picture as far as possible and adjusting expectations if gaps occur.
- Communicating successful fulfilment or failure.
- Checking customer satisfaction.

Research has shown that information exchange/intelligence gathering with key customers is very important in the development of tactical plans and overall account management. The key account manager therefore needs to consider from whom, internally, the information can be gathered and how it can be disseminated, analysed and applied in order to deliver greatest mutual benefit.

Development/adaptation processes
Analysis, approval and project management of requests for customization

This book has stressed that adaptation to customer need is an intrinsic part of KAM. In many companies there is a considerable degree of reluctance in making changes for individual customers, however important they may be. Common underlying causes include the following:

- The processes required to gain approval are ponderous and time-consuming.
- Barriers are erected by those who perceive tailoring as extra, unnecessary work and inconvenience.
- Fear that overall performance efficiency will be jeopardized.
- Capacity limitations: demand for customization can only be accommodated at the expense of projects for the rest of the company's business.

Often, rather than streamlining the evaluation of customization proposals, suppliers deliberately introduce stumbling blocks in order to discourage and cut down the number of special requests. While some of these obstacles reflect reasonable concerns, companies genuinely committed to KAM must be prepared to adapt to individual customer requirements: indeed, some of these adaptations should be regarded as valuable opportunities for researching new ideas and learning with the cooperation and, possibly, funding of the customer.

> Adaptations should be regarded as valuable opportunities for researching new ideas.

Once customization is accepted as a normal process, smooth and effective procedures can be established for evaluating non-standard customer proposals. The selection of approval criteria is a good way of defining the direction for customization projects and identifying inherent issues. The list of criteria should include strategic relevance as well as financial justification. The evaluation form shown in Figure 10.8 offers a simple approach to specifying and assessing a customization request.

To help in the evaluation of a customization proposal, management information systems should be set up in order to provide the

Cost source	Std offer accept-able	Requirement	Volume demand	Timing	Cost to change	Est unit cost change	Seen by Date
Products/services	No	High gloss metal surface finish on bearings	7m units pa	March 2001	R&D est. £130k	+1.8p per 100	
Packaging/ presentation	No	Bags in boxes labelled to customer spec	700,000 poly bags, 70,000 boxes	March 2001	Neg	+ 2.7p per 100	
Stock keeping	Yes		Ave. 5000 boxes	March 2001		Std	
Logistics	Yes		Est 250 pa deliveries to site	N/a		Std	
Financial	No	90 days	£250000 credit limit	From May 2001		Check finance	
Information	No	EDI, stock visibility.	Daily report	From March 2001	£12000 set up		
Technical support	Yes					Std	
Selling and customer service infrastructure	No	Customer site stock checks by our staff	Weekly, 4 sites: est 625 hrs pa	From March 2001	£2000	Est. £12500 pa	
Fit with criteria	Overall score		6				
	Size		7				
	Margin		5				
	Growth rate		3				
	Strategic direction		6			Priority	Medium / high
	Key customer		8				

Figure 10.8
An example of a customization request

information required in the form in which it is needed. Key account managers often find it difficult to wrest a few simple but vital statistics from reporting systems which are designed primarily for accounting and logistics purposes rather than for sales and marketing use. Decision makers quite reasonably demand fact-based proposals before giving their agreement and information systems need to respond with the right kind of facts.

Information systems need to respond with the right kind of facts.

At the outset, if possible, a proposal for customization should be sent to all relevant departments simultaneously, so that comments can be collected concurrently. Traditional methods involving fixed monthly meetings are too slow for business today and they are being replaced by electronic media which can help to expedite the process. The proportion of the authorization process which requires sequential examination and approval should be minimized. However it is configured, the process of obtaining inputs, iterations and approvals should be standardized and made clear to all participants.

'Tooling up is very costly in this industry. Now we have very clear criteria and an effective, well-defined procedure for requests for customization. Before we had a proper process, we could find ourselves committed to appallingly short runs of odd products. It cost us a fortune in some cases. Now, we do not buck the system, because it works and if the business case is not there, the strategic justification had better be brilliant or we do not do it' (automotive company).

Insight

Suppliers can lower the barriers to customization by making whatever they do easier to change. They should review their all their production, operational, logistics and transaction handling processes. Are core processes specified for flexibility as well as efficiency? Can the product/service be designed on a modular basis? Or would a common platform with variation built onto it answer the need? Modification post-design can add a great deal of cost if it has not been anticipated and provision for changes made.

Flexible and modular production and operations will become a critical determinant of KAM competence (unless the company has successfully opted for Porter's (1985) lowest-cost producer strategy, and such companies are few). Customers for Renault trucks or Dell computers can now design the exact specification they want through the company's website. If these companies can achieve this level and scale of customization, it should be possible for more companies to adapt to the needs of their customers, at least the most important ones. So what prevents them?

In fact, huge costs can be associated with customization, whether of products or processes, including management time implications. Customization is often one of the major culprits when large accounts become unprofitable, but erecting barriers against the call for customization is not the solution. Employing vigilance, creativity, transparency and a long-term outlook is.

Customization is often one of the major culprits when large accounts become unprofitable, but erecting barriers against the call for customization is not the solution.

Strategic adaptation through customization

Whereas some of a key account's requests for customization arise from nothing more than a desire for cosmetic differentiation from its competitors or a need for suppliers to fit in with its idiosyncratic way of doing business, others are driven by the fulfilment of its strategy and vision of the future. A supplier should be able to distinguish between these in order to give special attention to the latter. What a leading-edge key account wants in order to fulfil its strategy today, the rest of the market will want tomorrow, so its requirements of suppliers throw down useful indicators of future market developments.

While the supplier is working out how to respond to a strategic customization request, it is gaining valuable skills and experience, which it can later generalize. In fact, customization is a wonderful opportunity for reducing the risks and costs of innovating through learning from and with the customer.

Insight	'We have a menu of special services which only our key customers can have tailored to their needs. These accounts have been selected, not for size, but for their demand for value-added services, which we see as the future of the company. When we have tested these services and smoothed out the operational aspects, we will offer them to the rest of our customers. By then, we expect to have moved on to develop something else with our key accounts' (global services company).

An intelligent supplier should single out those customizations which fall in with its own strategic direction in order to give them special priority. Too often, the strategic opportunity triggered by the customer's request is overlooked and seen as separate from the selling company's own strategy. Even worse, it may be seen as an irritating diversion and cause of inefficiency in current, standardized processes and then be approached in a negative manner.

In an ideal world, the supplier will identify strategically important customizations at an early stage, so that it can consider from the outset how the customization might be further adapted for its own use and eventually adopted as standard practice. Alongside the normal approval process for considering a customization project in its own right, suppliers should operate a process to examine the value of adaptations for themselves, as shown in Figure 10.9.

Suppliers should operate a process for examining the value of adaptations for themselves.

To determine whether a requested customization should be adopted as standard practice it is necessary to decide whether the customization also has a value of significance to the supplier. This is accomplished by using a set of filters. The first filter eliminates customizations which serve only the customer's interests by identifying which of the possible drivers behind the request are specific to the customer and do not have wider implications for the rest of the market. If the customer's request is driven by a strategy which is only relevant to its own business, then the request should be treated on its own merits in the context of the relationship. If

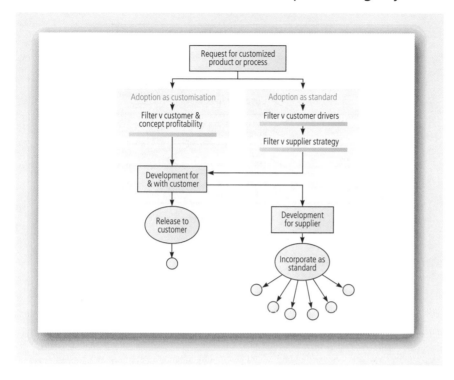

Figure 10.9
Process for selecting
and standardizing
strategic
customizations

instead it appears that the key account has found the optimum response
to market drivers, then the supplier should set a high priority on
developing the concept and eventually installing it as standard. Figure
10.10 shows some common customer drivers.

For example, a customer with a cash problem may want a different
payment plan from normal. The supplier may think it appropriate to offer
non-standard terms for them, but not want or need to change them for
everyone. If, on the other hand, all the customers in this sector are short
of budgets for capital expenditure, but have funds available for
operational expenses, then the need moves into the domain of the market
as a whole. In that case, it may well be worthwhile offering a creative
financial approach which, for example, allows equipment acquisition to
be bundled in with running costs.

To take another example, the arrival of global competition will affect all
participants in a market. Serious contenders will be obliged to transform
themselves into global competitors in order to survive and that will
involve expanding their operations geographically. In that case, the
supplier needs to gear up for global support or they will lose not only
the customer who first made the request, but others with similar needs
as well.

The second filter in Figure 10.9 compares the strategic implications of
the customization with the selling company's strategy in order to
eliminate mismatches. However, even if there is no apparent match with
current strategy, the origin of the request for adaptation should be
examined carefully in case it is flagging a shift in the market which
should prompt a change in the supplier's strategy.

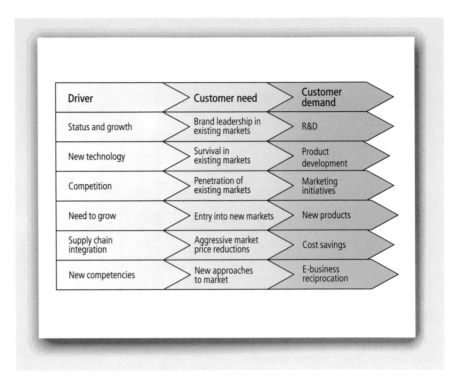

Figure 10.10
Expression of
common customer
driving forces

Subsequent parts of this process should be quite straightforward once the importance of the opportunity for basing development of the company and its products on customization requests has been recognized. There may be concern about how customers will react to this exploitation of their concepts, but usually they will be comfortable with this approach provided there is a sufficient lapse of time before an innovation becomes available to other customers.

Insight

3M's electronics business operates in a fast-moving environment characterized by continuous product development. Recognizing the strategic opportunity of joint R&D, they run a limited number of new product development (NPD) programmes with key customers that are not expected to reach fruition for three to five years. The products developed in this way will later become standard products sold through distributors, by which time their leading-edge customer will have moved on to the next generation of product.

Operational processes
Efficient and reliable delivery to a standard specification

It would be a mistake to suggest that everything a key customer buys is different from the company's standard offering: non-customized products and services often make up a substantial proportion of customer spend. It should therefore be possible for the key account manager to rely on the efficiency of regular, familiar processes delivering standard products and services and to concentrate instead on more strategic issues and business development.

Insight

'This is an immature industry and it has not really got its processes fully worked out yet. In my previous company we concentrated on developing the business and the orders just rolled out the door. Here, I have to get into everything, just to make sure it happens and I just do not have the time for strategy that I know I should' (key account manager).

Suppliers should not engage in KAM unless their basic operations are in good order. An average offer and performance will only achieve average results at best, so it might as well be sold in an ordinary way, because then at least it attracts only average overheads. It is a waste of money employing an expensive key account manager to stitch together cracks in fundamental processes or to win accounts which will be lost again through poor operational performance. Key customers are the kind of companies which expect sustained high levels of performance from suppliers. Furthermore, good key account managers will not stay with companies which cannot successfully deliver the standard offer, as a minimum, because neither the quality of the job nor the level of earnings will live up to their expectations.

> It is a waste of money employing an expensive key account manager to stitch together cracks in fundamental processes.

Insight

'We realize now that the previous key account manager must have done a lot of fixing for us. The new one does not see that as his role, so now we are seeing all the warts. We have said we are not happy, but he just does not seem to take it in. He wants to talk about new services and we want to know when they are going to sort out what they have already got' (global research company).

Many buying companies build relationships with selling companies in order to gain value through cutting cost out of the supply chain. Some supply chain costs are derived from protective mechanisms such as buffer stockholding and dual sourcing and, if the buying company believes it can trust the supplier's intentions and its performance, these costs can be removed. However, if safeguards are removed, the customer's ability to tolerate supplier failure is drastically diminished. Standard (as well as customized) operational processes must work at the highest levels of efficiency and reliability.

> If safeguards are removed, the customer's ability to tolerate supplier failure is drastically diminished.

According to a major retailer, sales and marketing set up the promise to the customer and operations and logistics fulfil that promise. If sales and marketing are excellent while operational delivery is poor, customers will 'visit' but will be disappointed and unlikely to repeat the experience. On the other hand, if quality and delivery are excellent while demand creation is poor, customer response will be poor anyway.

This visualization of the delivery of the customer promise is expressed in Figure 10.11, which demonstrates the relationship between the two functions and the importance of keeping them in balance. KAM and operations must work together side by side, but they should not get over-involved in each other's job or become so divorced from each other that they imagine that the two functions are independent. Customers want to deal with the supplier as a single entity, not as a collection of different departments.

> Customers want to deal with the supplier as a single entity, not as a collection of different departments.

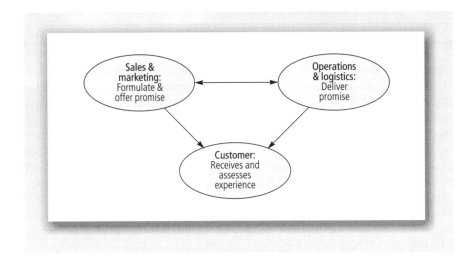

Figure 10.11
Delivery of the
customer promise

Even with standard processes, suppliers proactively manage and prioritize workflow. Requests will normally be handled according to the date of receipt, the size of the order or the level of pressure exerted by customers. Within this type of system, key account orders may not necessarily reach top priority, as they may be placed just in time rather than in advance, be frequent rather than individually large, and have an expectation of performance which does not include the need for progress chasing.

Key accounts expect to receive preferential treatment if and when they want it. That may not be all the time, but if they are in a hurry or if there is any rationing of supplies they do not expect to be treated in a 'fair' or 'first-come, first-served' basis. Most people have a basic sense of fairness and giving preferential treatment is not their normal *modus operandi*. For example, staff often talk about working to 'a level playing field', particularly in public sector organizations and privatized ex-public or not-for-profit companies. However, this approach is not commercially realistic and, in building close relationships with customers, suppliers have consciously signed up to some kind of preferential treatment for them.

> In building close relationships with customers, suppliers have consciously signed up to some kind of preferential treatment for them.

Key account managers need to secure acceptance of this principle from the people who are instrumental in making decisions about the priorities on the ground. This is not a one-off task either. The retention capacity of corporate memory is limited: reorganizations and staff turnover effectively require regular revisiting of the concept that the supplier company wants to practise positive discrimination in favour of its key customers.

Needless to say, such positive discrimination will not work if staff do not know which accounts are considered 'key'. It is often the key account manager's recurring task to placate key customers who have received offhand or even just standard treatment from a selling company employee who did not know that they should be treated differently. All employees must know who the key accounts are and how they should be treated, including switchboard operators, receptionists, truck drivers, order handlers, warehouse supervisors and everyone else who is in contact with customers or makes any kind of decision affecting them.

Key account managers cannot assume that even standard processes will run smoothly in delivering commitments to key accounts unless the way in which they should be handled has been communicated over and over again. People forget, people leave and new directives come out which are taken to over-ride previous instructions: the job of ensuring that all staff are engaged in delivering the promise never ends. Communication of key account identity, status and treatment is really a process in its own right (see section earlier in this chapter).

Efficient and reliable delivery to a non-standard specification

The key account manager's interest, more than that of almost any other company employee, is focused on the achievement of supportive, effective, dependable processes. As customization is likely to feature heavily in offers to key accounts, processes need to be sufficiently

Education	Ensure Key Account Managers understand their own systems, so they know what hurts and what does not.
Information collection	Develop a system to be used with the customer so the requirement can be properly understood and assessed.
Operations involvement	Involve Operations people early in the customer dialogue.
Regular format	Speed up request handling by chasing out all issues simultaneously: use standard format for requests for tailoring.
Assessment	Analyse and assess requests: identify where and how much core procedure used.
Agreement	Circulate for input, iteration and approval.
Capture	Ensure tailored process is properly specified and recorded.
Triggering	Ensure tailored process surfaces automatically whenever appropriate.
Communication	Brief all involved on tailored process and its significance.

Figure 10.12
Checklist for implementation for non-standard delivery

competent and robust in order to deliver to non-standard as well as standard specifications. Figure 10.12 gives a top-level checklist for non-standard delivery.

Operational people, not unreasonably, accuse key account managers and other salespeople of promising the customer a type of service that sounds simple, but is inappropriate for the supplier's systems and cannot be sustained. While key account managers do not have to become experts, they do need sufficient knowledge of operations to use in discussions with customers and in collecting information from them so that the experts can understand the request.

Insight	'We try to work on a stable, consistent, core delivery procedure allowing only for known differences, because variation equals error. We cater for customer variations through "post-tailoring" with value-added services' (logistics director).

Variation invites error.	Although variation invites error, many of the potential problems can be anticipated. The relevant functional manager should be involved at an early stage of discussions in order to work out how to deliver the customer's special requirements, in advance of commitments rather than afterwards.

The process of variation needs to be normalized as much as possible so that it does not become such an exception that it cannot be accommodated within the supplier's processes. When the supplier has reached agreement with the customer, it is essential that the final specification be recorded in a location accessible to anyone involved and not, as is sometimes the case, locked in the memory of the supervisor. Neither should the triggering of customization procedures rely on human alertness and intervention: it should be safely guaranteed by being made routine. However, if a problem does arise, it is worth noting that companies who avoid blame and use a problem to contribute to the organizational learning curve are more successful than those who feel obliged to cover up, disown and deny it.

Insight	'The good key account managers are the ones who come along and talk to us at an early stage, especially if there is a problem. The bad ones are those who do not talk to us until it's a crisis' (operations director).

Key account managers, on the basis of 'the buck stops here', are often tied down problem solving and fighting to prevent disaster on behalf of their customer. However, those who are constantly threatening, calling in favours and doing other people's jobs themselves in order to obtain the right result for their customer will just wear out quickly.

Performance monitoring of key accounts

One of a company's greatest concerns must be the monitoring of key accounts. Their share of the company's total revenue and profit is usually substantial, often 50–60 per cent and sometimes as high as 75–80 per cent. However, currently even blue-chip companies struggle to operate meaningful monitoring systems.

A stand-alone measurement is meaningless unless it is compared with a 'benchmark', so the first step in monitoring key accounts is the identification of appropriate benchmarks. Previous performance could be used, but this can lead companies to consider that small, incremental improvements constitute success. In fact, if other companies are improving more rapidly, these accounts could actually be falling behind and under-performing. The benchmark is therefore better set in terms of strategic requirement. Success or failure is then determined by performance against explicitly expressed aspiration.

> The key account manager needs to set the expectations of his or her organization in appropriate terms for each account individually. Not only should different levels of performance be anticipated, but different measurement parameters should be selected. For instance, the objectives set for an investment-strategy account, the way in which it is managed and the terms in which progress is reported are different from those for an account with a maintenance strategy. The former could be evaluated on growth, for example, and the latter on net cash provision.

Financial results can only represent outcomes: they do not predict the future. They are measurements of 'history' and, as such, it is too late to take any action to change them. Key account managers need other parameters for measuring if they are to keep track of action taken for their accounts. Indeed, the adage 'what gets measured gets done' is truer in selling environments than almost anywhere else. Therefore, monitoring criteria and procedures should adopt a wide focus and consider other measurements including the following:

- Financial: short-term, annual targets and profitability.
- Operations: key performance indicator achievement.
- Implementation of strategy: project progress and achievement of milestones.
- Relationship: customer perception of relationship value, customer satisfaction and retention.

Even the most common form of monitoring for key accounts, *financial* performance, is challenging. Traditionally, analysis has been based on products, and a comparable level of information on customers has not been available. The basic role of most companies' information systems is the tracking of goods and transactions and, hence, figures are produced at levels which are either too gross or too detailed for analytical purposes. Obtaining historical information beyond the previous year is usually very difficult as well. Key customers cannot be managed adequately without good information and, with the computing power now available, this situation is no longer excusable.

> Key customers cannot be managed adequately without good information.

Currently, few companies can assess the real financial profitability of their customers (see Chapter 7) and identify which areas of business with them are profitable or unprofitable. Standard reports may only cover revenue by customer and possibly gross margin, but not even contribution after attributable costs. In fact, as KAM involves longer term strategies and investments, standard and annual measures of results are inappropriate. Different financial measures, such as economic value added, should be considered as well, though these more sophisticated measures are more difficult to apply.

However, aspirations to be perfect should not be the enemy of doing better and most companies could quite easily improve their current monitoring systems with fairly simple measures. In addition, although many suppliers would be unable to cope with a sophisticated analysis across all key customers, they would gain valuable new insight into their profitability by digging a little deeper into just a few of them. Figure 10.13 shows the layout of a straightforward approach, which is nevertheless an improvement on those used by most companies. In addition to direct

Products/services		Month				Year to date			
		T-1 actual	T objective	T actual	T variance actual v obj	T-1 actual	T objective	T actual	T variance actual v obj
P1	volume								
	value								
	% change in value								
	cost of sales								
	gross margin								
	% change in GM								
P2	volume								
	value								
	% change in value								
	cost of sales								
	gross margin								
	% change in GM								
P3	volume								
	value								
	% change in value								
	cost of sales								
	gross margin								
	% change in GM								
Total sales	volume								
	value								
	% change in value								
	cost of sales								
	gross margin								
	% change in GM								
Less	discounts								
	refunds								
	cash payments/value of free goods								
	total payments								
	cost of internal time								
	- selling								
	- product development								
	- customer services								
	- logistics								
	- accounts								
	- IT								
	- marketing								
	- product customization								
	- other								
	total additional services								
Total contribution from customer	value								
	% change								

Figure 10.13 Monitoring key account financial performance

product costs, it shows attributable costs that should be logged against the bottom line for the account. A typical list of possible attributable costs is included, but each company will have a different list according to the nature of its business.

Second, *operational* performances should be monitored. These will generally be elements relating to quality, delivery, fulfilment and so forth. Suppliers should be aware that the buying company may have different key performance indicators (KPIs) from its own and may give them different priority. The supplier could be performing very well by its own standards, without realizing that it is under-performing on parameters which are important to the customer.

At the same time, progress in *implementing strategy* must be monitored. The simple action-planning tool shown in Figure 10.1 can be adapted in order to suit the individual situation. It contains the information by which progress can be monitored against both the action planned and the completion date. Implementation of key actions or other milestones should be identified as progress targets to help ensure that the programme overall is completed to schedule. As this kind of monitoring is more qualitative than quantitative, it is more easily overlooked than measures of hard data. However, implementation of key actions is extremely important, because if actual actions are delayed or never happen, then the results will undoubtedly be compromised. Of course, the effect is not seen until some time later and possibly too late to effect a rescue.

Lastly, the quality and stage of the *relationship* should be monitored as well, though not as often as the measures outlined previously. Customer retention is an objective measure of performance here, but it belies more complex issues. While customer loss might be considered disastrous, merely seeking to retain the customer will generally be considered a less than adequate goal at key account level. Success might be better set in terms of objectives for retention and growth or retention and improved profitability.

In contrast, the information needed to judge customer satisfaction and relationship value must be actively sought externally from the customer. Ideally, surveys should be conducted by a third party and so there is a cost associated with this type of monitoring. To save costs, many companies conduct their own surveys of customer perception and satisfaction, but many of these are flawed to the point that they do not provide either useful feedback or meaningful data. At the least, a company in need of customer satisfaction research which intends to carry out the survey itself should take advice from a professional market research organization on the questions to be used, their wording, the circumstances in which they are completed and the interpretation of the outputs.

The information needed to judge customer satisfaction and relationship value must be actively sought externally from the customer.

Summary

Some of the main elements of KAM success have been worked out through talking to practising key account managers about their experiences. They include the following:

■ High-profile support from senior management.
■ Appropriate organizational framework and organization-wide buy-in: beware of barons!
■ Well-rounded, highly-focused key account managers.
■ Customers with the right attitude and approach to business.
■ Supportive, effective, dependable processes.

This chapter has discussed some of the issues involved in achieving supportive, effective, dependable processes which can deliver key account strategies, and it has outlined some generic tools which can be adapted and used.

Communication is of great importance in KAM and in ensuring that other implementation processes work effectively. Communication, both within the customer's organization and within the key account manager's own organization, should be treated as a process itself, rather than a subcomponent of other processes. The techniques used in planning and executing consumer campaigns can be usefully applied to bring the whole process to a level of consciousness which gives it greater focus.

Suppliers should expect to customize products and processes for their key customers and they will need cross-functional buy-in and smooth-running processes for efficient customization. Successful selling companies examine the customization requests they receive and learn from them, incorporating beneficial changes into their own standard practice.

As key accounts become more dependent on supply chain partners, they become more vulnerable to any failure and, hence, they need and expect high standards of performance from a supplier's operations. However, the non-standard elements of their portfolio also make consistently excellent operational delivery more difficult, introducing fragility into the situation. While operations are not a key account manager's responsibility, it is very much in their interests to ensure that robust and reliable processes are in place. If they are constantly fire-fighting, the supplier's organization has failed the key account manager and the account.

Performance monitoring is a crucial process and one currently not well-executed in most companies. Monitoring generally needs to be more varied and extensive.

Implementation is always less fun and more demanding than strategy, but planning alone does not create value for customers or for shareholders. Implementation is reality.

References

Bonoma, T. V. (1985). *The Marketing Edge*. The Free Press

Gadde, L.-E. and Snehota, I. (1999). *Proceedings of the Ninth Biennial World Marketing Congress*. Academy of Marketing Science.

Krapfel, R.E., Salmond, D. and Spekman, R. (1991). A strategic approach to buyer–seller relationships. *Eur. J. Marketing*, 25(9), 22–37.

McDonald, M. and Woodburn, D. (1999). Key account management – building on supplier and customer perspectives. *Financial Times*, Prentice Hall.

McDonald, M., Millman, A. and Rogers, B. (1996). *Key Account Management – Learning from Supplier and Customer Perspectives*. Cranfield School of Management.

Porter, M. E. (1985). *Competitive Strategy*. The Free Press.

Chapter 11

Relationship development processes

Introduction

Of the key account management (KAM) implementation processes outlined in Figure 10.4, one type in particular deserves special consideration: relationship development processes. As discussed in Chapters 1 and 2, the growing importance of KAM is coincident with changes in the business environment and increasing emphasis on customer retention and, therefore, longer-term relationship marketing, as opposed to traditional transactional selling and marketing. Relationship marketing is a business approach which requires greater understanding of the nature and value of buyer–seller relationships, in order to maximize their potential by building sustainable, profitable relationships. The processes which underpin the links between trading partners must reflect this different approach to relationship development if it is to be implemented successfully. This concluding chapter seeks to highlight the ways in which specific features of key relationships can be targeted to serve as practical goals for an organized effort to develop valuable accounts.

Planned relationship development

Once the nature and substance of a key relationship has been identified, as discussed in Chapter 3, the relationship can be proactively developed as a conscious process. Some of the specific features of the various relationship stages can be addressed directly, and they can be used to provide a framework for relationship development activity, as outlined in Figure 11.1. Other features, such as supplier status (listed, preferred, sole or primary) or trust are actually outcomes of development activity, so they play a different role as valuable signals of progress in the relationship development process.

> The relationship can be proactively developed as a conscious process.

Targeted feature of key relationships	Devices for targeting relationship features
Mutual dependence	• Unique product/service • Joint activities • Commitment of resources • Barriers to exit
Joint strategic planning	• Add to agenda • Exchange of strategic information
Adaptation	• Products/services • Processes • Organization
Exchange of information	• Identification of information owners • Information inventory assessment • Creation of need to know
Contacts	• Contact mapping • Target roles, number and strength
Interpersonal relationships	• Contact mapping • Key account manager selection • Social activity

Figure 11.1
Framework for relationship development activity

The list of techniques given in Figure 11.1 for targeting key relationship features is not exhaustive, nor are the activities mutually exclusive: using a device to improve one particular area will often have positive benefits in other areas (and occasionally, a negative impact). While the development of relationships has considerable benefits potentially, it also has costs attached. Application of these devices will involve time and money, both of which should be fully attributed to the individual customer in order to ensure that the selling company maintains a proper understanding of the customer's profitability (see Chapter 7). In particular, the costs of joint activity and the commitment of resources to the customer can be substantial. Indeed, the key account manager will need extra skills even to be able to formulate and cost proposals for submission to senior and financial management.

Mutual dependence

Mutual dependence usually results from a mix of positive and negative drivers. The positive drivers are the competitive advantages achieved through a unique specification, joint activity and commitment of resources which pull the companies together, so they want to work together. The negative drivers are the barriers to exit which stop the companies from separating from each other, such as cost, disruption and loss of competitive advantage, so they feel they cannot escape from each other.

A unique product/service

On the positive side, there are numerous ways suppliers can develop mutual dependency. Traditionally, suppliers try to develop a unique product which is embedded in the customer's offer and cannot be substituted. This is an important approach and one which underlies joint initiatives in research and development, and product development. It is far easier to reach this position through working with the customer than working in isolation and, with cost sharing, it is cheaper as well. Indeed, one of the key differentiators between a *cooperative* relationship and an *interdependent* relationship is admission to the customer's new product development activity. The supplier benefits from the security of ongoing business to which competitors are effectively denied access.

Joint activities

While developing a unique product or service is one of the most powerful ways of developing business, it may have intrinsic limitations. The advantage only lasts as long as the customer makes the product which depends on that component, which could be a long time or a very short time indeed. Suppliers should look for other positive techniques to use as well, such as the creation of joint activity. Joint marketing campaigns, for example, work to develop the business and link the two companies together in the public's mind. Suppliers might offer training for the customer's staff, which not only improves their knowledge of the supplier's products, but can also serve to develop positive contacts with a new contingent of customer staff. Involving staff from both supplier and customer in any project will improve the quality of output and the level of understanding of each other's capabilities, and build the relationship.

> The advantage (of a unique product/service) only lasts as long as the customer makes the product which depends on that component.

Commitment of resources

Commitment of resources to an individual account is another powerful device, though potentially one of the most costly. The range of possibilities here is enormous. Information technology (IT) companies, for example, may set up dedicated help desks for their customers, or their customers' customers. Other suppliers may locate their own staff on the customers' premises to carry out processes that the customers would previously have executed themselves. For example, Procter & Gamble (P&G) staff who manage the stocks and ordering of P&G products on behalf of Wal-Mart, the huge US retailer, work from Wal-Mart's offices, not their own. Again, manufacturers may buy equipment purely to fulfil the specific needs of a major customer. Supplier and customer may jointly contribute to premises and facilities, particularly if the customer is outsourcing a function they previously carried out for themselves. Inevitably, as more and more innovative ways of doing business together are proposed, dedicated resource is required to support them.

However, not all dedicated investments build the relationship. Customers expect that a substantial amount of business will receive special support from the supplier anyway, so to develop the relationship the

> Not all dedicated investments build the relationship.

customer must perceive that the investment and value exceeds its expectations (Lohtia and Krapfel, 1994). Nevertheless, it is here that the selling company can be most creative, adding exceptional value for the customer and securing a closer relationship as well.

> The supplier should be aware of the fact that closer relationships will generate expectations of further investment, and that it is not at liberty to select the ingredients in the recipe for a successful relationship to suit itself. A committed customer will expect a positive response from its supplier on a majority of occasions when a mutually beneficial proposition is mooted, even if it requires investment. The supplier therefore needs to be prepared to view investment as an ongoing commitment rather than a one-off expense and, if it cannot do so, it should consider whether its other efforts at relationship development are sufficiently likely to succeed to be worth pursuing.

Moreover, selling companies should realize that they are quite unlikely to achieve any cost savings for themselves until the relationship has reached a fairly advanced stage (see Chapter 4). At less advanced stages, although the supplier may benefit from a higher volume of business, the savings tend to be heavily weighted towards the customer's side. When the relationship has achieved a level of significant trust and commitment, the customer should be prepared to work with the supplier to achieve mutual cost reduction. Normally, projects and activities aimed at cost saving will require prior investment from the supplier.

Barriers to exit

Many companies are experts at creating barriers to exit for their customers, which we earlier called 'negative' drivers. Identifying them as negative drivers does not necessarily mean that the customer views them in a negative light. If the customer perceives that the exit barrier is simultaneously a substantial benefit to its business, it can accept the position with equanimity. For example, the carrier UPS offers its customers computers and software which automatically label and track the customer's despatches (Berger, 1996). The customer saves money on equipment and labour costs and gains access to better information. Before long, reverting to its own systems becomes difficult and disruptive. Customers are aware of the underlying motive, to lock them into doing business with UPS, but the benefits are sufficiently substantial to allow them to view the deal comfortably.

Suppliers should maintain a careful balance of positive and negative drivers in creating mutual dependency. In some cases negative drivers predominate to the point where the supplier has become the customer's jailer. Needless to say, those customers are waiting for a chance to escape and, if they do, they will not return. Customers are aware that becoming more closely tied to a supplier makes them vulnerable to opportunism (see Chapter 4). They are constantly on the watch for abuses of position and suppliers should monitor their own behaviour carefully from the same angle to make sure they do not transgress, either deliberately or inadvertently.

Insight

In the 1980s and early 1990s (and still today, to a lesser extent) IT hardware and software suppliers developed their products to be incompatible with systems and software from other suppliers. Customers who wanted to add to their systems had to buy from their original supplier's range, even if the item they wanted was clearly not the best on the market. Some customers were so frustrated with the situation and with the poor quality of some of the products they were effectively obliged to buy, that they discounted the advantages of the main system and made a point of buying from another supplier when their equipment was due for replacement.

Joint strategic planning

Add to agenda

Before embarking on a joint strategic planning exercise, which will itself raise customer expectations, the supplier should first be sure that it is prepared to meet a higher level of expectation. However, unless the supplier's products are an important purchase for the buying company, joint strategic planning will not get off the ground anyway. In fact, attempting to put a discussion on strategic, longer-term planning on the agenda is a good way of determining the customer's strategy towards the supplier. A genuinely positive response from the customer would involve the dedication of an appropriate amount of time from a range of people (more than just the purchasing manager) of sufficient seniority.

It is advisable to enter the process with a strong idea of the form it will take, agreed together in advance. The structure of the process by which the supplier has identified and classified the customer as a strategic key account could be used (see Chapters 5–7), particularly because this approach has a strong focus on the customer. Customers respond with appreciation when they see that effort has been applied to discovering what they need, rather than what the supplier needs from them. The emphasis should be on listening to the customer, sharing information and working together to reach a mutually beneficial plan. Customers often discover that the 'strategic planning initiative' is really a thinly disguised sales pitch, and they do not react well to it.

> Customers often discover that the 'strategic planning initiative' is really a thinly disguised sales pitch.

Exchange of strategic information

If the supplier does not already have access to enough information to prepare for strategic planning, the beginning of the process will be a good time to ask for it. This alone is a real benefit to the supplier and there will be further exchanges of strategic information during the process of planning together. Companies who are currently short of information might initiate the process as a way of gaining a greater insight into the customer, but they should remember that, in successful planning, information flows in both directions, including disclosure of their own strategies.

Insight

BOC developed a process of strategic planning for its key customers for industrial gases, which called for a good understanding of the customer's business. Key account managers were introduced to the process in a series of workshops in which they analysed the customer. They took this analysis out to their customers, all of whom responded positively to BOC's approach, some very enthusiastically. The customers adjusted any incorrect assumptions and then contributed to the final plans that were developed. The plans were more focused and more realistic, and gained the buy-in of both the customer and BOC's key account manager.

Adaptation

Key customers expect their key suppliers to help them gain competitive advantage, so they expect to receive something different from the average customer. Adaptation to the specific requirements of key customers, whether of *products/services, processes or organization*, is therefore a very important part of KAM. Chapter 10 has already discussed the implementation of customization for products and services or processes, while Chapter 8 focused on the processes involved in organizing for identified key accounts.

Exchange of information

Relationships are developed through the process of exchanging information and also using the resultant knowledge. Research has shown that selling companies who had not progressed beyond the *cooperative* relationship stage were 'in the dark' compared with those who had reached the *interdependent* stage, and this put a serious crimp on their chances of making new offers in ways which were likely to win more business (see Figure 3.7). As emphasized in Chapter 9, the key account manager carries much of the responsibility for supervising communications and building the knowledge base on behalf of the selling company.

The key account manager carries much of the responsibility for supervising communications and building the knowledge base on behalf of the selling company.

Identification of information owners

The first stage in the process of exchanging information is the identification of information owners or at least those who may be a conduit for it. This can be part of contact mapping, which is described in the following section. Clearly, if the originators and principal 'owners' of information are identified, appropriate ways of obtaining the information required can be devised. It may not always be possible to go direct to the source, but at least an understanding of who holds the key to what will suggest more efficient and successful approaches.

Assessment of the inventory of information

If the selling company is to target information exchange actively, then it should start with an assessment of the inventory of information about the customer that it currently possesses. Undoubtedly, it will find that it has good contacts and a good supply of information on certain subjects and is poorly served elsewhere. Therefore, the first step is to establish what kind of information is lacking and the second step is to determine what other information is also required.

Information requirements depend on the strategy and plan for the account. For example, if the objective is to achieve a level of revenue and margin which cannot be reached on basic product offering and depends on selling value-added services, then the supplier's strategy might be to persuade the customer to outsource a complete area of activity to it. In order to make such a proposition, the key account manager would require a good deal of information on the current scope of the activity. However, if the strategy were different, there might not be any point in making the effort to collect and assimilate that information.

> Information requirements depend on the strategy and plan for the account.

Creation of a need to know

The selling company must demonstrate or create a need to know, otherwise the buying company will be either suspicious of their request, or just dismiss it as a waste of its time. The supplier needs to identify and prioritize the information it wants and develop its case for having access to it. For example, a joint strategic planning initiative provides a good reason for requesting strategic-level information.

Once a strategy has been developed, it can be used to identify the information gaps, as suggested earlier, and that ensures that a coherent, sound reason for requesting the information does exist which can be justified to the customer. Of course, buying companies will expect to receive information of comparable value or sensitivity in return. In fact, it is quite likely that the supplier will need to be the first to volunteer information in a pump-priming approach, signalling the degree of trust it places in the buying company.

> Buying companies will expect to receive information of comparable value or sensitivity in return.

Contacts

> The development of intercompany bonds through individual contact points in the buying company can be subjected to explicit targeting and activity as much as any other part of the relationship.

Contact mapping

Contact mapping (see Figure 11.2) is a valuable process in expanding a contact portfolio or, conversely, introducing new staff from the supplying company to customer contacts. It would normally be based on the customer's organizational chart. It highlights who within the customer's organization is responsible for what and what kind of decisions they make relevant to the buying process, or what influence they bring to bear on it, and what information they hold. The selling company then identifies who within its own organization should have a relationship with whom and with what degree of involvement. Mapping contacts in this very visual way is a valuable process of identification of areas of current strength and weakness. For example, it may be that most contacts are at too junior a level or, perhaps, that there are no contacts at all with certain functions or locations.

It is worth emphasizing the need to have good contacts at both the strategic and operational levels. Selling companies commonly have difficulty in penetrating the account at a sufficiently high level and this problem needs specific focus. It should be noted that tactics for reaching strategic decision makers can be very different from those for reaching operational people. For example, it may be that the selling company's managing director needs to be involved, so an effort has to be made to set up an occasion with the kind of 'hooks' which interest senior people.

> Suppliers who had close, *interdependent* or *integrated* relationships with their customers had more contacts inside the customer, while others had fewer contacts and not enough of their attention either (McDonald and Woodburn, 1999). Selling companies need to use relationship development processes consciously in order to increase the number and strength of their links with contacts in the other company so as to escape this self-perpetuating rut of being 'out in the cold' and 'in the dark'.

Having identified the people and their positions, the strength and quality of the relationship can be superimposed onto the map. The relationship 'owner' within the selling company can be identified as well. Once the map of the current situation has been constructed, it is a short step to planning the desired level of relationship in each case and then to ways in which that might be achieved. Some companies even measure the strength of the relationship between individuals on a scale of one to five and set a numerical target on improvement.

In the example in Figure 11.2, with the exception of the production director, the selling company has only weak links with directors in the customer organization and none at all with the managing director. However, they have a good relationship where it matters most, that is, with the production director: he ultimately controls the budget for components, which includes this supplier's products. The supplier would like to be more involved with product development at an earlier stage, which requires developing a better relationship than they currently have with the research director. Relationships within the finance function are not good at any level.

This framework, which is based on the formal organization, is only one of those that could be used. The contacts could be replotted in other structures, such as the customer's internal value chain or decision-making units or internal personal networks, and those would reveal other significant strengths and weaknesses.

Selling companies commonly have difficulty in penetrating the account at a sufficiently high level.

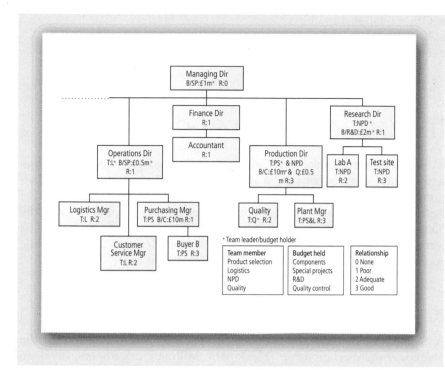

Figure 11.2
Relationship
mapping by formal
organization chart

Target roles, number and strength

In real life, the picture gets messy very quickly when mapped on paper, but on a database the targets and their influences can be logged systematically and then matched with a parallel database of selling company staff. Having set up the links on the database, the current and desired stages of the relationship can be logged and staff tasked to work on developing greater involvement. Following is a list of some of the data which might be logged in the individual contact's database record to provide information which may be used to identify those customer contacts who could be most useful in developing the relationship. Such an analysis of the people involved also helps to a keep focus on what is the purpose of that relationship development.

Details of customer contact database record
- Name and title.
- Contact details.
- Role in organization.
- Role in account.
- Team involvement.
- Authority and budgets held.
- Contacts in selling organization.
- Current relationship level.
- Targeted relationship level.

- Other relationship objectives.
- Key messages for transmission.
- Relationship development strategies.

Interpersonal relationships

A key account relationship which has developed beyond the *basic* stage will include contact between a number of people in the two organizations, and not just the key account manager and purchasing manager. As described previously, contact mapping enables the supplier to view the picture of its contacts within the buying company and examine them in terms of the personal relationship as well as their decision-making ability, access to information, budgetary discretion and so on.

Key account manager selection

A change of personnel is one of the most common reasons cited for the breakdown of a relationship (McDonald, Millman and Rogers, 1996), so interpersonal relationships matter a good deal in key account pairings. It seems self-evident that the selection of a key account manager for a particular account should consider personal suitability and compatibility as well as more objective factors. However, many companies find it difficult to appoint their key account managers to accounts on intangible, personality-based parameters. Most often, staff are allocated to an account according to their experience, knowledge, location, position in the organizational structure of the selling company or, occasionally, their management approach. Personality factors are only taken into account when a breakdown occurs and there is a danger of losing the account.

It should be possible for selling companies to specify the profile of the buying company quite objectively and match it with a profile of the skills and qualities required of the key account manager who will be successful in the account (see Chapter 9). It is unlikely that the perfect person will be available, but a systematic process at least gives the greatest chance of achieving the best fit. Selling companies have to be realistic about the specification, however, and an element of realism can be introduced through giving each factor a weighting in order to determine its importance relative to other factors.

> Many companies find it difficult to appoint their key account managers to accounts on intangible, personality-based parameters.

Insight

'We sat down and wrote the specification of the ideal global account manager. Then we looked at it and realized that this guy could be our chief executive. Well, we were prepared to pay good money, but not that much, even if the people had been available, which they were not. So we had to go back and decide what really mattered' (global services company).

Social activity

Attempts to find a measure of personal interaction have tended to look at the amount of social activity between participants outside the workplace, but the link between this activity and the business relationship is not at all clear. Therefore, there is no guarantee that promoting social events will enhance the relationship, although a lot of companies obviously believe that it does. The focus, rather, should be on the ease and quality of the working relationship. Many people do not have time or want to make time for social activity with business contacts, despite having a genuine regard for them in the work context. In fact, some companies and some sectors, such as the public sector, actively discourage social contacts between buyers and suppliers.

> The focus, rather, should be on the ease and quality of the working relationship.

Nevertheless, a supplier's approach should consider the style of the industry, and a well-chosen social event in the right context can be productive. Events should be carefully selected to suit the people to be invited and planned well in advance. Turnout rates can be embarrassingly low if the timing is wrong or customers are given too little notice to arrange time in their diaries, particularly the most senior people. The organization of an event has to be impeccable if the occasion is to enhance the relationship: if it is not, it could actually inflict damage.

Layers of relationship involvement

Relationships can and have been looked at from a multitude of perspectives. Figure 3.1 presented an additional angle which saw them as constructed of layers of involvement, defined as activity links, resource ties or people bonds, aimed at different objectives (Gadde and Snehota, 1999). These three elements offer a different foundation on which to build an approach to the development of the relationship.

> From this angle, activity links are those where supplier and buyer carry out tasks together. The main aim of these activities is coordination, for the synchronization and good management of the business they do together. On the other hand, the principal objective of resource ties is adaptation to the specific needs of the customer. After all, if the customer could be served by the supplier's current, standard offer, then there would be no need to dedicate resources to them, so it must be adapting to their differences which requires investment. Lastly, the main reason for developing bonds with the people in the customer organization is the need to secure positive interactions with them. All decisions and action taken is, of course, mediated by or enacted by people, and so they clearly cannot be removed from the equation even when the customer is considered collectively as a company.

Layer of involvement	Principal objective	Examples of development initiatives
Activity links	Co-ordination	Interlinked processes
		Installation of new procedures
		Training exchanges
		Joint marketing activity
		Product development
Resource ties	Adaptation	IT & telecommunications
		Dedicated equipment
		Outsourced services
		Joint facilities
		Staff implants
		R&D projects
		Financial investment
People bonds	Interaction	Strategic level
		Operational level
		Social level
		Contact portfolio
		Customer-interacting staff

Figure 11.3
Relationship development initiatives by layer of involvement

Source: Developed from Gadde and Snehota, 1999

Figure 11.3 shows some common examples of initiatives which could be offered to customers which would help to develop the different layers of the relationship. Instinctively, it seems sensible to ensure that a balance across these three layers of involvement is maintained, though this approach has not been confirmed by research. We suggest that these layers of involvement be applied when new initiatives are proposed, whether by the customer or by the suppler, to consider what effect they will have in the relationship and how they will shape the business.

Summary

Well-developed relationships display certain characteristics which are not seen at simpler stages, or which are seen to a lesser extent. We suggest targeting those characteristics which can be addressed directly as a reasonable approach for a supplier to take, in order to encourage the development of the relationship, even though it is not clear which is cause and which is effect.

Relationship development requires the investment of time and money in a plethora of directions and selling companies who want to achieve levels beyond the transactional, *basic* stage need to be prepared to invest in their key customers. Those who have not recognized the demand for investment are likely to disappoint their important customers and fail to build the relationship.

A visual form of mapping for contacts is helpful in a number of processes of relationship development. Ultimately, all the activity and interaction with the customer will be channelled through these contacts and, therefore, a good understanding of them is fundamental to success. In a large account, the number of contacts and volume of information captured requires that it be kept in a database in order to hold, manage and manipulate the information in different ways.

Key relationships display different layers of involvement, which are described as activity links, resource ties and people bonds. Different kinds of initiative will impact on each of these layers and it would seem sensible to pursue some of each kind in order to maintain a balance within the relationship.

The insight gained from understanding the relationship in depth can be used to aid planning and implementation of key customer development at both the strategic and tactical levels. Managing key customers profitably requires a perspective on business relationships which moves beyond the simple commercial transaction, to the complex interchange born of a multitude of tangible and less tangible links and benefits.

References

Berger, M. (1996). How a new automation initiative is helping UPS deliver even more services to its customers. *SMT*, December.

Gadde, L.-E. and Snehota, I. (1999). Proceedings of the Ninth Biennial World Marketing Congress. Academy of Marketing Science.

Lohtia, R. and Krapfel, R.E. (1994). The impact of transaction-specific investments on buyer–seller relationships. *J. Business Indust. Marketing*, 9(1), 6–16

McDonald, M. and Woodburn, D. (1999). Key account management – building on supplier and customer perspectives. *Financial Times*, Prentice-Hall.

McDonald, M., Millman, A. and Rogers, B. (1996). *Key Account Management – Learning from Supplier and Customer Perspectives*. Cranfield School of Management.

Mini-cases

The following mini-cases are offered to readers as a way of considering just some of the complex issues which face all organizations who are serious in their intentions of building profitable and lasting relationships with customers. Please 'role-play' the characters in the mini-cases, but also consider what would happen in your company if it were faced with the situation described and how you think your customer would react. We have also included some case studies from the customer's point of view, which may be used as training scenarios for 'boundary spanning'.

Each of these mini-cases is based on real cases, but the names and some of the circumstances have been changed. Any name similarity with existing companies or people is entirely accidental and unintended.

We have included a brief discussion at the end of each mini-case. We stress that these are not answers, as there is never a perfect answer to any problem in life. Please compare our thoughts with your own and please discuss them with colleagues, as this is the best way to learn.

Case 1: diversification dilemma

Smith & Jones Systems plc (S&J) provided a 'turnkey' information systems solution for a major government department five years ago, which they continue to support. Relationships between the board of S&J and the senior civil servants in the department are very positive. However, the key account manager absorbs most of the stress inherent in the business relationship. He has had to mediate in disagreements between S&J and government technical staff on the few occasions when the system has not met user expectations. In addition, the system now needs a major upgrade, which has been delayed because of budget constraints. The perceptions of users are that the S&J system is creaking at the seams and S&J are not responding to their needs to squeeze more out of it.

The government has now decided that it wants to contract out all the information systems operations of this department, which will mean any bidder taking on all the civil service technical staff in the unit, as well as being given the challenge of upgrading the system and keeping it up to date. The opportunity will be advertised in the *European Journal* and will be subject to all the usual public sector tender approval procedures designed to ensure fairness and objectivity.

As an existing supplier, S&J are invited by the senior civil servants in the department to a meeting in order to be informed of the new situation (the grapevine had already got to the key account manager). The meeting involves the managing director and the key account manager from S&J and, from the customer, the head of department and head of information technology (the latter will probably be transferred to the employment of whoever wins the bid). Officially, the department staff are only one small part of the decision-making procedure for the new contract, but they can influence the brief. Meanwhile, S&J have concerns about whether it is strategically appropriate for them to bid for an 'outsourcing' contract and whether they can compete with the two big players in public sector outsourcing. However, they do not really want to lose this flagship customer.

Q: **How should they conduct the meeting?**
What did they decide to do as a result of it?

A: S&J have clearly had problems integrating their operations with the customer's and have not developed the network of contacts seen at the mid-KAM stage. Consequently, they are starting at a disadvantage. Nevertheless, at the meeting both representatives from S&J should show real enthusiasm for the proposal and should act as if they were extremely keen to proceed with this outsourcing opportunity and put the relationship on a new footing. The objective should be to collect as much information as possible about overheads, including salaries, terms and conditions and details of all fixed and variable costs. Crucial to any potential bid will be a deep understanding of all the tasks undertaken by the customers information systems department. The purpose of this is to establish whether there is likely to be sufficient margin in such a contract to warrant starting what will, in effect, be a new business venture.

Having done these calculations, the company should decide how it is going to respond to the trend towards outsourcing of information systems work. There are three options:

- Ignore it and continue to be a software house.
- Form alliances with outsourcing specialists.
- Diversify into outsourcing.

In order to be an outsourcing company or even an alliance partner of one, S & J would have to invest a great deal in relationship building and understanding how to manage in different company cultures.

In the event, even the one-off opportunity was considered to be such a radical departure from S&J's core business that they decided to forego the opportunity. They worked with the large consultancy which won the bid and were eventually taken over by them.

Case 2: taking a key account for granted

Excellent Process Products (EPP) was spun off from a large manufacturing conglomerate in 1994. The former parent, Gloss plc, is still the dominant account in the EPP portfolio, representing 40 per cent of business.

Old loyalties are beginning to break down. The financial controller of Gloss plc has recently complained to the purchasing director that he has had to allocate senior staff to spend days sorting out EPP invoices. Apart from being arithmetically inaccurate, which is just pure sloppiness, the invoices are presented in a way which makes it very difficult for people approving them to reconcile them to products which they know have been received.

The purchasing director himself is aggravated because he perceives that the new key account manager his senior buyer is dealing with is inexperienced in comparison with his predecessor and cannot always make decisions without referral to the sales director. There is no doubt that the services of EPP are first class and good value and he does not want to seek an alternative supplier. However, the company is making itself difficult to deal with and he wants to take a relatively hard line in order to ensure that they improve.

He decided to request a one-to-one meeting with the sales director, but discovers that he is on holiday. The purchasing director is in no mood to wait, but refuses the offer made by the sales director's personal assistant (PA) of a meeting with the key account manager. He does not say so, but he does not believe that the key account manager could initiate the changes he wants.

The sales director's PA informs the key account manager for Gloss plc that the purchasing director has tried to contact the sales director. The key account manager has had little contact with the purchasing director as his main contact is the senior buyer.

Q: **What should he do to resolve the immediate need to identify the purchasing director's concerns?**
What ought to be done in the long term to improve relationships between EPP and Gloss plc?

A: EPP has obviously made one of the cardinal mistakes in key account management. Putting a comparatively junior manager into such a pivotal key account in the mistaken belief that old loyalties will see the relationship through is irresponsible in the extreme. Major accounts must know that their business is in the hands of a senior person who can take decisions as and when necessary.

In this particular case, no doubt EPP's key account manager for Gloss plc by now understands some of the reasons for the purchasing director's concern. His pressing task must be to reassure Gloss plc, probably by getting another EPP director to visit the purchasing director immediately, so that the operational concerns may be attended to as a matter of urgency. This will at least allay fears until the return of the sales director. The more difficult issue concerning the nature of the relationship and representation issues can then be tackled by EPP. Clearly, however, the status of the key account manager for Gloss plc needs to be raised.

Besides this, there is a need for involvement of more EPP staff in order to resolve process issues. For example, a focus team of EPP sales ledger and Gloss plc bought ledger staff must be set up to sort out the invoicing problems. The key account manager must ask the sales director to support him and apply pressure to other functional managers in order to support such initiatives. The sales director must also lobby the managing director in order to ensure that the key account manager has a permanent team of named functional professionals who will have some objectives placed on them related to his account. Those objectives must be set by the key account manager, so that he has authority to get things done for the customer.

(You may think that this case is far-fetched, but it is based on a real situation!)

Case 3: demanding flexibility

All Components plc is a key target for Special Raw Materials Ltd (SRML). Although they are not the biggest company of their type, since they have been dealing with Japanese motor companies in the UK All Components plc have been looking to replicate the partnership agreements they enjoy with customers with their critical suppliers. This means that some suppliers will be assured of 100 per cent of their business for five years at a time (assuming excellent performance). All Components plc's declaration of interest in 100 per cent partnerships has meant considerable competition among the suppliers who might be eligible.

A key account manager, Damon Riley, was assigned in April 1996. Damon has worked very hard, at significant cost to SRML, in convincing All Components plc that they would be their best partner for strategic raw materials. The effort included pilot deliveries at special prices which demonstrated the quality of SRML products. Now, eighteen months later, the big opportunity of gaining 100 per cent of All Components plc business is on the table.

However, All Components plc are looking for terms and conditions which are not common in the business. For example, they want to be able to choose their own key account team including technicians, they want SRML to manage the raw materials stocks on a consignment basis and they want up to forty success criteria to govern the ongoing relationship.

They also want extended credit from SRML. Damon quickly assures them that consignment stock and their forty success criteria are acceptable. He tells All Components plc that he must take their other requests to the board. SRML takes equal opportunities very seriously and the board would be worried about allowing a customer to choose their own key account team. While accepting that a good personality fit is important, normally team members would be chosen by SRML on the basis of their career development not a customer's preference. Changes would only be made if a team member made a mistake which caused serious customer discontent.

SRML is also reluctant to extend more than thirty days credit, even to the most strategic of customers, due to effect on cash flow and the cost of working capital.

Of course, the board will be expecting Damon to make a recommendation.

Q: What will Damon's recommendation be?

A: Damon recommends to the board that SRML offer All Components plc a team somewhat more highly skilled and experienced than the account might expect. Their request for choosing the team might well come from insecurity and the offer of a top team should diffuse it. If the team members were to be introduced to their opposite numbers by an SRML director at a social event, this would provide an opportunity for building mutual liking and respect and demonstrating high-level endorsement of the people chosen for the account.

On the credit issue, SRML could hide behind proposed UK legislation to ensure prompt payment, although the partnership is also likely to operate in countries where extended credit is not only legal, but business as usual. An alternative would be to make an exception, provided interest is paid. Nevertheless, since the volume of business which could flow from the partnership is substantial, All Components plc would doubtless be disappointed with such a compromise. Damon recommends that sixty days credit be formally agreed with them for an initial twelve-month period. SRML should reserve the right in future years to vary credit terms in line with exceptional economic conditions or local legislation.

He also recommends that, assuming his recommendations are acceptable to the board and to the prospect, that board members become involved in the formal signing of the partnership agreement with the directors of All Components plc. Assuming it is agreeable to both companies, the trade press could be invited. Both companies would gain favourable publicity for their flexible, partnership approach.

Case 4: learning to look a gift horse in the mouth

Jo Young, who works for Punch Financial Services, is key account manager for Clover plc, an innovative fertilizer company. Punch Financial Services is well-known for its coordinated approach to customers' risk management – key account teams consist of a variety of specialist underwriters.

She is approached by Brian Dale, the borough finance officer of a very large London local authority. He has heard about Punch Financial Services and Jo herself from someone he knows at the golf club who was at university with her. His local authority has a myriad of suppliers of financial services and he would like to start consolidating with fewer suppliers as contracts come up for renewal. Because of public procurement procedures, he cannot promise a full partnership and he makes it clear to Jo that Punch Financial Services must compete with incumbent suppliers on price.

Jo listens politely, thanks the borough finance officer for his interest and says she will come back to him to suggest how they might proceed.

Punch Financial Services operates very proactive prospect target-ing and one of the key criteria used is that companies of strategic interest to Punch Financial Services are likely to be in high-risk businesses. Punch Financial Services has never done any work in central or local government. Although the company has never turned 'bluebird' business away in the past, Jo is not entirely sure that it would do either party any good to do business on a transactional basis. The borough council would never be key to Punch Financial Services, whereas it might be key to another financial services company.

Then she considers the fact that the nature of government in the UK has changed significantly during the 1980s and 1990s and that there are new opportunities for shared risk. Perhaps Punch Financial Services ought to rethink its aversion to public sector business?

Q: What does she decide to do?

A: It is always very flattering to know that a contact has recom-mended you to another organization and it is only natural to want to do a good job for the person who is approaching you on this basis. Jo could treat this as a test case, in order to explore whether opportunities really do exist for building some kind of profitable partnership with local authorities.

However, difficult choices do have to be made in key account management. Punch Financial Services cannot afford to be all things to all people and must be pragmatic. This London local authority is likely to be in the bottom right-hand box of Punch Financial Services' account portfolio matrix. The reason is that the profit opportunities are likely to be minimal and Punch Financial Services' strengths compared to others are also likely to be mini-mal. While Jo might want to do a good job for Brian Dale, he is working in a political environment where his professional judge-ment could be over-ruled. Learning the formal and informal decision-making structure of a big local authority would be a major challenge.

Jo decides to supply the minimum information necessary to ensure that Punch Financial Services is included on the tender list. If invited to tender, she would submit a standard proposal, but would make no allowances for Brian's warnings on price. In fact, she would probably have to include a substantial contingency to compensate for the risk to Punch Financial Services of taking on non-core business. This means that she keeps faith with Brian and the contact which recommended her while also keeping faith with Punch Financial Services. In the unlikely event of the tender being successful, the business would be treated as incremental and transactional, a one-off. It could generate useful cash for Punch Financial Services, without having to tie up too many scarce resources chasing low margin business. Punch Financial Services has a special department for looking after tactical business.

Had an invitation to tender been received without the personal contact and apparent keenness of the borough finance officer, Jo would definitely have decided not to submit a proposal.

The situation would have been quite different had it been a food or chemical company (i.e. high risk). Punch Financial Services would have seen an opportunity for at least a twenty-year relationship and would have invested considerable resources and effort into learning about the prospect and their risk management challenges. They would have ensured a highly competitive, value-based proposal was presented to them.

Case 5: a family feud

The logistics division of Well & West plc (LogFast) distributes extremely high volumes of low-value products for X Market Trader Ltd (XMT). XMT is exceedingly entrepreneurial in style, which has caused one or two culture clashes with the more conservative LogFast. However, the relationship seems to thrive on the challenge and both supplier and customer demonstrate significant commitment to each other and work very closely together. Focus teams involving personnel at all levels from both companies have been formed in order to examine ways in which mutual cost reduction and quality improvement can be achieved.

Well & West plc has a number of other divisions. One of them, HighShift, is the market leader in the distribution of high-value goods.

XMT deals in high-value products as well as low-value products, although the volumes of high-value products are quite low. The distribution director of XMT wants to do business with HighShift on the same basis as LogFast.

To date, LogFast's key account manager has been avoiding the issue, as the internal rivalry between LogFast and HighShift within Well & West plc is not something he particularly wants to or is able to explain. The sales director of LogFast has been pleading with his counterpart in HighShift to join the very positive business relationship they have with XMT, but without success.

The distribution director of XMT is becoming impatient and the key account manager and sales director of LogFast know that they have to make a case to the main board of Well & West plc. Even if they succeed, the sales director of HighShift might be infuriated and obstructive, which might not help the customer.

Q: **What case do they make and what happens next?**

A: This is a fairly typical problem which customers have with their suppliers. Indeed, what emerged clearly from our research was that the customer is intolerant of internal conflict within the supplying organization, so this issue needs to be resolved quickly.

It is clear that Well & West plc run the risk of losing the XMT business unless their own group's internal divisions can be resolved.

The issue has to be escalated to board level in a purely objective way. A cost–benefit analysis is required, so that no-one is in any doubt how much business will be lost if HighShift does not cooperate with LogFast. Furthermore, the same document should raise the general issue of how the group should deal with customers requiring one policy.

One possible solution would be the creation of a key accounts division which can be seen as independent of the functional divisions. Of course, key account team members would still have to be drawn from other divisions. They must have objectives placed on them which relate to achievement for the key account. In practice, this often leads to the erosion of divisional 'tribal' rivalries, which delivers benefits for the customers and the company overall.

Case 6: practise what you preach

The sales director of Workwise Uniforms has just had a meetings with the key account manager for their top client and her identified successor who announced that they were both leaving to join a top competitor.

They complained about lack of status and authority, a situation which the sales director has known about for some time, but has been unable to rectify, despite attempts to convince the managing director that key account managers and key account teams should be more empowered. (He also knew that the key account manager had been disappointed because the market position of her client had slipped from number one in their sector to number three and she had wanted him to move her on to a client on the way up their league. This the managing director had also blocked because of her popularity with the company's top account.)

The irony is that Workwise Uniforms encourages empowerment, among other positive employment practices, in their clients. It would be hugely embarrassing if their competitor were able to boast about the defection of key staff because Workwise Uniforms did not practise what it preached. It was the sort of story which certain business magazines might be delighted to get their hands on.

Needless to say, the sales director would also have to deal with the client. The top decision makers would be devastated to lose not only their popular key account manager, but the team member who had been presented to them as her eventual successor. It would be difficult to match someone else to their exacting requirements at short notice.

Q: What should the sales director do next?

A: The sales director has two issues to address here. First, there is the immediate problem of the defection of the key account manager and her number two. Here, the only solution would appear to be for the sales director to take on the account personally until replacement staff can be recruited. He should also be totally honest with the client, explaining what has gone wrong and informing them that any future key account manager will be given more reassurance about their status and authority.

The second issue is of course the issue of empowerment generally in Workwise Uniforms. The company needs to establish the general principles and a framework for decision making more formally. Consultation should take place with staff and key accounts in order to find an optimum solution which will provide all-round satisfaction.

Case 7: jealous partners

Ideally, Jellox SA would like to ensure that their partnership suppliers do not work with their competitors. However, since competition law precludes them from being able to enforce such a demand, they have placed on their suppliers the burden of convincing them that no possible cross-fertilization can take place between what they do for Jellox and what they do for their top rival, NV plc.

Q: How should the suppliers respond?

A: As has been explained, competition law in the UK and Europe states that anything offered to one customer by a supplier must theoretically be offered to all. Key account strategy offers the opportunity of tailoring products and processes so closely to an individual customer that no key account will obtain the same formula. They will obtain what offers them best value.

Most suppliers faced with this challenge from customers are careful to ensure 'Chinese walls' between key account teams. Confidentiality agreements are signed, which include the pledge that no member of the designated key account team will work in the competitor's team, even for a certain period after their duties may have changed.

Case 8: healing wounds

Winston James is the technical manager for HighRisk Products Ltd. The company has just installed new processes and received training from ProcessMaster plc. While the new processes are still running parallel with the old, something goes terribly wrong with them. The operatives claim that they have been following ProcessMaster plc instructions to the letter.

The failure attracts top management attention. Winston calls in the consultant who delivered the training, who, in front of the human resources director, accuses the operatives of sabotaging the new processes because of their resistance to change. Winston, fuming, asks her to leave the premises and declares that the purchasing director will have to sort out some compensation with the key account manager while he concentrates on making sure that the customers of HighRisk Products Ltd get what they have ordered using the old processes. However, Winston is worried that the human resources director might just have seen some justification for the accusation of resistance to change.

A large postmortem meeting is called, involving all interested parties from HighRisk Products Ltd and ProcessMaster plc. Meanwhile, Winston works all the hours he can to keep products flowing to customers while also finding out more about the failure of the new processes. He concludes that there had been flaws in the delivery of the training, but it also seems to be the case that one or two 'opinion leaders' on the shop floor have been fomenting discontent.

Winston knows that, whatever the outcome of the meeting with ProcessMaster plc, he has a huge problem on his hands restoring the morale and motivation of the workforce, but it is one that he feels very unwilling to admit to anyone else.

Q: What happens at the meeting?

A: What *does not* happen is the trainer repeating her accusations and there is no 'banging of the table' which will ensure ProcessMaster plc is blacklisted forever more. . .

Q: What does happen?

A: The key account manager of ProcessMaster plc has to be empowered in order to offer compensation and training alternatives. He needs to secure the opportunity of talking to the HighRisk Products Ltd workers to find out what their problems are and trying to arrange more training for them. He can probably second-guess Winston's anxiety and he needs to ensure that technical expertise is available to him full time in order to offer support and make sure that he comes up smelling of roses!

The board of HighRisk Products Ltd know that they need the new processes and are unlikely to chuck ProcessMaster plc off-site, unless they are offensive. If they demonstrate appropriate humility and a genuine desire to put things right, they are likely to be given the chance to do so.

Ironically, it is often in the context of putting problems right that stronger relationships can be forged between suppliers and customers. Problem accounts have been transformed into reference accounts!

Case 9: pride comes before a fall

John Uplook, general manager of 234 Services (UK) Ltd, a market leader in office services, thinks that his company has a very good record on key account management. In fact, he thinks that they are masters of best practice in key account management.

One of 234 Services (UK) Ltd's prize accounts is Telephony (UK) Ltd. The managing director of Telephony (UK) Ltd, Rod Lines, has appeared in 234 Services (UK) Ltd's national magazine advertisements praising their services. Privately, however, Rod is irritated by what he perceives as a cultural fault – their market leader arrogance – and a tendency to quote prices which they then lower when he challenges them.

The public closeness of 234 Services (UK) Ltd and Telephony (UK) Ltd has not stopped 234 Services (UK) Ltd's nearest rival, Green and White (UK) Ltd, from targeting Telephony (UK) Ltd and Rod Lines in particular. Green and White (UK) Ltd are offering him better prices first time, without time-consuming negotiation. They display eagerness for his business rather than condescension and their products are just as good. Rod feels obliged to let them pitch for his business, but he does not welcome the hassle which changing suppliers will cause. He would prefer 234 Services (UK) Ltd to be more like Green and White (UK) Ltd in their approach. He knows that the culture of 234 Services (UK) Ltd comes directly down to the key account teams from the very macho general manager.

Q: What can Rod do, short of changing supplier, to convince John Uplook that he ought to change?

A: The first action that Rod Lines should take is a thorough analysis of the value that his company receives from 234 Services (UK) Ltd rather than concentrating solely on price. If the same value can be achieved from Green and White (UK) Ltd at a lower price, then it is his duty to change suppliers. Before doing this, however, he should insist on a bid from both companies for a 100 per cent partnership arrangement, not to help him decide on price but to help him decide on value.

If he really prefers to keep 234 Services (UK) Ltd having done this, he should have a frank meeting with 234 Services (UK) Ltd on the basis of total value and the nature of the desired relationship. In this case, he was reassured that they would respond to his requirements.

If, after this, he had still been unsure about 234 Services (UK) Ltd's cultural capability to adopt a partnership approach, he would have had two options:

● switch 100 per cent to Green and White (UK) Ltd or
● manage the status quo.

Many purchasing decision makers feel the need to ensure some degree of competition for their business because they associate risks with single sourcing, such as the complacency of the supplier.

Case 10: going global

XYZ Global have announced their plans to the world to reduce their lines to a few global brands and to reduce their supplier base from 500 000 to 50 000. All existing suppliers have to bid for the global business. ION Services will no longer be able to serve XYZ Global separately in the UK, Belgium, Brazil and the USA. ION Services has no problem in demonstrating a presence in all the countries in which XYZ Global operates, but whether they can offer a consistent standard of service globally is quite another matter.

ION Services has to be a front-runner for XYZ Global's property services; they already have a majority share by being their supplier in four out of the twenty countries in which they have major plants. Most of the competitors do not have offices in other countries, just alliances with other independents.

XYZ Global have given their potential suppliers three years to build up to the global bid. ION Services has to win. The company might not stand the shock of losing a key account in four countries at once. Apart from that, it is obvious that achieving the global coordination required by XYZ Global will stand them in good stead for winning business with other global companies.

Q: What sort of plan do ION's strategists start to put into place?

A: This is a problem faced by most global suppliers today, as more and more of their global customers seek to reduce the complexity of decentralized, multisupplier contracts.

Fortunately, ION Services has all the pieces already in place. What ION Services must do is call a meeting of subsidiary principals and relevant headquarters' personnel in order to deliver a strategy for global key account management, as many of their potential problems will stem from ethnocentric attitudes in the subsidiaries. The authors ran such a conference for a decentralized, country-based supplier of services using a business game to test out the decisions which would be made by delegates in respect of a hypothetical global key account. The results were surprising to all and hammered home to all the need to subjugate local interests to the good of the global account. More importantly, it changed attitudes and paved the way for constructive teamwork across national organizations supporting global customers.

ION Services has to address the following challenges:

- process excellence,
- cross-cultural management,
- thorough and effective communications, internally and externally,
- attention to detail over a huge scope of work,
- ensuring the whole team can see the whole picture (there may be hundreds of people devoted to a key account worldwide).

Case 11: the power of persistence

Jeanne Étoile, general manager of Étoile Consulting, has just awarded the trophies in the annual Étoile & Clients' doubles tennis tournament. She has been extremely proud to see the Étoile–customer doubles teams playing together – a mirror of the way her company works together with clients. It was particularly pleasing this year to see twenty-six nationalities represented in the tournament.

Q: **She spends her next day in the office thinking deeply. Étoile is recognized as the best practitioner of key account management in its sector. The company could be finished if it lost that accolade. How can Étoile keep up the momentum?**

A: Étoile needs to keep abreast of developments in the industry and seek continuously in order to provide solutions which provide superior value to its clients. Apart from this, however, Étoile could join a best practice key account management benchmarking club at one of the leading postgraduate business schools, such as Cranfield. This way Étoile will always be at the leading edge of key account management best practice.

The company will also invest effort in the following activities:

- Process integration.
- Continuous communication with clients in between projects.
- Recruiting specialist skills.
- Strong marketing communications and promotion.

Case 12: the frustrations of a 'basic' relationship

Peter Piper has been the account manager for Discount Retail Ltd for three years. Discount Retail Ltd keep all suppliers of goods and services at arm's length. All business is bid for on a one-off basis. Social invitations from suppliers are rebuffed. Account managers are very unlikely to meet a purchasing manager regularly, let alone a decision maker in another department.

Peter works for Contract Employees Limited (CEL). The company has been successful in regularly supplying temporary staff to Discount Retail Ltd's warehouse. Recently, a few vacancies were filled by another agency, which undercut CEL's price. In fact, the warehouse manager was furious with purchasing because the staff supplied by the competitor were incompetent.

Peter is keen to persuade his managing director to take Discount Retail Ltd out of his portfolio and give the company to a junior account manager.

Then word gets back to Peter from one of the temps who had done an assignment at Discount Retail Ltd about the dispute between the warehouse manager and purchasing.

Q: **Should it change his mind?**

A: This knowledge should probably not change Peter's mind. Discount Retail Ltd is clearly not the kind of key account with which a value-creating relationship can be built. It would be in the bottom right-hand box of the account portfolio matrix (see Figure 4.12). There is not much potential for profit growth here and the relationship is poor. Accordingly, the relationship should remain transactional, with each transaction done on the basis of generating cash.

Peter may decide to stay just long enough to discover whether the Warehouse Manager wins his argument with purchasing and gains higher level support for preferring CEL. This could establish a special status for CEL within the account, which might enable the account to be reclassified in the account portfolio matrix. Peter could then move on to his next account, having achieved some progress in difficult circumstances. The reclassification of the account would influence the choice of the skills required in the new account manager.

Case 13: surviving market testing

Components GmbH has won a contract to supply newly developed sealants to a European manufacturing consortium, KFG. They are the only supplier of these parts to KFG. The entry costs were high, due to the unique customer requirements, but it is now unlikely that any competitor could follow. The sealants are performing very well and Components GmbH has the opportunity of demonstrating more of its products. More importantly, the customer is very interested in the company's keenness to set problem-solving targets to be jointly addressed and met.

Components GmbH has been given the opportunity of demonstrating its expertise in a very specialized aspect of its manufacturing process. An expensive, inefficient and dangerous cleaning method has to be changed. Components GmbH recommends an ultrasonic cleaning system which fulfils all the customer's needs. KFG are now convinced that Components GmbH is a business partner which they must work with.

Q: **How can both parties proceed, given that KFG insist that their requirements must be met through European Union tendering procedures?**

A: It is not clear why KFG need to advertise in the *European Journal*, but perhaps there is a public sector element in the consortium. If KFG are required to advertise contracts in the *European Journal*, then they must do it and they must be very specific about their requirements. They can of course encourage Components GmbH to respond.

Components GmbH need to proceed as follows:

- They need to use their special expertise in order to influence the specification.
- They need to use their existing knowledge of KFG in order to ensure they meet all the common requirements.
- They need to provide extra, convincing information and analysis which should establish a competitive edge over any other tenders submitted.

Many selling companies with a partnership approach are averse to customers going out to tender. Nevertheless, they must remember that the customer will be required to market test their performance from time to time and, if they truly are offering the best solution, an objective tendering process should recognize it.

Case 14: disaster recovery

You are the key account manager for the customer XAN. XAN have ordered 100 per cent of their requirements for an essential raw material (ZAP) from your company (SZM) for some years. The business is moderately attractive to SZM. XAN's enthusiasm for SZM is, unfortunately, taken for granted.

XAN has recently taken over QES. The purchasing manager of XAN has discovered that one of your colleagues has been giving QES a lower price than he has been getting. You try to retrieve the situation, but the financial director of your company blocks the lower price and compensation package which you propose. The purchasing manager of XAN, who is now the chief executive of the merged group, punishes you by giving 20 per cent of the business for ZAP to your main competitor (BLK). He has also told you that he has discovered that BLK have a new product which he wants to pilot.

Despite everything, communications with the ex-purchasing manager (now chief executive) are still cordial. The new purchasing manager is more sceptical. You are determined to rescue the situation.

Q: What steps are you going to take to re-establish the company as a 'partnership' supplier to the XAN/QES Group?

A: First, the key account manager together with the key account team should review the positioning of the account in the relational development model and consider the high risk of disintegration. The candidate should identify 'breach of trust' and 'complacency' as reasons for disintegration. They should also identify that there were aspects of 'delusion' about the relationship – the strategic intent of buyer and seller were not aligned. XAN thought they had a partnership, but the breach of trust on price and the attitude of the financial director indicates that, corporately, SZM was not managing the account as an 'interdependent' partner.

Second, the key account manager must re-examine the positioning of XAN/QES in the customer portfolio analysis. The indications are that the attractiveness of XAN and QES together is greater than XAN alone. Unfortunately, the customer's perceptions of SZM versus the competition have deteriorated and investment will be required in order to restore their confidence. Thus, the candidate might describe the movement of the account from the 'maintain' box to 'selectively invest'.

Third, if communications are still cordial, the customer will probably be willing to explain what they want SZM to do. The key account manager must prepare a strong case for the SZM chief executive to meet the XAN/QES chief executive to hear his views. If SZM is committed to key account management and XAN/QES is strategic to them, the chief executive must put his commitment behind a joint strategic plan to innovate jointly and add value in the supply chain.

A student should get extra marks for suggesting a reconfiguration of the value which SZM is delivering to XAN/QES in order to get away from directly comparable prices, such as managing stock for the customer, managing the use of the product in the customer's processes, reducing the quantity needed by improving quality, etc.

Case 15: promise unfulfilled

RDT is a glamorous brand name in fast food catering and is regarded by your company (UYT) as a key account. It has a high profile and commands management attention. The company has bought some of its equipment from you in some European markets, but at very low prices. The promise of opening the door for global supply has never been fulfilled.

You have just found out that RDT is losing market leadership and is planning to close hundreds of branches worldwide. The expected announcement is causing panic in the industry and a trade journalist tells you that she expects all companies to be running around looking for lower grade equipment.

Q: You are the key account manager for RDT. How do you respond?

A: RDT's intentions towards UYT are 'basic', since they promised wider scope in return for lower prices and never delivered. Therefore, RDT ought to be managed in a tactical way. Its elevation to 'key account' has more to do with status than profit potential.

The key account manager would check any rumour about his or her account. He or she would usually check with the customer if the relationship is strong but, in this case, checking with industry sources might be more successful. Attention should then turn to the customer portfolio matrix. RDT's position should be reassessed on the basis of a decline in status and volume potential. The account is clearly less attractive than originally thought. The key account manager should be proposing a 'demotion' of the account to 'maintain' or 'manage for cash'. Candidates should present the arguments they would use to justify that to the board of UYT and members of the key account team.

Extra marks should be awarded to the candidate who also considers where new business is going to come to replace the RDT volume. Some might consider the lower grade products which seem to be attracting attention. Others might suggest going upmarket to avoid price competition.

Case 16: parochial pains

You are the manager of the global accounts division of a worldwide information systems supplier (WHIZZ). The national account manager for a famous US retail company (G-Stores) sends you an e-mail. He comes from the same hometown as the chief executive of G-Stores and they both still live there. G-Stores' headquarters is in their hometown. Apparently, G-Stores is planning pilot stores in South America and Europe and he cannot persuade the relevant country managers to give the new stores any local support.

Q: How do you work with him to maximize the opportunity for WHIZZ?

A: The creation of a global accounts division is one of the ways of over-riding local variations in service. Candidates might discuss the different ways in which companies can organize themselves in order to 'go global' with relevant accounts.

The answer should also discuss the nature of the relationship with G-Stores. It sounds like the relationship is at least cooperative, but it may be rather over-reliant on the personal relationship of the key account manager and the chief executive, rather than WHIZZ company capabilities.

Next, a consideration of the global attractiveness of G-Stores to WHIZZ and their perceptions of WHIZZ's global capabilities should be undertaken. The customer portfolio matrix is likely to show G-Stores as a 'selectively invest' global account.

The national account manager seems to realize that he is 'out of his depth'. The manager of the global accounts division needs to appoint someone with international experience in order to make sure that WHIZZ business growth is closely interlinked with G-Stores' expansion. In addition, in the short term he is likely to have to organize intercompany payments to the countries in which G-Stores has pilots in order to ensure that the proper service levels are provided.

Extra marks can be awarded if the candidate discusses how a joint strategic plan might move the supplier–customer relationship forward in order to maximize mutual benefit and potential for 'integration'.

Case 17: driving change

You are the financial director of a multinational chemical company (ChemCo) with manufacturing plants in Belgium, Argentina and India and sales units in sixty countries. Competitors have been publicizing the cost advantages they have gained from concentrating on a few key suppliers who can service them globally and offer a global price. You have known for a long time that this is the only way forward for your company, but you have been hampered by a hierarchy which allows country managers and plant managers to buy locally. Although the company has a worldwide purchasing policy, it is largely ignored. You have just had a heated conversation with the plant manager in Belgium who has bought some 'dumped' supplies from a company with a poor quality record. He was only interested in making his short-term profit objectives.

This has prompted you to check on insurance cover and you realize that there are too many different levels of cover with different companies in different geographies. You feel that the company's risk is not being handled consistently and that the company may be highly exposed in the event of major claims. You telephone the company which deals with insurance matters for corporate headquarters. The voice-mail system asks you to wait if you do not know the extension and plays you some music by Vivaldi. After an irritatingly long wait, you ask for the name that is on the system as a main contact. He has left the company. You ask for whoever is dealing with your account. You are transferred to his mobile telephone. Over a very crackly line you ask about global cover. He does not know the answer, but thinks they may not have global scope.

Q: Where do you go from here?

A: When you have done your research on potential global service providers and built a business case for supplier rationalization, then you can approach the chief executive officer. You can show him the article about your main competitor and their supplier rationalization and global purchasing programme. You must also show him, on one sheet of paper, a list of quantitative and qualitative reasons why your company should follow the trend and go further than the competition, rationalizing suppliers of services as well as raw materials. You can cite the example of the dodgy raw materials in Belgium and the subsequent insurance issue. You can show him a list of potential service suppliers who claim that they have global scope.

The chief executive officer will probably be convinced that it makes sense, but will be concerned that people who currently have purchasing power around the company will not give it up to a central department. Even if they did, does the company have the capability to manage the change?

This is where you can test out the mettle of the service companies who claim to have global scope. Make contact with them and ask them what their customers are doing and how. They may be able to introduce you to non-competitive companies who are globally sourcing their services and can give you some ideas for a way forward.

Case 18: homework failure

You are the information technology (IT) director of a fast-growing, UK-based, mail order company (MoCo) which is in the process of implementing a new customer relationship management system. Customer relationship management was needed because of the Internet-based sales which have vastly increased the number of customers and varied the location of customers. Your senior systems analyst rushes into the office to tell you that the new system has hit another glitch. She expresses concern about the skill levels of the software engineers who have been supplied by XYZ Ltd. XYZ Ltd is a 'business partner' of ABC Computing plc, whose brand of hardware they use. An ABC Computing plc consultant introduced XYZ Ltd to you. (The hardware is installed by another 'business partner', MNO Ltd, who were also introduced by ABC Computing plc.)

ABC Computing plc do not know it, but you are about to take over your nearest rival, a German company. The acquisition will give you a significant market share in Europe and enable you to form an alliance with a US company. What they should know is that your Internet-based business is doubling every month and has driven sales up 20 per cent overall. ABC Computing plc is still treating you like small fry. Since IT is absolutely crucial to your business, you need something more sophisticated from your preferred brand.

You call a named contact at ABC Computing plc who is responsible for your account and dozens of others. He visits about once a year, usually with the MNO account manager. A gatekeeper tries to put you off speaking to him – surely MNO or XYZ could deal with your query?

Q: How do you respond?

A: Clearly, your contact/representative has a short-term approach to your business and has not bothered to learn anything about your company. A sale is made and then the installation is chucked 'over the wall' to a third party. While consortium solutions can be appropriate, you expect the brand you trusted to take charge of owning the relationship, even if they do not own the day-to-day technical details.

Unfortunately, you are stuck with the systems you have bought and you have to find a way of leveraging some power in order to ensure that you obtain the value you need from them. Because the supplier is treating you tactically, you will probably need to escalate the matter above the contact/representative to a senior manager, using your Internet success as a 'carrot'. A threat to tell your story to the computer press could be the 'stick'!

In the long run, since the systems are strategic to you, a more cooperative relationship is desirable. However, should you really invest time and resource in trying to develop the supplier?

Case 19: telling is not selling

You are the operations director for a major European manufacturer. You are sitting in a room with the managing director and the purchasing director waiting for a presentation from a supplier of an important subassembly. There are four of them fussing over a personal computer and a projector trying to get the best focus. There is the key account manager, the production engineer, a customer service specialist and someone new. Eventually, they announce that they are ready and the key account manager flashes up the title of the presentation: 'Pushy Plc and Key Plc – Partnership Plan 2000'.

He starts to talk.

'Excuse me', you say. 'I would just like to do some introductions, just so that everybody knows everybody.' It turns out that the new person, who looks nervous, is an account management trainee.

The account manager raves on about the increase in demand for this sort of plant around the world and how their subassemblies can be used in virtually any model you might have thought of making, as well as how the future looks bright for both companies. The slide show has mesmerizing animated cartoons and sound effects. You try to ask a few questions, but the account manager does not seem keen on straying too far from the script. The engineer occasionally interjects a few wise words on their technical excellence. The customer service person offers a few platitudes about good relationships between the two companies. The trainee continues to look nervous.

The account manager finishes his presentation with a flourish.

Q: **What is your response?**

A: You thank him and get up to respond. You have one humble black and white overhead with a few bullet points.

'It is true that we have made the right choices about market segments and are doing better than most manufacturers of heavy plant and machinery. It is true that we could use your subassembly in some of our new models. We could use someone else's just as easily. So what do you say to

- our engineers auditing your shop floor processes,
- joint work scheduling,
- joint research and development and on-line data sharing and transactions and
- oh – and after we have helped you save money on all of that – how about a price reduction?'

Case 20: turf wars

You are the human resources manager for SDY Ltd, a relatively small company serving some very big, powerful customers. The managing director met a few key accounts a year ago and they expressed a wish for wider contact within SDY Ltd, so he set up a number of departmental contacts for them and asked the account managers to brief the contacts for their accounts monthly. The key accounts seem to like their departmental contacts very much in some cases, more than they like the account manager. You are observing a 'team meeting' called by the account manager of the biggest account, PUG Retail. She talks about how much volume the customer wants for the next few months.

'Great news! PUG Retail want 100 000 extra units next month for a special promotion in their new hypermarkets in France.'

The factory manager folds his arms and sucks air through his teeth. 'That wil be difficult with the big order from Hollo due any day.' He looks to the cost accountant. 'Will you authorize overtime?' She shrugs. 'I suppose I will have to.' She looks at the account manager. 'You do realize that agreeing this volume with PUG Retail will make the Hollo job less profitable? You know we always give them priority at this time of year because it is their high season.'

'We would all be out of a job if it was not for PUG Retail!' She retorts. 'I slog my guts out to keep them loyal to us and you are all supposed to support me. I get the orders. I'm not here to sort out your departmental difficulties.'

'They are loyal to us because they get a silly price. They may keep the factory running, but do we actually make any money out of this account?', the cost accountant mumbles.

The account manager bangs the table. 'I hope you do not say that sort of thing to their accountants when you are reconciling the invoices with them?'

'Of course, I bloody do not! Anyway, what else do you have to brief us about?'

'They want regional delivery instead of central warehouse delivery. So I said that would be alright.'

Suddenly the logistics manager leaps into action. 'You did what? Whereabouts in France do we have to get to? It is a big country you know. Do they want an artic every time or a seven tonner?'

'You have a contact in their logistics department – talk to them directly,' the account manager replies.

'Never mind that – how much extra is it going to cost?', the cost accountant fumes.

After a pregnant pause, the customer service manager pipes up: 'Did anybody sort out the new labels? There was a translation mistake. I did send the new copy to the print room.'

Q: **What is the role of human resources in such a situation?**

A: Setting up key account teams may not be enough to make sure that they flourish. Hostility has even been known to break out between different functions in one department, even in quite a small company. This is probably a job for specialists. Team members need to be confronted with the effect of their behaviour and attitudes on others as individuals and on the company and its customers. In addition to the training cost, you need to be aware that rebuilding the team will take time.

Case 21: plunging into the unknown

You are the managing director of a medium-ranking US advertising agency. Your relationship with a fast food chain which grew from being a kiosk in a poor town in Virginia to being a national flagship is a famous case study in what supplier–customer partnership should be.

You are playing golf with Ol' Joe Dollopin, the founder of 24hrBreakfasts, when he says he has made the decision to go into South America and Europe and can you provide advertising services for their pilot stores in Argentina and The Netherlands. You have no idea and you have no idea if any of your colleagues have any idea.

Ol' Joe says he can see you need some time to come back to him with a proposal. He will be really sorry to lose you and have to go to a bigger agency which is already established worldwide, so he hopes you can do the business. The truth is, without the 24hrBreakfasts account, your agency will probably become a takeover target.

You discuss the matter with the other four directors who agree to come forward with well-reasoned arguments to support their proposals for the way forward.

Two directors argue for going global with 24hrBreakfasts because of the following:

- It makes the company competitive with the big boys.
- 24hrBreakfasts will provide some security.
- Alliances can be formed with local agencies that want some exposure to the US market.
- It is a big growth opportunity.
- Profit will follow eventually.

Two directors argue for selling up to an existing global player because of the following:

- The market has already got as many global advertising agencies as it can support.

- You can use the growth of the 24hrBreakfasts' account as leverage in the negotiations.
- Each director can take a wad of money from it and start rediscovering leisure time.
- It is easier to do.

Q: You have the casting vote. What do you decide?

A: Taking a plunge into unknown territory on the basis of the requirements of only one customer is very high risk. The rewards could also be very high, but it would require very strong motivation plus bought-in expertise to realize them. It seems that not all your team are very highly motivated. It may be more appropriate for you to seek a sympathetic global player to take your company over. The potential of the Dollopin account will ensure a good price and you and your colleagues could either take early retirement or pursue a career in the new company.

This selection of mini-cases has presented just a small part of the myriad of problems which result from an organization's efforts to become more customer focused. We hope that you enjoyed thinking about these problems and are better prepared as a result for dealing with the challenges inherent in your key account relationships.

Now that you have read this book!

It should be clear by now that key account management is a complex, multifaceted process which lies at the very heart of an organization's revenue and profit generation. It is far more complex than just selling and negotiating, involving, as it does, the skilful management of all the people and processes of the supplying organization, as well as exploring in depth the processes of the key account and producing a strategic plan to bring together two organizations in order to create value for both parties. No organization does this perfectly, otherwise all key accounts would be at the synergistic stage. Please therefore complete the questionnaire once more and compare your scores now with those in you earlier attempt. They will almost certainly be lower the second time around. This is quite normal and indicates that you have learned some valuable lessons from this book. It would be a wonderful bonus for the authors if you were to join your colleagues in making some significant improvements to your key account processes.

How advanced is your key account practice?

How well do you know your key accounts?

Do you

Score out of ten:

- Know your company's proportion of customer spend?
- Know their financial health (ratios, etc.)?
- Know their strategic plan?
- Know their business process (logistics, purchasing, manufacturing, etc.)?
- Know their key customers/segments/products?
- Know which of your competitors they use, why and how they rate you?
- Know what they value/need from their suppliers?
- Allocate attributable (interface) costs to accounts/customer groups?
- Know the real profitability of the top ten and bottom ten accounts/customer groups?
- Know how long it takes to make a profit on a major new customer?

Index

Consider Critical success factors, key decisions, info that you need in key sectors... to make info, key factors, key decisions in key sectors...